Swaraj ka Shankhnaad

AF660374

Swaraj ka Shankhnaad

(Ekal Abhiyan)

Siddhartha Shankar Gautam

PRABHAT PAPERBACKS

No part of this publication can be reproduced, stored in a retrieval system or transmitted in any form or by any means, electronic, mechanical, photocopying, recording or otherwise, without prior permission of the author. Rights of this book are with the author.

Published by
PRABHAT PAPERBACKS
An imprint of Prabhat Prakashan Pvt. Ltd.
4/19 Asaf Ali Road,
New Delhi-110002 (INDIA)
e-mail: prabhatbooks@gmail.com

ISBN 978-93-5521-069-2
SWARAJ KA SHANKHNAAD
by Shri Siddhartha Shankar Gautam

© Reserved

Edition
First, 2022

Translation
Birch India

Price
₹ 300.00 (Rupees Three Hundred only)

Printed at
R-Tech Offset Printers, Delhi

Contents

Our Ekal vii
Ekal Geet ix
Foreword xi
Complimentary Message xvii
Man Ki Baat xix
Reflections on My Ekal Journey with Shyam Ji xxiii
Expressions of My Self xxv

1. Insemination of a Silent Revolution 1
2. A Dream That We Made Our Own 22
3. Amazing Ekal 35
4. Expansion Through Self-dependence 56
5. A Powerful Movement for Social Change 72
6. An Inspiration to Becoming Sanjivani (Panacea) 101
7. Ekal Brahmastra Se Gram Swaraj 125
8. Encouragement and Enlargement Through Social Connect 147
9. From Sanskar to Expansion of Service 173
10. Turning Adversity into Opportunity 194

11. Ekal on the Way to Becoming a Mass Organisation 212

12. Vanvasi Ka Shyam 242

13. Address of Prime Minister Narendra Modi 259

Details of Statistics about Ekal Abhiyan (Till November 20, 2020) 265

References 268

Our Ekal

1. Our Aim:
    - We Are the Sons and Daughters of Bharat Mata
    - Today, Our Mother Is Shedding Tears of Suffering
    - We Resolve to Wipe Her Tears
    - We Will Awaken the Power of Mother Earth
    - We Will Bring Happiness and Prosperity to the Country
2. Our Plan:
    - We Will Focus on the Four Lakh Small Villages of the Country
    - The 40 Crore Residents of These Villages Are the Backbone of the Country
    - We Will Strengthen Them Through the Implementation of Our Panchmukhi Yojana
    - We Will Free the Land of Chemicals and Liberate the Gramvasis (villagers) from Addictions
    - We Will Persuade All Our Brothers and Sisters to Adopt Ekal as Their Mission
3. Stages of Change:
    - Through Seva, We Will Connect with People
    - Through Our Network of Connections, We Will Organise People
    - Through Our Organised Collective Power, We Will Strengthen the Society
    - We Will Generate Pride in the Society by Making the Villages Self-reliant
    - The Self-esteem of Villages Will Be the Key to the Strength of the Country

4. Our Resolve:
    - We Will Convert Our Villages into Ideal Villages
    - We Will Transform Village Panchayats into Units of the Bharat of Our Dreams
    - We Will Organise Daily Satsangs in the Villages
    - We Will Generate Harmony in the Villages
    - We Will Evoke in People's Hearts the Sentiment That 'We Belong to the Country, the Country Belongs to Us'
5. Our Dream:
    - We Will Build the Bharat of Swami Vivekananda's Dreams
    - We Will Realise the Gandhian Concept of Gram Swaraj (Rural Self-rule)
    - We Will Ensure that Dr Ambedkar's Vision for the Country Is Given Due Respect.
    - We Will Build a Splendid Bharat as Envisaged by Dr Hedgewar
    - We Will Form Ourselves into Lord Rama's Army and Will Bring about Ram Rajya in the Country (an Ideal Government)

Bharat Mata Ki Jai!

Ekal Geet

(The Song of Ekal)

Ekal is our identity
Ekal is our true identity, Ekal is our slogan
We are the children of Bharat Mata, Bharatvarsh is ours (2)
Ekal is our identity (2)

In every single village we'll kindle the light of education
The sacred land of Bharat will be a paradise once again.
We pledge to impart education to every village child.
We are the children of Bharat Mata, Bharatvarsh is ours (2)
Ekal is our identity. (2)

Our country will be clean, and free of suffering and disease
It will reach its zenith when all, young and old, are healthy
Dynamic will be our youth, this is our single goal
We are the children of Bharat Mata, Bharatvarsh is ours (2)
Ekal is our identity (2)

Organic farming we'll adopt for the well-being of our country
Fresh, sweet fruits and vegetables, will make everyone healthy
We will protect our mother, the cow, we have taken a vow
We are the children of Bharat Mata, Bharatvarsh is ours (2)
Ekal is our identity (2)

Villages will be honoured; self-rule will be brought.
A bridge of love between village and city will by us be wrought.

All will live with self-esteem, that's our solemn pledge
We are the children of Bharat Mata, Bharatvarsh is ours (2)
Ekal is our identity (2)

Value-based education to every doorstep we will take
By generating harmony, Ram Rajya we will create
Determined are we to make Bharat the crown of the world
We are the children of Bharat Mata, Bharatvarsh is ours (2)
Ekal is our identity (2)

Foreword

Today, plural and harmonious India is facing myriad problems that are relatively new. Yet, India is unique in the world; our past is traditionally measured in the form of eras. According to scholars, India has witnessed 14 eras thus far. All these eras may span various centuries and therefore all 14 eras may expand into lakhs of years. Now, the question is: Which is this era that we are currently living in? Have we been careful to record it? Only the experts and scholars may exactly know the methods of this evaluation. An ordinary Indian only knows that every age witnesses a change because that is the unalterable principle of nature.

People hope that any change must be constructive. In fact, social reformers of every age step up to effect such a change. They take many initiatives. There is a long chain of such social reformers who have made their contributions in various eras. Our country has preserved memories of some of them and people remember them with respect. Since our society always has room for reforms, social reformers initiate the necessary changes and work to ensure that their efforts come to fruition. Then, every epoch-making reformer passes on their mantle to the next generation of followers.

There could be an umpteen number of ways to bring about a change in society and the usability of such methods is determined by the success of the experiment and the type of change required in society. This is how any social change occurs in any time period. There cannot be a single formula for it. Its criterion is set by the demands of changing time. The successful efforts of one era cannot be a prototype that can be emulated in any other era. Any new experiment will only determine how something could be done at a particular time.

In India, there has been a historical tradition of social reforms. Almost every walk of life has been touched by reformative endeavours. We have a long list of social reformers who made social reform the foremost goal of their lives and sacrificed everything for its sake.

The idea for social reform first takes shape in the mind of the reformer. Then, it takes the form of an experiment. This cycle continues. Not all experiments succeed. Only a few of them are adopted by society and they go on to set a trend. They register their own identity in the annals of history. Such efforts are popularly known as 'social reform movements'.

In this historical backdrop, Indians will now begin to understand the Ayodhya Movement in its entirety. Until now, the Ayodhya Movement has been seen through the prism of a controversy or a tragedy. The controversy had a rainbow of hues. Similarly, the tragedy had its centuries-old agonising background. Today, there is neither any presence for a controversy nor any trace of a tragedy. Both have been completely forgotten. The Ayodhya Movement today is on the threshold of a change in the narrative. This is the time when a multi-dimensional campaign will start highlighting it through different lenses and the mirror will show its future. In fact, such an exercise is already on the anvil.

The question of Ayodhya has been more difficult to answer than the epic Yaksha Prashna (a question that requires deep and versatile knowledge as elaborated in the epic, the Mahabharata). But now, as it has been answered by Yudhishthir (a key character from Mahabharata), the cycle of history has turned from the Mahabharata towards the Ramayana (another Hindu epic, whose hero is Lord Rama, the king of Ayodhya). The cycle of history moves in its own particular way. It is beyond any explanation or interpretation.

Everyone at least agrees that the Indian psyche underwent enormous churning as long as the Ayodhya issue was alive. It passed through an uncountable number of stages. Every stage came with a new question of a far-reaching nature. Each question seemed as huge as the Himalayas. Has the Ayodhya Movement crossed this Himalaya? Only a braggart can claim it has. The reality is that a new stage of the Ayodhya Movement began on 5 August 2020. This date is memorable not only because the Bhumi Pujan (foundation laying ceremony) was conducted on the Ram Janmabhoomi, but because of what Rashtriya Swayamsevak Sangh (RSS) chief Mohan Bhagwat said on the occasion: 'By the time Ram Temple is erected, an Ayodhya should be built in the heart of every Indian.' Mr Bhagwat is unique in the line of sarsanghachalaks (RSS chiefs). He symbolises the confluence of modern thoughts and ancient traditions in his thinking, conduct, body language, and personal behaviour. If my estimate is correct, Mr Bhagwat has adopted a new working mantra to achieve significant results utilising the commitment of his team. It will prove to be a very valuable guiding force for his successor. I have also witnessed that he has built an entire structure of his working methods.

All those who agree with this observation, will also admit that people who listen to or have worked with Mr Bhagwat closely, can sense that he has the rare ability to articulate positively and in a non-controversial manner, according to the demands of any situation. He is a dharmic (religious) person in the true sense of word. Here, 'religious' doesn't denote any particular religion. It only suggests that a person, who occupies a top position in a prominent organisation of the country, is devoid of any personal ambition or attachment. Only such a selfless person can be truly religious. With this context of his personality in mind, the above-mentioned line spoken by him is the soul of the Ayodhya Movement. It is full of religiosity. It is full of Indianness. We have to imbibe the message of that sentence. The day when the Ayodhya Movement will reach its destination, its everlasting slogan will be this mantra. Though it is a mantra, it could also be considered a sutra (set of rules or formula).

A formula has to be well defined. It should be explained clearly. We must avoid the dilemma of comparing mantras and the formula. Bhagwat ji also quoted two couplets from the epic Ramcharitmanas to explain his point. The real meaning of these couplets was made clear when he gave an interview to a monthly magazine, *Vivek*, wherein he said, 'We should imbibe the ideals set by Lord Rama and live the way he lived, adopting all the values he endowed upon us. Once you achieve this feat, you will see that an Ayodhya lives inside you.' It really seems easy to say and to listen to these words. The challenge is to make them a part of our personality. It is no doubt utterly difficult, but it is not impossible. Bhagwat ji has given us the formula for attaining the state of mind where this becomes possible.

This book takes you on a parikrama (circumambulation of a sacred entity) of just such a state of mind. It is like a pilgrimage to a holy site.

The more the sites, the more the pilgrimages! One such known pilgrimage is called 'Ganesh Parikrama' (pilgrimage of Lord Ganesha). There is a popular folk tale behind it. Folktales carry memories from one generation to another. Folktales can even be called a part of Puranas (mythological writings other than the Vedas). Puranas are not history; Puranas and history are in fact as opposed to each other as the East and West. They do not cross each other, rather they flow as two separate streams. Their origins lie in different viewpoints of life. Indians have developed a specific method of writing history. It has been constant for ages and has been unaffected by the flow of time. The tradition of Puranas originated from the writing of history.

Now, the question is whether this book is a pilgrimage of Lord Ganesha or does this book follow the pattern of creating Puranas in the style of history writing? This will eventually be decided by the reader. A reader has their own independent mind and may not be interested in these two questions. They will judge the book as per their study, experience, and perception. In my view, this book deserves a new category. This book depicts that the Ayodhya Movement has presented a new and an innovative approach to social reform and in this light, the Ekal Abhiyan has completed three successful decades. When the Ekal Abhiyan was conceptualised, the Ayodhya Movement was in its infancy. The Ayodhya Movement was launched amid humongous challenges. Its parallel branch was the Ekal Abhiyan. Had there been no Meenakshipuram Mass Conversion-like incident, renowned Hindu leader Ashok Singhal ji would not have endeavoured to unite the Hindu society. How did he become the first pracharak (preacher, or RSS volunteer) to sense the danger lurking in Meenakshipuram? Once, Mohan Bhagwat ji himself revealed the answer to this question on the occasion of the first and last birthday celebration of Singhal ji in Delhi. Meenakshipuram took place in 1981 and it was in its aftermath that the then RSS chief Balasaheb Deoras tasked Singhal ji to unite the vast Hindu community.

This book can be called a travelogue as well as an account of a pilgrimage. Any journey that leads a traveller's life towards a purposeful destination is a pilgrimage. Any voyage that puts an individual's psychology in a positive state and helps in soul-searching is a pilgrimage. Any effort that makes a person feel a sense of fulfilment is a pilgrimage.

Pilgrimage is unlike tourism. This needs to be emphasised here, as both are being understood to be the same these days. In India, pilgrimage has always been a tradition. In the West, tourism is a tradition. Pilgrimage is regarded as one of the four difficult tasks prescribed to human beings as per ancient Indian traditions. The Ekal Abhiyan has discovered many such pilgrimages that should have been found much earlier. The Movement has reached places far away from urban life, in forests, and found purpose in uplifting the lives of the residents there. Hence, all these faraway places are our new pilgrimage sites. If this Movement keeps up its successful pace, all those living in distant lands, dissociated from mainstream life, will soon intermingle with mainland India. All those backward colonies that have aligned themselves with the Movement have themselves become pilgrimage sites.

This book is divided into 12 chapters. As the reader finishes one chapter, they will feel eager to read the next to delve into the depth of the Ekal Abhiyan. Each chapter is a journey in itself and at the end of the book, the reader realises that they have lived all those years to make the Ekal Abhiyan a successful venture. The first chapter is titled 'Germination of a Silent Revolution'. This chapter narrates the incident that paved the way for the Ekal Abhiyan. Whoever paves the way, is the first link of the chain. Then, people join them as second, third, fourth links, till a full-fledged movement is built.

—Ram Bahadur Rai

Complimentary Message

I consider myself fortunate that I got the opportunity to become a volunteer of the Sangh, got to know its teachings and adopt them in my life. In 1989, the Vanbandhu Parishad (The Friends of Tribals Society) was established in Kolkata with the goal of improving literacy and health among the vanvasis—the rural tribal people of India. I was one of those who were roped in to work with the Parishad as an active member. Within a few years, on the suggestion of my late father, Sadhuram ji Bansal, the Shree Hari Satsang Samiti came into being. It was because of his blessings that I became a volunteer of the Ekal Abhiyan. And my association has continued for the past 30 years. I am witness to the fact that there has been no other public movement as wide, distinguished and wonderfully planned and executed as the Ekal.

This book summarises all those innovative endeavours and methods that led to its phenomenal rise, depth and continuous march into the future. All these efforts resulted from the extraordinary talent and farsightedness of the Ekal's founder, Shyam ji. This book will no doubt inspire and provide immense insight to prospective nation-oriented thinkers, organisers and devoted social workers. I heartily welcome this book and wish it the very best. I hope this book will guide genuine and result-oriented workers devoted to nation building.

—Sajan Kumar Bansal

Man Ki Baat (Musings of the Mind)

I am sitting on a chair, pondering how to express my train of thoughts? When and how did the idea of this book enter my mind? As I ruminate on these questions, my mind travels swiftly across the 31 years that it took for the transformation of the Ekal Vidyalaya to the Ekal Abhiyan (Movement). On this journey, the kaleidoscope of my memories reveals to me a variety of experiences, brainstorming sessions, numerous events, spellbinding scenes, impossibilities turning into possibilities, the sunrise of hope from the horizon of hopelessness, the love of co-workers, the chastisement and encouragement from seniors, childlike mischief and laughter followed by calm and serious discussions. Looking at this panorama, I realise that the Ekal is not just a movement, but also a complete and profound philosophy of life. The story of Ekal may be said to enfold within itself both the Ramayana and the Mahabharata. Every aspect of this story reverberates with the same echo. Every aspect makes the same clarion call. When I think of all this, a sudden urge tells me that I must begin with an incident of 6 December 2019.

The occasion was the inauguration of the 1,00,000th school that was opened as a part of the Ekal project. The school was situated in a remote village of Gujarat, and was to be inaugurated by Chief Minister Vijay Rupani ji. When we learnt that PM Modi would address us on this occasion, we were both surprised and overjoyed. He spoke with such warmth and concern for us, and was so familiar with all our future projects that it seemed as if he was actually a senior Ekal functionary working among us. His speech filled us with great determination, and with elevated spirits we started preparations for the Parivartan Kumbh (transformation fair) to be held in Lucknow from 16-18 February 2020.

This fair was initially planned for November 2019, but was postponed because of some unavoidable circumstances. Everybody had been downcast because of the postponement. It had seemed then that it would prove to be difficult to motivate the Ekal team to organise the festival on the next date. However, a veritable miracle was in store. The PM's speech proved to be the nectar that intoxicated every young worker and fired them with enthusiasm. The Lucknow festival turned out to be a grand, magnificent show. For all of us present there, the writing that seemed to be emblazoned across the horizon spelled, 'Look, the change has descended from heaven! Ekal has made it possible.'

On the humongous stage erected for the occasion, we witnessed the senior office-bearers of the Movement passing the torch of Ekal to the younger ones. It seemed to be the culmination of devotion for the Mother Land. The universal and palpable feeling present in the massive gathering was that something new and unique was poised to happen. It was like a bugle being blown, and being echoed in the thousands of voices emanating at the venue. The moment had cast its spell. Some were speechless, while some had gone numb. Some were speaking ceaselessly and hysterically, but others were falling short of words, despite being flooded with emotions.

I began to wish that some sage would come and collate everything that was transpiring on that momentous occasion in its totality, leaving out nothing. It was at that exact moment that the idea struck me: that this outpouring of voices, this bedazzling occasion, this effulgence of various concepts and philosophies, the planning for the future, and thoughts about their execution must all be amalgamated, and woven into words by a skilled wordsmith. A book must be published which would serve as a diary for the future generations of thinkers and nation-builders, and they would draw ideas and inspiration from this historical, world-level revolution of thoughts, ideas and their execution.

Unfortunately, by March 2020, the coronavirus pandemic gripped the world, and suddenly, everything came to a halt. All our schemes lost their momentum and got stalled. Now, the question was: how should we take care of our vast Ekal family? How should it be kept vitalised at a time when all physical activities were prohibited? All of us were disturbed and searching for ways to win over the pandemic woes. Suddenly, a familiar celestial guiding light and spiritual awakening emerged in the form of a messiah called Shyam ji. He made us fearless and suggested ways to take the Ekal from villages to cities and from our country to foreign lands. He filled us with renewed vigour and determination to integrate all the people associated with Ekal: old and young, male and female, and take the Movement to new horizons. The source was one, but the streams emanating from it were multiple. To our great surprise and satisfaction, the Ekal became more active in the following 10 months than it had ever been.

Now, the old urge surfaced yet again. It told me that this miraculous movement deserved to be recorded in a book form. All its dimensions ranging from its mastermind, indefatigable workers and their guides, ever-moving philosophy and ever-widening periphery must be detailed in a book. I sincerely believe that the spirit of the highly respected late Shri Ashok Singhal ji has become infused into the consciousness of Shri Shyam ji Gupt, and is constantly reminding him: 'The Ekal is a Brahmastra. Stay put in the battlefield and continue to wield it.' It is a fact that when Shyam ji speaks from the stage of 'Kranti Ram Ki' (revolution for Lord Rama), he becomes the living personification of Hanuman's (monkey god and close associate of Lord Rama) awakened powers.

Sometimes we feel that Shyam ji is expecting too much from us, and we are too exhausted to fulfil his injunctions. But, for inexplicable reasons, we find ourselves in agreement, and plunge ourselves into the tasks entrusted to us. Late Chitlangaya ji used to say, 'When Shyam ji plays his flute, everyone is mesmerised into following his tune. All the senior and junior workers of the Ekal feel highly privileged that Shyam ji is our guide. The inimitable leader that he is, he makes us feel that we are one family. He commands and reprimands us to develop our original thinking and to trust our own decisions. He grants us the right to make mistakes.

I was lost in all these thoughts when the idea of the book took over me again. Whom should I speak to about this? Who could do justice to writing such a book? I did not have the courage to broach this with Shyam ji. I knew he would chastise me sternly. Then one day, I received a call from Ramesh Saraogi: 'Jiji (elder sister), the Ekal is doing a marvellously fine job. I think a book should be written about the passion, capability and miraculous imagination of Shyam ji.' I was listening to him spellbound. I told him, 'This is what I have been thinking over since ages. You have just given voice to my wishes.'

And that was the exact moment when both of us decided that we would be the ones to take this work to its culmination. Ramesh later exhorted me to meet the challenge single-handedly by saying, 'I am unfit for this job. It is for you to take it up.' Now, I knew that the sole onus for the book rested on my shoulders. I began my search with a discussion of my plans with the veteran, most respectable journalist Shri Ram Bahadur Rai. Rai Saheb listened to me very patiently, following which he gave his go-ahead. I entreated him to support the project thoroughly, to which he agreed. I was overjoyed and content that I had his backing. Rai ji himself selected Siddhartha Shankar Gautam to be the writer-editor of the book, under his personal supervision. Throughout its writing, he lent every possible support that was needed for the project. For me, this was a cause for the highest fulfilment. However, now when the book is ready, I am still perturbed with a query: 'Do we even possess the scale required to measure the depth of passion and the expansiveness Shyam ji's thoughts?'

Perhaps, more such books will be written in future and the readers will themselves decide the answer to this question.

—Manju Srivastava

Reflections on My Ekal Journey with Shyam Ji

I have known Shyam ji since 1982. He was an RSS pracharak in Cuttack and I had gone there to work as a supervisor in a factory that manufactured fans. In a few days, on coming to know that an RSS volunteer had come from Kolkata, he visited me, riding on a motorbike. We had a long, meaningful conversation, after which he urged me to shift residence to the RSS office in Sheikh Bazar, instead of living alone. He helped me pack my suitcase and took me to the RSS office on his motorbike. That was the first time that I witnessed his intrinsic quality of reaching out to the swayamsevaks (volunteers) and showering his affection on them. In a very short time, he became so close to me that he even offered to share his room with me.

That was when I got the opportunity to observe Shyam ji's working style from close quarters. I saw that whenever he returned from a tour, he would hold discussions with his comrades late into the night. He would also, without fail, prepare notes. In fact, I found him always busy with activities associated with his mission. I had never seen such a workaholic person in my entire life.

In 1989, he was transferred to Kolkata to take on the responsibility of the Akhil Bharatiya Vanvasi Kalyan Ashram, in which I held the charge of General Secretary. While in Kolkata, he always stayed at my home and very soon became a very dear part of my family. This was natural, considering his ability to mingle with everyone anywhere, and make all his own. At my home, our discussions on the ways and means of expanding our work would begin at night and often continue till the wee morning hours. We would evaluate the capacity of every volunteer and then chalk out our roadmap. When my father died in 1988, he counselled and guided me in ways that were unique to him, and are beyond the capacity of an average person. With utmost gratitude, I can say that it was this guidance that laid the foundation of my future familial and social life.

The Vanbandhu Parishad, or The Friends of Tribals Society, was founded in the year 1989. Since then, it has been Shyam ji's farsightedness, his ability to plan, his hard work and dedication to his goal that has made the present Ekal Abhiyan a mammoth and powerful force, capable of re-establishing Bharat Mata's status as the Vishwa Guru (world leader). And this has happened despite all the adversities that Ekal has faced in its journey from zero to zenith. The credit for this also goes to the thousands of dedicated karyakartas working for the Ekal cause under the leadership of a role model like Shyam ji.

I think for a person to be accepted by people as their guide and leader, his thoughts, words and deeds have to be noble, and in harmony with each other. Shyam ji is just such a person. Therefore, I felt that his daily routine, his extraordinary working style and his thoughts and ideals should be preserved in a book form, so that future volunteers can seek inspiration from his example. I shared these thoughts with my colleague Sajan Kumar Bansal. He readily agreed. But the problem we faced was the manner in which to carry our intention to its completion.

Shyam ji was a pracharak of the Sangh. Had we asked for his permission or sought help from him, he would have firmly refused. We knew that both obtaining his permission, as well as the writing of the book would prove to be difficult tasks. With all these things churning in my mind, I spoke one day to Manju Srivastava ji, who I regard as my elder sister, and she shared a similar plan she had been nurturing about just such a book. It was the result of her toil and her persuasive prodding that Ram Bahadur Rai ji agreed to guide this endeavour, and finally Siddhartha Shankar Gautam wrote and edited this volume.

I hope that this written journey of the Ekal Abhiyan, and the account of the inspirational personality of Shyam ji will definitely impress readers and it will also prove to be a highly useful document for future volunteers.

—Ramesh Saraogi

Expressions of My Self

Before writing and editing this book, I had never seen Shri Shyam Gupt ji, nor been introduced to him. Though I was connected to the RSS and kept meeting its office-bearers, somehow my path had never crossed with his. Perhaps his philosophy of 'never resting until Ram ji's work (creation of an ideal society) was completed', did not create an opportunity for someone like me to reach him.

He was 78 and yet possessed the vitality of a young man. He would keep touring distant places and organising programmes throughout the year, ostensibly signalling to all belonging to Ekal the message that the Movement should keep progressing without any pause. But I did finally manage to meet Shyam ji in person, without which the writing of this book would have been inconceivable. This was made possible entirely due to Ram Bahadur Rai ji's affection for me and the trust that he reposed in my abilities.

Let me trace for the reader the journey that led me to adopt this noble initiative as my own. Not so long ago, before the advent of the coronavirus pandemic, I had been working in close association with Rai Saheb. It was around the same period that Manju Srivastava Didi, a mother-figure of the Ekal Abhiyan, gave Rai Saheb the idea of this book, and Rai Saheb, in his benevolence, handed over the execution of the task to me.

Though I had heard about Ekal before, I honestly had no clue about its functioning and administration. Hence, I was a little hesitant about taking on this responsibility. One day, while Rai Saheb and I were travelling towards his home, he broached on his desire that I write the book. When I confessed my ignorance of the Ekal Abhiyan to him, he calmly replied, 'You don't need to worry about that. If you doubt whether the Ekal will be worth your while, you just take a hint from the fact that it was Shyam ji, the main force behind Ekal, who had introduced me to the Sangh.'

This statement of Rai Saheb filled me with surprise and curiosity. I knew that a man who could convince an intellectual like Rai Saheb to work for the Sangh must surely be an evolved soul. After some time, I met Manju Didi, again through Rai Saheb, and with her, the background for the book was rolled out. Manju Didi kick-started the process by providing to me all the existing published work about Ekal so that I could develop a good understanding about the Movement.

Then suddenly, the whole country came under an unprecedented and complete lockdown because of the fast-spreading Covid-19. I used this period of being restricted at home to study the published literature given to me. Once I was through the whole written material, I was full of confidence that I could complete the project with the cooperation of the concerned people. So far, I hadn't met the most important of them all: Shyam ji. It was only after the government gained victory over the coronavirus pandemic due to its all-out efforts that I came to Delhi and my desire to meet Shyam ji in flesh and blood was finally fulfilled.

The meeting was a momentous one for me. His residence was a small room. Wearing thick spectacles, he was sitting on a cot, from where he warmly welcomed me into the room. The moment I set my eyes on him, I was totally awe-struck. He was in an advanced stage of life yet there was a child-like smile on his face. The pure, unsullied expression on his countenance reflected self-less, paternal love. This very first meeting influenced me so much that I instantly became his follower. Our discussions began, and continued with no signs of ending. All this time, I kept observing the luminous aura around him that seemed to convey that 'Ekal is Shyam and Shyam is Ekal.' This meeting also provided to me an understanding of how Rai Saheb was introduced to the Sangh by Shyam ji and came under his spell.

Shyam ji explained the Ekal to me in a very eloquent manner, in his highly cultured language. I spent three days in his charismatic presence. We had long discussions about many issues in those days. He answered all my queries about Ekal. We also discussed issues apart from Ekal and

Sangh. By the time our interactions concluded, I felt that Shyam ji was a part of my family, and I was a new member of his Ekal family.

As I see it, this book is not mine at all. No, this book is the labour of Shyam ji and his team of thousands of Ekal workers and it will belong only to them, always. The book chronicles the organisational structure of the Ekal, its working style, background and future schemes. It also highlights the life of Shyam ji within the Ekal Abhiyan, and his thoughts about the Movement. I am merely an instrument through which the book was written, with the blessings and encouragement of Shyam ji, Rai Saheb and Manju Didi.

It occurs to me that had Rai Saheb not chosen me for this task, I would have been deprived of the knowledge about an extraordinary dimension of the Sangh—the Ekal Abhiyan—that has taken education to every neglected part of our nation, and convinced people to live with values, become self-reliant and become agents of social harmony and reform. This Movement has, very importantly, taught the vanvasis (residents of our forests) to live with self-respect and honour. All this was made possible only because of Shyam ji's persona, and his passion and efforts towards the cause.

I dedicate this book to the lakhs of nameless volunteers who toiled under the guidance of Shyam ji, followed the true teachings of Sanatana Dharma and made them a part of the social fabric. They have assimilated the teachings of Ekal in their lives in a way such that Ekal has become their lives. It would not be an exaggeration to say that the success of this mission was possible only at the hands of 'Vanvasi Ka Shyam'. I am fortunate that though I began as an outsider, I was given the opportunity to sit beside the yagya vedi (sacrificial altar), watching with wonder the sacred rituals being performed by Shyam ji for the betterment of the society.

I humbly acknowledge the contribution of my wife, Mrs Seema Siddhartha Gautam in this project. I only wish that she had tried to understand Ekal with more depth while going through the drafts. It would have given me greater satisfaction if one more member had joined the Ekal family. Khushboo Mishra, thank you very much for your valuable assistance.

Finally, I dedicate this creation of the Ekal and Shyam ji to society at large and to the memory of late Shri Ashok Singhal ji. I hope that the Ekal Abhiyan continues to achieve more milestones in the future for the upliftment of society.

—Siddhartha Shankar Gautam

1
Insemination of a Silent Revolution

'Stop your speech, Sir. Have you come here only to deliver a speech or do you also have any concrete plan to do some constructive work?'

It was in the middle of RSS veteran Bhaurao Deoras ji's speech. Stunned and tense, he stopped promptly. His comrades were equally surprised as well as angry. Who could dare stop a senior RSS functionary's lecture midway? It was unprecedented. No one has yet dared to stop an RSS veteran from speaking. A silence prevailed. Would this silence herald the insemination of a revolution that would result in the uplift of tribals? It was such a compelling scene that Bhaurao Deoras ji, who was the first line office-bearer of RSS, got overwhelmed. After some meticulous thinking, he announced the launch of 'One Teacher, One School' scheme to be started from a forest village in Gumla district (125 km from Ranchi) in South Bihar (now Jharkhand).

At that time, Deoras ji was a regional pracharak of the RSS and in-charge of Bihar. Since he was naturally gifted with original thoughts, he would always keep creating ways to actualise plans. The development of the tribal society living in deep forest areas was his first priority for piecing together a Hindu organisation in Bihar. For this purpose, he ensured that whenever he would visit any distant rural area, he would ask local office-bearers to visit the tribal areas and listen to the problems of tribals. Deoras ji even brought many experienced pracharaks from UP to Bihar to make the welfare of the tribal people an effective project. One of those transferred pracharaks was Shankar Tiwari, who was working as in-charge of Ranchi. Deoras ji lovingly called him 'Shree Shankar'. At the urging of Deoras ji, Tiwari ji organised his tour to Garu village in Palamu district. This village falls in the forest areas of Mahuadanr.

It was a long trip. The roads and pathways were bumpy. It turned out to be a tortuous journey. Bihar and Jharkhand are still notorious for their roads; you can imagine their conditions in those days. Worse, it was a forest area. Though it was a car journey, Deoras ji had to ask many times, 'How long still do we have to go?' When the caravan finally reached Garu, it was evening. It was also the time of shakha (gathering). Deoras ji had to be present there too. He was tired, but he was disciplined in the Sangh teachings. He proceeded straight towards the shakha venue.

The scene of the evening shakha was startling, bizarre and yet pleasing. Around 30-35 teenage volunteers had assembled to attend the shakha. They were all tribals and wore only one loincloth.

Suddenly, Indra, the god of rains, decided to make it more difficult. But, this difficulty was like the labour pain before a new birth. It started pouring heavily, but the head teacher, who was a determined teen volunteer, started the class of physical demonstration. Deoras ji was extremely satisfied with this show of commitment. He admitted later that it was the best physical demonstration he had ever seen in a Sangh shakha. And it was meant to be like this. Tribals live in the midst of Mother Nature, they suckle its natural milk and grow right among lush green thick forests. Their physiques are moulded in the best possible natural exercises.

When the shakha programme ended, villagers from nearby villages came to discuss their issues. This meeting took place in a small room. It was full of volunteers and villagers. Since it was raining outside, everyone wanted to get in. Even Deoras ji and his associates didn't have a place to sit. The meeting was ushered in somehow. After formal introduction of all those who were present, Deoras ji started sharing his intellectual insights about the importance of welfare of the tribals or vanvasis. He spoke about the supremacy of Hindu religion, the importance of Hindu organisation and the conspiracies being hatched by the Church to convert Hindus… Suddenly, an old man rose from a corner and asked him to stop his speech.

An old, weak and illiterate vanvasi demonstrated the courage to stop a senior RSS functionary's speech. However, it's not surprising. Only a vanvasi is worthy of such courage as he is miles away from formalities. He was born in the lap of nature, suckled its original milk and lived in the culture of courage. So, why should he feel afraid? Who can stop him from calling spade a spade? His hackling followed with a spell of absolute silence. All the volunteers were just waiting—what will happen now? Deoras ji himself broke this eerie silence. He asked the old man, 'Bhaiyya ji, what do you want? What can we do?'

The affection in Deoras ji's tone melted the tension in the atmosphere. That old vanvasi (forest-dweller) shunned all his inhibitions and poured his heart out. He began to say, 'Sir, we are vanvasis. Who can sacrifice more than us for the protection of Hindu religion? My village is very far away from here. There is no pathway from there to here. It's deep inside the forests, but the Christian missionaries have reached there and established their network. They wanted us to convert by hook or by crook. But, we refused. I used to tell my co-villagers that someday, even a Hindu priest would come to our village. When children of the village told me that a senior leader of a Hindu organisation is coming to the neighbouring area, I came to see you despite my poor health. I think the Hindu priest I was waiting for is you. So, it is my humble request that you should do something concrete so that our people can be protected.'

As the vanvasi finished the sorry tale of his people, a compassionate calm followed for a few seconds. Even tears rolled down some eyes. This vanvasi was a complete picture of faith and confidence. Perhaps, the whole forest-dweller community was speaking through this man and was challenging the Sangh to come out to defend them. Deoras ji listened to him very carefully, but asked him politely, 'Please, you yourself suggest a way out.' The vanvasi said, 'We are disturbed by two ghosts. You get us rid of them. We'll be safe.' What??? Everyone was puzzled. Where did these ghosts suddenly come from? Deoras ji was known for losing his temper on the very mention of ghosts, etc. But he himself was flabbergasted. He asked, 'Bhaiyya ji, we are unable to fathom this story of ghosts. Please explain further.'

Actually, no one was at fault. Deoras ji was also dealing with the symbols of forest language for the first time. So, it was puzzling for him and others. The vanvasi came to their rescue and explained these terms: 'Sir, the two ghosts that have made our lives hell are illiteracy and malaria. These two are also the tools of the Christian missionaries. They make full use of them and convert a lot of people. In our village and surrounding villages, there does not exist a single school or dispensary. The government mostly operates only on paper and the Hindu community is obstinately oblivious of us. The Christians run whatever medical and educational system is available in the forest areas. Like all human beings, we also want our children to be healthy and educated. Tell us where we should take our children if not to these Christians? They teach the Bible in their schools and hand over the cross before giving the medicine in their dispensaries. Hence, if you really want to do something for us, you must first make arrangements for education and medicines for our people.' The meeting ended on the suggestion of that brave vanvasi. Deoras ji looked radiant with determination. It seemed a plan had germinated in his mind.

That night, Deoras ji couldn't sleep. He was eager to do something and was lost in contemplative thoughts. A vanvasi had shown the biggest Hindu organisation a practical way to reach into the heart of the distant and loneliest Indian. After this connection to the heart was made, an India of Swami Vivekananda and Dr Hedgewar could be built!

While returning from this tour, Deoras ji kept saying, 'Do anything Shree Shankar… we have to do this—take education and medicine in every village.' Later, Deoras ji proposed this idea in the meeting of RSS volunteers. And thus originated the plan for 'Ekal Vidyalaya' alias 'One Teacher, One School' and 'Gram Aarogya Yojna'. Who knew this was the beginning of a new era? A silent revolution was being inseminated? Possibly, Deoras ji had caught the wind of the arrival of Hindu century in years to come. It seemed that the Ganga that flowed from Gangotri of that vanvasi's speech found a Bhagirath in the form of Deoras ji. Finally, when this Ganga knocked at the door of that vanvasi, he woke up from his slumber in a way as if he was waiting for this moment to take on all anti-Hindu forces. It seemed Deoras ji was addressing all volunteers and forest-dwellers: 'All the workers dedicated to Hindutva have found a purposeful path now. Now, what do you wait for?'

The fundamental capital of any nation is the wisdom of its ordinary citizens. This wisdom emanates from the knowledge or education the citizen has acquired. If we divide the population of India into parts, one part lives in villages. These villages are untouched by the government, have no roads, no school, no electricity, no safe drinking water and neither any powerful society. Whosoever stays close to nature and his soil, he is equally culturally rich and is guardian of his moral values. Those who stay away from nature and are uprooted from their soil, suffer from moral decline. What an irony! Wherever there is education and luxuries, morality is absent. And wherever there is morality, people are forced to live in penury. Here also lies the solution to the problem. If we link these worlds through a bridge, one will be enriched with morality and culture, while education will arrive in the life of another. This purpose is served by the Ekal Abhiyan that is also called Gram Siksha Mandir (The Temple of Rural Education).

The research says that the informal education policy has been found more productive than the formal one in most of the countries of the world. But, in India, the government claims to have opened one school for about 3-4 villages and the country is nevertheless educationally backward. Its 30% population is illiterate. 'One Teacher, One School' is the most successful prototype of the informal method of education. This scheme is popularly known in India as the Ekal Vidyalaya, but it's more suitably called as 'Gram Shiksha Mandir' in the villages.

This Vidyalaya or Mandir is run for three hours every day in the remotest village inhabited by tribals, vanvasis or backward villagers. The teacher for this school is mostly selected from the village itself—anyone who is educated from Class 8 to Class 10. This school admits those boys and girls who help their parents in various domestic tasks and field works and thus are unable to attend the government primary school. This school primarily aims to teach children in the age group of 6-14 years. It teaches them primary syllabus up to Class 3. Besides teaching, students are also endowed with knowledge about values and the importance of being clean and healthy. A consciousness is also kindled in them about the love for their country.

The Ekal Vidyalaya is no more a project now. It has grown into a complete working system in rural areas. It is not only educating villages of India, it is resurrecting the lost cultural values of our society. It is helping rural folks how to beat illiteracy, poverty and exploitation. Moreover, these schools are helping in generating social and cultural values in urban areas as well. Villages and cities are equally illuminating with teaching methods and values are effectively endowed through this unique programme. These schools are in fact laying the foundation of an energetic future generation of educated Indians who will neither serve India but will also take the world towards new horizons of enlightened development.

There are two fulcrums of the Ekal Abhiyan. One is the army of workers who have devoted their lives to run the Ekal Schools in the villages. The other one is horde of workers that are active in urban areas and guide and support the rural workforce. We can learn from the Ekal's success how the insemination of a silent revolution finally resulted in the form of a mammoth banyan tree.

THE INSEMINATION OF THE EKAL THAT GREW INTO A BANYAN

Let's re-visit the 1893 Parliament of World Religions in Chicago, USA. The speech of India's young saint, Swami Vivekananda. 'My brothers and sisters of the world, I represent a country that has assimilated all the religions of the world.' These words of Swami ji made him a known name in the world. He was supposed to speak for three minutes there. However, only the ovation for his words lasted for more than three minutes. It was a welcome surprise for all. That day, Swami ji was hosted in the mansion of an elite family. When it became night, the husband and wife in the family heard someone crying upstairs. They rushed towards the room. They saw that Swami ji was lying on the floor and crying like a child. They humbly folded their hands and asked, 'Swami ji, did we commit some fault or was there anything lacking in our hospitality that made you cry like a child?' Swami ji replied, 'Friends, it's none of your fault. You are wonderful hosts. It's just that I am reminded of my country. Crores of people in my country will be sleeping without food and I am enjoying this luxurious hospitality here. How can I sleep peacefully on your splendid bed?'

It is said that Swami ji kept writing letters to his friends the whole night. In a letter to one of his friends in Madras, he writes, 'I am seeing that Mother India is ensconced on the throne of Vishwa Guru (World Leader) and is guiding the world towards a prosperous future. I see India is rising via its agriculture and villages. India is rising from the house of a *bhangi* (sweeper) and the shop of a *chamar* (cobbler). India is awakening because of those who don't have proper food and clothes. Why? Because they have been enduring the insult since ages and now they have become human bombs of endurance. Give them affection. Once they are awakened, they will illuminate the world. But, how will they be awakened? Education, education and education! But O fellow Indians, the son of a farm labourer will not come to your school because your school is a factory of manufacturing brown Englishmen. So, you will have to take the school to him. He will only have free time in the night as he works during the day. You will have to carry a lantern and teach him History, Geography and other subjects.'

This was actually the germination of the Ekal Abhiyan that Swami ji visualised in 1893 and around 100 years later, in 1989, the first sapling sprouted in a vanvasi village in Dhanbad district of undivided Bihar. Its architect was saintly businessman Madan Lal Aggarwal. The mentorship was on the shoulders of Bhaurao Deoras ji. His lieutenant Shyam Gupt ji oversaw the whole project. There is a saying that a tree that remains inseminated for about 100 years is destined to grow into a giant banyan.

So, this book chronicles this story of a seedling attaining the form of a large banyan.

THE ADVENT OF MADAN BABU, MANGILAL JAIN AND SHYAM GUPT

Now, the question before Deoras ji and his comrades was that the villagers should not wear a cross for the sake of admission in schools and treatment at a rural dispensary. In fact, that old vanvasi had passed on an important input to Deoras ji who clearly understood the pain of the vanvasi society. He resolved to make it his own pain thenceforth. The first decision he took was to open a hospital. Someone donated some land after a lot of persuasion at Lohdarga in Jharkhand as people didn't have a positive opinion about the Sangh then. In the aftermath of the first ban (1948), the Sangh was having a hard time. Its finances were in doldrums. First Prime Minister Jawaharlal Nehru had unsuccessfully conspired to frame the Sangh in the assassination of Mahatma Gandhi. All pracharaks were told to withdraw from their working stations. Later, when the ban was lifted and the organisation reassembled itself a bit, there came the Emergency of 1975. It rattled whatever was built in the last few years. Thousands of volunteers were incarcerated. Despite such intense confidence-shaking setbacks, the Sangh was determined to rise again. Its workers were plotting ways to clean its image in the society and sustain its existence. In these circumstances, the Sangh didn't have that much finances that it could support the project of Deoras ji right away.

During the period between 1986 and 1989, some events were happening side by side for the development of the vanvasis. On November 13,14, 15, 1986, the RSS and its offshoot organisations called for a joint meeting in Gumla district of South Bihar. Deoras ji shared his concerns and plans for the vanvasis in this meeting. He said that only a conducive atmosphere and quality education system could ensure the multidimensional development of the vanvasi society. He proposed that an Ekal Vidyalaya must be opened in every village of the area and that these schools must run with the cooperation of rural and urban workers so that the gulf between village and city could be bridged. He added that these schools also had to inculcate values in students. As an experiment, Madan Lal Aggarwal ji was tasked to open the first such school in Dhanbad.

Now, Dhanbad was set to see and uplift the compassionate power of the vanvasi society. Before Independence, the Church had raised an organisation called 'Jharkhand Mukti Morcha' here. The objective of this organisation was to secede the vanvasi society from the fold of Hinduism. The missionaries used the excuse that the Hindu society was exploiting vanvasis. They even widely spread this misinformation through different mediums. Since the Hindu society was indifferent towards the vanvasi society, this flame of blame remained afire. The nadir was reached when some vanvasis showed black flags to Prime Minister Jawaharlal Nehru as he visited the vanvasi belt in 1948. The vanvasis even demanded a separate 'Christian State'. This demand was raised before PM Morarji Desai in 1979. Once, a violent outrage in Singhbhum district turned so intense that the Army was called out to quell it. Madan Babu visualised a blueprint to neutralise this malignant movement. He wanted the vanvasi society to understand and then free themselves from the dependence on the Christians. Madan Babu though was known as a renowned businessman, he led the life of a sanyasi. Like his wealth, he had also inherited the volunteership of the RSS. He took active part in the Freedom Movement in the leadership of Gandhi ji and also invited Bapu to spend time in his residence.

In 1986, Dhanbad reeled under a severe drought. Madan Babu also felt the pain of sufferers. In order to work on a larger plan for the welfare of the vanvasis, he set out to study the problems faced by people in a village. Being a big businessman, he carried a consignment of relief materials with him. When he studied, he found that the lives of vanvasis resembled those of the downtrodden. There was acute paucity of resources with them and the drought had brought upon them a gigantic calamity. Madan ji was filled with grief and grit to do something for these woe-struck vanvasis. He assembled some vanvasis and asked them lovingly, 'What problems do you people face? What do you need? Please tell me. How can I help address your problems?' But, no one from the crowd said that they needed money or food. It surprised Madan Babu. Then, an old and very weak vanvasi came forward and said, 'Babu ji, we ask for nothing. This is the cycle of nature and it will remain in rotation. If you want to do something for us, please arrange education for our children.' Madan Babu went into a trance of pleasant silence! How can a man of forest be so aware of education? He assured all the villagers that he would start a school there. Another old man came forward and said politely, 'Many people come to us and promise bombastically. But they never return. Will you come back?' Madan Babu's eyes brimmed with tears at this request and he promised, 'I will definitely come back.' In his heart and mind, he felt that it was both the request and challenge for him, for vanvasis are clear in their aim—they want nothing but education for their children.

Now, Madan Babu had found the direction for the welfare he had planned for the vanvasi society. He made the final decision to educate the vanvasis. As a first step, primary schools were started in many villages. Interestingly, he wisely got urban rich families involved in this venture. Many such families adopted the newly opened village schools and they also regularly visited to assess their progress and enquire about their requirements. They would religiously arrange whatever these schools required. Madan Babu was popular among the moneybags of Dhanbad and wielded considerable influence upon them. He successfully found 60 sponsors for 60 schools in the first stage. And thus, Dhanbad laid the foundation of the vanvasi education through avant-garde 'One Teacher, One Village' schools.

During this time, in Kolkata, a senior worker of the Vanvasi Kalyan Ashram and volunteer of RSS, Mangilal Jain, was also busy in charting out the nature of welfare programmes that could be launched for the vanvasis.

He would reach Ranchi from Kolkata, while Madan Babu would come from Dhanbad. Then, both of them would proceed to Jashpur, Raigad in present day Chhattisgarh. The headquarters of the Vanvasi Kalyan Ashram was in Raigad. The office-bearers used to meet there to do appraisal of the Ashram's work and plan future roadmap. The Ashram earlier ran a hostel for vanvasi students. They stayed in the hostel away from their parents. The students would reportedly get bored in this hostel as they were parted from their families. Once on the way to visit a place, Jain ji paused at this hostel to check its condition. Everyone in the Ashram was startled. Jain ji was curious to know about the condition of the hostel, its teachers and the students. He called a student in a classroom and asked him to name the man in the picture on the wall. The student nodded with 'don't know'. Similarly, the third and fourth students did the same. Jain ji became perturbed. He now asked a teacher the same question. He was also clueless. Now, Jain ji felt very disappointed. The picture was of a great man of India, Guru Govind Singh. Neither students nor even a teacher recognised him. Even this was pardonable. But, the teachers never bothered to know about the picture. This was unfathomable. He shared his disappointment with Madan ji that Guru Govind Singhji's picture is unknown not even to students but also to the teacher of the hostel. The rot is in the foundation here! Nobody knows how to move into the future? They are merely following the people in their next row. The teachers are in fact misleading the students. It was heart-breaking for Jain ji. He knew that something would have to be done to stem the rot. Otherwise, the Ashram would not reach any destination.

The next meeting of the Ashram was chaired by its general secretary Rambhau Godbole. Jain ji shared his assessment of the hostel and that both the teachers and students were not properly educated. The standard of the hostel was of very low quality. The teachers, therefore, needed rigorous professional training. Godbole ji noted this proposal and promised that it would be acted upon soon. The meeting of the Ashram used to take place after three months. Jain ji waited for three months to know the progress of his proposal. As the office-bearers sat to discuss issues, Jain ji shot his query: 'What happened to my proposal?' The general secretary replied, 'A plan is being chalked out.' He waited for three months more. The next meeting took place. He was again curious to know: 'My proposal…?' This time, he got a different reply. He was told that the money had been collected in Mumbai and the plan was in its last stage. Now, Jain ji was elated and full of hopes that his and Madan ji's efforts would bear fruits. The development and welfare of the vanvasis would turn into reality from dreams. He waited for the next three months as if it were three years. Finally, the day of the meeting arrived. All the members assembled. Jain ji enquired about his proposal. He was told that a patch of land was purchased in Dadra and Nagar Haveli. Some mud huts were constructed for the training camp. Jain ji said, 'Sir, our campus has ample space for the training. Two vacant rooms will serve the purpose. Why should we go so far for this?' The reply was negative. The enthusiasm of Jain ji vapourised. He felt dejected. Why would anyone go so far away and stay in mud huts? He boldly made it clear before the Ashram office-bearers that such planning will not bring vanvasi welfare. He went to his friend Madan ji and persuaded him: 'Babu, we will ourselves have to do something now.'

Thus passed days, months and several seasons. Jain ji's volunteer friend, Ashok Modi, was establishing a factory of fans in Cuttack those days. He was facing some roadblocks. So, he invited Jain ji to help him. Jain ji examined the factory and then suggested some remedies. Jain ji was an RSS volunteer from a very early age and hence, wherever he went, he would try to meet local RSS cadres. Jain ji asked Modi ji to take him to the RSS office in the city. Fortunately, that very day, Shyam ji had returned from a tour and had reached the RSS office. Jain ji felt very impressed with Shyam ji in the very first meeting. He was curious to know how Shyam ji operated. He asked Shyam ji how RSS was working in Odisha? Shyam ji's reply cast a spell on him. Shyam ji presented a whole panorama before him. It was summarily like this—we would have to organise these many shakhas and hold these many weekly meetings to attract these many volunteers and this much fund would be required. Shyam ji's plan was a blueprint for five years. Jain ji was completely in awe of Shyam ji's clarity and working capacity. He had met hundreds of Sangh workers in the past, but no one had the vision and workability as Shyam ji had. Jain ji felt content and shared it with Madan Babu, 'Babu, we have found our guide for vanvasi welfare. If possible, bring Shyam ji into the Vanvasi Kalyan Ashram.'

Madan Babu and Shyam ji knew each other, as both were Sangh volunteers. When he saw Jain ji's trust in Shyam ji's abilities, he started trying to get Shyam ji inducted into the Ashram. Then, Madan Babu was prant sanghchalak (regional in-charge) of Bihar state and Rajju Bhaiyya ji was sah-sachiv (general secretary) of the Sangh. His order was set to be universally obeyed in the organisation. Madan Babu was close to Rajju Bhaiyya. He discussed his Vanvasi Welfare plan with Rajju Bhaiyya ji in detail and also sought Shyam ji's participation as a guide and executioner in the project. Rajju Bhaiyya was gifted with luminous insight. He immediately sensed the importance of this project and green-lighted the new mission. And Shyam ji was relieved from Sangh's Odisha branch and deputed to the Vanvasi Kalyan Ashram as its regional head.

Now, Madan Babu, Jain ji and Shyam ji began to brainstorm over the modalities of the project. They were now only seen engrossed in mulling ways to launch the project. How to go about it and what should exactly be done? To seek further guidance in this regard, they approached RSS chief Bhaurao Deoras ji. They presented the whole panoramic view of their planning. Deoras ji was familiar with the conditions of the vanvasis. Coincidentally, the government of the day had just released its new Education Policy report and it had recommended the Gurukul Model of education system in the country. According to the report, it was imperative for the moral and practical development of Indian society. Deoras ji himself was thinking over this. Finally, he suggested a powerful and affordable method and it was 'One Teacher, One School'. It was powerful as it was capable of producing results in every village and it was affordable because it needed limited resources. Such schools could be opened anywhere and under any circumstances. After Deoras ji's guidance, Madan ji started some of such schools in limited places. This proved to be an inspiration to Jain ji and Shyam ji. Thus, the project of 'One Teacher, One School' for the vanvasis took birth.

THE PRESENCE OF HONOURABLE ASHOK SINGHAL JI

Who was Ashok Singhal? He was a multi-dimensional man. He was a mother, father, guru, spiritual personality, source of inspiration, epoch-maker, a warrior and a priest. Perhaps, he was even more than all these adjectives. He was so dedicated and insightful to expand the work of the

Sangh that he would go to any extent to find and convince talented people to work for the organisation. One example of his dedication is that he took his elderly mother to the family of Shyam ji so that Shyam ji should be allowed to devote life for the Sangh. He would enquire and attend to even the trivial problems of his junior colleagues. Shyam ji was sent to Odisha. Odisha was, and is even today, one of the poorest states of India. So, Ashok ji was concerned how Shyam ji would work there in absence of required resources. He wanted Shyam ji to succeed in any circumstance and the first requirement for this was money. For this purpose, Ashok ji contacted many moneyed people and kept a regular supply of resources for Shyam ji. He helped an uncountable number of workers in the same way. That's why he was renowned as guruji among RSS-related folks.

You could go to discuss any problem with him and he would listen to it and then close his eyes. After some moments, he would suggest a sound solution to the problem. It seemed that he was linked to some divine source and received guidance from there. Sometimes his method appeared unworkable, but they would always work in the end.

His spiritual powers were confirmed when he shared a life experience. Bhanu Pratap Shukla was a former editor of RSS mouthpiece, *Panchjanya*. He suffered from cancer and the doctor said that he would die soon. When he himself realised that his days were numbered, he went to see Singhal ji one day. He shared a secret with Singhal ji. 'There is one very extraordinary conversation with the late Guru Golwakar ji that I wished to share with you before I die. It was 1972 and Guruji had undergone a cancer operation. Then, he went to tour UP. I was one of those who were appointed in his service. One day, I went to talk to him when he was alone. I dared to ask him blatantly: "Now since your life has been decided (because of cancer), who will protect Hindutva after you?" He went into silence like a yogi and then he said, "I will continue this work even after I am gone. I will work as a revenant." Then, I asked who would be the apparent being of this revenant? He said in a feeble but firm voice, "Ashok Singhal".'

So, Singhal ji, for us, was an incarnation of the late Guruji. In a divine coincidence, Guruji died in 1973 and in the same year, Singhal ji miraculously defied death and started life anew. Then, he worked as a representative of the late Guruji and magically united scattered saints and spiritual leaders of Hindu community. It was an achievement that was a watershed in the annals of Hindutva movement. He became an indefatigable warrior on the front of Ayodhya Ram Janmabhoomi movement. He became a shield of Hindus when the conversion threat raised its head anywhere in the country. His heart would bleed whenever he heard of atrocities on cows in cow shelters and slaughterhouses. He would worship cows in the shed of the organisation office daily. And with similar enthusiasm, he would protest and sit on dharna against slaughterhouses like Al Kabir slaughterhouse. On the issue of saving river Ganga, he almost put his life on sacrifice and sat on fast unto death. With another great man, Govind Dev ji, he set up a chain of Ved Vidyalayas. His energy made him capable of taking light of Vedas from his paternal village to the office of Mahesh Joshi in Denmark. He was active with passion till his last breath. On November 16, he was preparing for a grand yagya in Delhi. Alas, on 17 November, he passed away to be part of the celestial yagya that was waiting for him in the heaven.

Singhal ji was the lodestar of the Ekal Vidyalaya movement. It was his grandiose efforts that have pulled the movement to such gracious heights. When the Sangh turned 40 years old, Guru Golwalkar ji established the Vishwa Hindu Parishad (VHP). When VHP turned 25, RSS chief Deoras ji conceptualised the Ekal Schools. And as soon as the Ekal Abhiyan reached the age of 10 years and started walking on its own, Singhal ji planned to form an army dedicated to Lord Ram. In 1999, he set a target of 1,00,000 Ekal schools before the movement and he christened this plan as Brahmastra. He took out the movement from Jharkhand and took it to all across India and then to overseas shores like the United States. Whenever he met any cooperative rich person, he would discuss issues of funding for the Ekal schools. His close associates recall that during his last days, he always spoke about the future of Ekal schools in every meeting he attended. He would hopefully say, 'See, the Ekal schools will one day solve the problems of the country.' Whenever Shyam ji would go to meet him, he would first ask, 'Are you facing any problem? Are you getting enough finance or teachers for the Ekal schools?' Like all the movements, the Ekal also faced setbacks and roadblocks. But whenever such an urgent situation arose, everyone saw Ashok ji standing to as a rock behind the movement. He never let Shyam ji feel disheartened. He would advise him, 'Never feel let down by adversities. This is the testing system of Ram ji. He checks his followers. These tests are bound to happen, but you will see that Ram ji will help you in miraculous ways.' He had nothing in his life and heart except Ram Janmabhoomi, Cow, Ganga, Ved Vidyalaya and Ekal Vidyalaya.

Parinam Kumbh was scheduled to take place in Dhanbad on March 1,2,4 (2015). A year ahead, Singhal ji himself had wished to be present in the Kumbh on all three days. Singhal ji's followers would keenly wait for opportunities to see and listen to him. They always wanted him to spend some time with them. And now he himself was desirous to be among them. Shyam ji was overjoyed. However, the programmes of various conferences and gatherings of Hindu organisations for the Golden Jubilee celebration were readjusted in lieu of the Delhi Assembly polls. The Delhi conference was very important for Hindu organisations. But, no one had an inkling of the idea that Singhal ji would not be around by then. Assuming on their own that Singhal ji would not be able to attend events in Dhanbad, the sponsors announced his absence and this information also reached Shyam ji. He was naturally very sad. When Singhal ji came to know of such an announcement, he was livid and declared, 'I have promised to the Ekal and am committed to it.' Shyam ji received a message three days before the scheduled programme that Singhal ji would participate in it. All the workers of the Ekal exulted when they heard this news. It was felt that when Singhal ji would be part of the programme and naturally would also speak on the occasion, no one else needed to talk about the Ekal. Shyam ji himself had prepared the names and timings of the speakers. When this was handed to Singhal ji some moments before the programme, he asked in wonderment, 'Why is Shyam ji not speaking?' The workers told him that Shyam ji had excluded himself of his own volition. Shyam ji came to him and humbly explained, 'When you are speaking, the Ekal would automatically echo in your words. Perhaps I don't need to elaborate on it separately.' Singhal ji became angry and told Shyam ji, 'Will I explain your Panchmukhi Shiksha (five-faced education)?' Shyam ji replied with respect, 'Whatever you will say will be like Panchmukhi Shiksha to us.' Singhal ji became angrier and warned Shyam ji, 'Your speech is a must here. If you are not listing yourself as a speaker, I will call your name from the podium and you will have to speak.' Shyam ji read Singhal ji's affection for him and gave in to his order. Singhal ji spent three full days in Dhanbad and took very keen part in every session. He would descend from the podium and mingle with workers, sit with them and listen to them in detail with full attention. If he would not understand anything, he would ask about it. His activeness and spending so much time among people would make Shyam ji worried that it might impact Singhal ji's already feeble health.

Once Shyam ji dared and asked Singhal ji that he must rest at home and others would take care of the workers' programme. He again took offence and said, 'Then why have I come here?' Shyam ji took a liberty and said, 'Then we will seek your blessings and force you to speak with us more.' But Singhal ji said sternly, 'I will not say a single word other than what is listed for me.' Shyam ji was unable to understand why he remained present in the whole programme? Yet, for Shyam ji and workers, Singhal ji's presence was a direct blessing from Lord Ram. Shyam ji had panicked by the lack of arrangement but in the end everything fell in order and he was showered with praises from all sides. He was still at sea how it happened so successfully despite so many paucities? He thought it was Ram ji who was managing through his divine powers. But who was the agent of this divine power at the gathering? Shyam ji recalls those moments and Singhal ji, 'Today, when Singhal ji is not among us, I am reminded of another spiritual dimension of him. It became evident in those 3 days in the Kumbh. He was the divine connection with Ram ji there.' Such was the passion and love of Ashok Singhal ji for the functioning and success of the Ekal Abhiyan!

A SOURCE OF INSPIRATION FOR THE WORKERS

A farmer always ensures that the plant he has sowed must sprout perfectly, with its various parts like leaves, flowers and fruits blossoming into fine products. And for this purpose, he works hard to irrigate and supply nutrition to the roots of the plant. Similarly, the aim of the Gram Shiksha Mandir alias Ekal is to ensure that this farmer or vanvasi is awakened to new enlightenment and unity through basic education. The most important role in this movement is that of the teacher who devotedly teaches villagers or vanvasis. Such teachers need resources to be an important part of this mission. Dr Rakesh Popli took it on himself to manage resources for Ekal teachers. Dr Popli is a living example of devotion in life to the young workers attached with the Ekal. Dr Popli left a lucrative job as a scientist in the US and returned to India to serve his motherland. He joined Kanpur IIT as a professor. But, he soon realised that it was impossible to work for the motherland while being in a government job. There is only one route to take the country on the course of greatness—through villagers and vanvasis living in distant rural and forest lands. So, he quit his job and set out for a rural hinterland Vishunpur in Gumla district of Jharkhand to conduct his experiments on child education among the vanvasis. His wife Rama Popli was with him in this endeavour. They brainstormed for years to find out the most appropriate education system for the vanvasis. The conclusion of their study ultimately became the pattern of the education system of vanvasis. Later, Dr Popli taught at BIT Engineering College, Ranchi, for years and also kept working for the education of vanvasis. His wife Rama ji also opened a Navin Vidyalaya for small children and conducted many valuable experiments on children's education. The Ekal family was proud and blessed to have such hardworking and able people working for it and guiding it.

The Ekal teachers are trained by a group of senior teachers at regional levels. This training is organised in the supervision of a high-powered central council of the organisation. When Dr Popli was the chairman of this council, he was focussed on quality-based training of these teachers so that the Ekal schools always maintained a high standard of education. He studied meticulously the efforts being made by various nationalist organisations and independent workers on rural and children education. Based on this study, Dr Popli wrote two books—*Ekal Vidyalaya Pathyakram and Prasikshad* (Ekal Schools Syllabus and Training) and *Acharya Margdarshika* (Guidebook for Teachers). This is the peculiarity of the informal education that students are not merely invited to schools to study but to take part in various extracurricular activities. The education system of the Ekal is inclusive of recreation along with education. That's why it is also known as 'entertaining education'. This is not an easy task. It was exactly because of this reason that Dr Popli wrote those books to pass easy and valuable tips to teachers in the forms of symbols about numbers, language, science and general knowledge. These books also teach how local resources in vanvasi areas can be utilised to teach kids new forms of folk dances, singing, storytelling and various forms of sports. Dr Popli's wife Rama Popli, Srinivas Panda and Seema Ajgaonkar assisted him in writing these extremely valuable books. Wherever these four people gathered, they mesmerised their listeners. Their style of mixing education and entertainment was magical. And when this magic will turn vanvasi kids into capable Indians of tomorrow, who can stop India from becoming a strong nation? When India becomes a strong nation, it would help in the welfare of people all over the world. Today, Dr Popli is no longer physically present with the Ekal Abhiyan, but his books will always guide the Ekal community and he will remain a source of inspiration.

THE MILESTONE OF EKAL'S FOUNDATION

We have mentioned earlier that the Ekal originated in Jharkhand (then South Bihar) in 1989. Its seed properly flowered in 10 years. In the last 20 years, it has grown into a full-fledged tree. The Ekal community hopes that it should grow further and become a large banyan in the next 10 years. The journey of the Ekal has been very thrilling so far. There are three stages of this journey—first, the experimental stage (1989-1998) that was limited to Jharkhand; second, when it crossed the boundaries of Jharkhand and began to be called the Ekal Abhiyan; third was 2001 onwards, when the Ekal crossed the frontiers of India and became international. In these three stages, many devoted people, apart from RSS pracharaks, nurtured this movement and its foundation still rests on such people. Even in the future, the contribution of such people will be its guiding torch. The lords of the mind who injected lifeblood into the Ekal are followings:

JHARKHAND PARV

1. **Shree Mangilal Jain (late)**- He was with Shree Madan Babu as one of the founders of the Ekal and remained with him since the initiation of the movement. He was also the founder member of Vanbandhu Parishad. He was a volunteer of the Sangh since his childhood. He mostly worked in Kolkata.
2. **Shree Vimal Lath**- He was an industrialist, social worker and a patron of literature. His residence became the first office of Vanbandhu Parishad.

3. **Shree Suryaprakash Sharma**- He completed his education from Mathura in 1978 and was sent to Jharkhand by the Sangh. He started kindergartens in the forest areas and prepared the ground for the Ekal Vidyalayas.
4. **Shreemati Manjushree**- She was introduced to the Vanvasi Kalyan Ashram in 1986. Her first sojourn in the vanvasi area was in Jharkhand. She dedicated herself to expand the organisation throughout India since the inception of the Vanbandhu Parishad in 1989. She was a teacher. In 2002, when she felt that her profession was hindering her devotion to the Ekal, she took voluntary retirement and devoted herself completely to the Ekal Abhiyan. She at present is guiding the women wing of the movement and is the chairperson of the Ekal Institute.
5. **Dr Harish Anand**- He finished his education from Moradabad in 1987. The Sangh sent him to open a dispensary in a remote area, Goyalkera in Singhbhum district of Jharkhand. In 1998, he took the Ekal Abhiyan to Northeast states.
6. **Shree Amrendra Vishnupuri**- He completed Master's degree in Sociology and then was trained in Mass Communication and Journalism. As a member of Sangh's Vidyarthi Parishad, he joined the Ekal Abhiyan in 1989 and then onwards devoted his life to this movement only. He became the first-row man of the movement and is currently with the Publication Division of the movement.
7. **Shree Sanjay Sahoo**- He was introduced to the Ekal Abhiyan when he was a Zila Pracharak of the Sangh. Then, he devoted himself to the movement and became the first-generation member of the movement.
8. **Shree Kameshwar Sharma**- He became part of the Ekal Abhiyan as a member of the team that was given to the movement by Vikas Bharti. He shouldered responsibility of many Ekal projects in Jharkhand.
9. **Shree Umashankar**- He has been with the Ekal since the organisation of the first Harikatha camp in Ayodhya in 1995.

AKHIL BHRATIYA PARV

10. **Shree Srinibas Panda**- Pandaji took the reign of the Ekal Abhiyan outside Jharkhand and took it to Odisha. He conducted many

experiments about moulding the children's education as per demands of the modern time. He is guiding the Ekal's Combined Training Department. As the head of the Ekal's Primary Education Department, he is credited with introducing the syllabus for the education of vanvasi children.

11. **Sushree Seema Ajgaonkar**- After completing her project, she became the wholetimer of the Vivekananda Centre. Then, she became the director of Koswad Project near Mumbai. In 1998, she took charge of the Training Department of the Ekal Abhiyan.
12. **Shree Lalan Sharma**- He was a qualified professional in Forestry Sciences. He was attracted towards the welfare of the vanvasis under the influence of Vikas Bharti. In 1998, Vikas Bharti had given many valuable human assets to the Ekal and Lalan ji was one of them.
13. **Shree Prashant Sahoo**- He was a young man from Odisha who had come to do BMTC and in recognition of his talent, he was entrusted the responsibility of evaluation of the working mechanism of the Ekal Abhiyan.
14. **Shree Ashish Mishra**- As the Ekal expanded, it was felt that its cadres should be properly trained. In 1998, a first experimental Basic Management and Training Centre was opened in Prayag. He contributed to the movement as the fourth batch student and also became a guide in the Evaluation Department of the movement.

INTERNATIONAL PARV

15. **Dr Trilokya Nath Satpathy**- In 2001, the Ekal Abhiyan crossed the Indian border and arrived in America. There, it started the Aarogya Yojna (Health Mission). Dr Satpathy devoted himself to make it a success.
16. **Shree K.E.N. Raghavan**- In 1980, he was a member of the Sangh's student wing, Akhil Bharatiya Vidyarthi Parishad (ABVP) and amassed a lot of experiences. He joined the Ekal Abhiyan in 2001 and was instrumental in conceptualising the gram vikas (rural development). His deep research in the field resulted in the invention of bio-fertilisers.
17. **Shree Ganesh Shenoy**- He left his banking job in 1998 and became a lifetime member of the Vivekananda Centre. He joined the Ekal

Abhiyan in 2001 and laid the foundation of the movement for the entire South India. He deserves the credit for the Ekal's overall success in South India.

18. **Shree Madhvendra Singh**- He started his journey in the field of education as a teacher with the Vidya Bharti. He became principals in many RSS-linked Shishu Mandir schools. In 2005, he joined the Ekal and soon won everyone's heart by his devotion and working capacity. Today, as the head of the movement, he is leading the team of thousands of full-time volunteers.
19. **Dr Satish**- He began his active social service as a lifetime member of the Vivekananda Centre. He married Hema ji and became renowned as an expert physician and simultaneously worked for various Sangh projects. He played a key role in opening new chapters in big cities of Tamil Nadu. In 2008, he worked as the coordinator of the Aarogya Foundation. Now, he is no more physically present among us.
20. **Shreemati Hema Malini**- When the Aarogya Yojna travelled to South India, it was felt that an able woman leader should join the initiative so that women of the state may also be part of it. Hema ji took this responsibility. She has earned the credit to establish Aarogya Vibhag in South India.
21. **Dr Paran Gauda**- Dr Gauda did his Masters in Nuclear Physics from IIT, Mumbai with a gold medal. He then earned his PhD from the prestigious Bhabha Institute. Later, he joined the Vivekanada Centre as a lifetime member. He also served as the advisor to the rural development programme of the Indian government—CAPART.

The above list of luminaries is a galaxy of dedicated people that speeded up the Ekal Abhiyan and put it on the road leading to achievement after achievement. Most of these devoted men and women have their own team of 4-5 independent people who keep guiding the movement as per their expertise in various fields. These people make the central team of the Ekal Abhiyan. This team takes decisions about every contour of the rural development, formulates its policies and ensures that they are effectively operationalised.

□

2

A Dream That We Made Our Own

'However arduous the circumstances may turn, however big the challenges one may face, the road to solution will be easy and simple. You will have to just make a start.' These words of Shyam ji define the uninterruptible journey of the Ekal Abhiyan.

The culture of India distinguishes it in the comity of world nations. Swami Vivekananda had 125 years ago proudly said that the Hindu culture has taught the world both tolerance and universal acceptance. This is also called the Aranya Sanskriti (forest culture, or green culture) as it originated in the laboratory of forests where values grow side by side with flora and fauna. We have all been proud of this culture and will keep doing so in the future. Unfortunately, our vanvasis (forest-dwellers, or tribals) are poor, illiterate and live in horrible conditions. Almost half or more than half of India's population lives in villages and small towns. If this population is empowered properly, India will be a powerful nation. This is the crux of Swami Vivekananda's 1893 address at the first World's Parliament of Religions in Chicago, USA. In his message, he had even suggested a method to realise this dream—easy access to education for every ordinary Indian. The Ekal Vidyalaya is nothing but a practical form of Swami ji's vision.

In the 1980s, Jharkhand (then South Bihar) was on fire. The secessionist movements were raging. There was violence everywhere. It was in the middle of this rage that Bhaurao Deoras ji proposed a solution to end the atmosphere of strife—it had to be done by educating the rural population. He had basically developed this idea to douse the raging fires among the vanvasis who were agitating for various demands and had even resorted to armed struggle. He thought that once mainstream India would be able to educate tribals and help uplift their standard of living, the anger of tribal would automatically subside.

The Ekal Vidayalaya was born from this spark. Whenever Madan Babu was asked what he would achieve by opening the Ekal Schools, he would answer, 'I will raise an army of Ram ji.'

In 1989, the movement was formally initiated. Madan Babu saw this seedling sprouting into a tree in his lifetime. The movement matured under the leadership of PD Chitlangaya ji. When it got patronage of great Ashok Singhal ji in 2001, the movement began to fly.

Then HRD Minister, Dr Murli Manohar Joshi, knew Chitlangaya ji very well. He invited Shyam ji to give a presentation on the Ekal education system before well-known educationist and director of NCERT, Jagmohan S. Rajput. One of the books written by Shyam ji had already reached Rajput ji. He had suggested some deletions from the book, but he had liked it and proposed to implement the prescribed education policy in the entire country through government programmes. Joshi ji also agreed with this proposal and he instructed Chitlangaya ji to prepare a lecture on this topic. The lecture was to be delivered before the education ministers of all states in the Vigyan Bhavan in Delhi. However, the introduction of Chitlangaya ji stirred a controversy and the people questioned: 'Why has a businessman been selected to speak on the subject of education?' Joshi ji thought of a plan to placate the people. He asked Chitlangaya ji and Shyam ji to wait outside and once Joshi ji called their names, they were to enter the hall. However, when the programme started with Saraswati Vandana, the education minister of Bengal created a ruckus on its recitation and in the hullabaloo that ensued, Shyam ji and Chitlangaya ji could not be called in. They kept waiting outside. However, this occasion catapulted the Ekal Abhiyan to the national stage and it hogged enough limelight. Thereafter, taking cue from the Ekal education system, the government launched its much-acclaimed Sarva Shiksha Abhiyan (SSA).

When the Ekal went national from its Jharkhand laboratory in 1998, it caught the attention of all notable educationists. In 2001, this movement crossed the border and registered its presence overseas under the patronage of Chitlangaya ji and because of Singhal ji's guidance. Its dream of one-lakh schools seemed imminent. The confidence of all those who were working for the Ekal skyrocketed. For the first time it seemed like Ekal would realise its real potential.

A thoughtful pracharak called Shyam ji weaved new dreams for the Ekal as if it was his personal dream. He made the Ekal his lifetime mission. We will keep discussing his journey with the Ekal from time to time, but let's take an account of the nine-year-old journey of Ekal itself. In these nine years, the Ekal has become a toddler from the infant it was and it can run on its feet now. This has been possible because of Shyam ji's unshakable devotion.

Let's turn back a few years. It is 1975. Shyam ji was then a worker of the Sangh in Agra. He had no clue about vanvasis and their lives. In 1978, he was deputed to Odisha and it was here that he came to know about the vanvasi community. He came into contact with veteran Sangh leaders like Bhaurao Deoras ji and Rajju Bhaiyya. When Shyam ji was bracing up to go to Odisha, Deoras ji and Rajju Bhaiyya tried to inflate his confidence and told him that if he were able to open 500 new branches of the Sangh, he would contribute immensely to the cause of the organisation. Shyam ji took it seriously and made it his target. Even though, given the prevailing circumstances in the country in those days, the target of 50-60 branches was more than enough. And here was someone dreaming of 500 branches! But yes, the Sangh never teaches its cadre to back out from their determination. Thus, Shyam ji employed himself and his comrades like maniacs. They distributed their tasks judiciously. Shyam ji was assigned the Phulwani region. It is presently the municipal and administrative headquarters of Kandhamal district. Historical grapevine has it that Phulwani was named after a woman called Phuldai. She was sacrificed by the locals as a part of a religious ritual. The Phulwani region is on the banks of the Salunki River. Its surroundings are utterly beautiful and full of medicinal plants, wild shrubs, small hillocks, waterfalls and a simple vanvasi community living on the feet of small hills. This place is a paradise for nature-lovers. But despite such abundant natural beauty and wealth, the vanvasi community residing here was totally oblivious of the natural treasure around them and their own potential. Worse, they were being enticed by the Christian missionaries to convert to Christianity. They had no alternative for survival except to embrace Christianity.

Shyam ji and some other Sangh volunteers visited few of the shakhas (gatherings) being run in Phulwani. Since all the activities in the Sangh are regulated through these shakhas, it was imperative to review their functioning. The shakhas are organised every evening at some selected public place. The volunteers who attend these shakhas are trained in self-protection, basic medical know-hows and the process of rehabilitation. In Phulwani, a shakha was organised in a school so that youngsters could learn some social service skills. In total, 25-30 people would attend this shakha, including Class 9-10 students. It was evening. The Sangh karyakarta had called the shakha. It was organised in the campus of a school. As soon as Shyam ji walked into the room, he was stunned to see the large number of youths in the gathering. Most of them wore merely loincloths, while Shyam ji and others were properly clothed. The scene in the room was like a painting of two group of people—one wearing clothes, while the other wearing their own skin. Those semi-clothed men looked happier and were eagerly waiting for Shyam ji. This meeting with young vanvasis was going to be a memorable one. Shyam ji first introduced the purpose of his arrival. He told them that the Christians working among them were converting them from their original religion. 'Christians are invaders. They are bamboozling you as you are very simple and trust them easily,' he told the vanvasis. Suddenly, two boys in the back row started talking. Shyam ji was a typical Sangh disciplinarian. He called out both of them and asked them to stand up. He asked them what they were talking about. They both were terrified. Shyam ji thought he was unable to speak proper Odia to communicate with them. The boys were more afraid now. The situation was now a picture of hesitation and suspicion. Neither Shyam ji nor the boys had any clue. One of their teachers, who was sitting nearby, sensed the predicament of Shyam ji and explained: 'Sir, both these boys were discussing that perhaps the guest (you) are Katki (from Cuttack).' Now, Shyam ji was perplexed by the word Katki. The teacher further explained, 'Cuttack is a big city in Odisha and people in this village call every urban-dweller a Katki. It's sort of a slang here.' Now, Shyam ji felt insulted as he had come for their welfare and they were calling him Katki. Out of his anger and curiosity, he asked the boys, 'Why did you call me Katki? Only because I am planning something good for you?' On hearing this, one of the boys came forward with courage: 'You are calling the Christians names. Yet, they have built schools, hospitals and churches. They will not take these buildings to England. Aren't they all for us? We will be educated, cured and work in these institutions. Why are you then worried for us? What's wrong if we wear the cross?'

Shyam ji was left speechless. He had come to rescue these vanvasis from Christians and they were telling him that there was nothing wrong in wearing a cross. He asked them, 'It's perhaps alright to wear the cross. But why are people being converted. Why are people becoming Christians?' No one mustered the courage to answer this question. After the exchange of some more ideas, the meeting dispersed. But the questions of the youth kept echoing in the mind of Shyam ji.

Shyam ji was agitated. He wondered if the youth had so much courage and clarity of thought, why were they being converted? The vanvasi society living in that area identified as Kui. The Sangh karyakarta suggested to Shyam ji, 'The head of Kui society lives nearby. Let's discuss this issue with him.' Shyam ji took some of his co-volunteers along and went to see this gentleman. Evening had descended and this was the time when every vanvasi would turn to the bottle of alcohol. Shyam ji was introduced to the Kui chief. He was told why Shyam ji had come to meet him. The karyakarta asked him politely, 'Brother, we have come to learn from you that if youths of your society are so courageous, then why are they getting converted to Christianity?' He remained silent. When the karyakarta prodded him again, he lost his cool. 'It's all because of you bloody Katki people?' Shyam ji and everyone else felt very disturbed. He told the karyakarta, 'He is again calling us Katki and abusing us. Tell him to cool down.' Somehow that vanvasi chief regained some of his senses on his own. Though he was still inebriated and struggling for words. He nevertheless began to explain the dilemma faced by his society. Whatever he said opened the eyes of everyone sitting before him and it also reflected the resourcefulness and helplessness of the Kui people. He said: 'You know that there is a law here to prevent religious conversion. If a conversion happens, it'll be a crime and the perpetrator will have to go to jail. But it has to be proved in court that the conversion really took place. It demands hiring an able lawyer. All the big lawyers are in big cities like Cuttack and Berhampore. Christians can hire any top lawyer, but we can't find any. Why? It is because Christians have money and we don't have it. If we get a good lawyer from Cuttack, we can teach the Christians a lesson. But how can we send the Christian priests to jail without the services of good lawyers? You people from Cuttack complain against our conversion, but you never care for us. You never help us with the resources.' After this, the Kui chief began to sob. Everyone consoled him and assured that everything will be better soon. Then, the Sangh delegation took leave of the vanvasis. But Shyam ji became more agitated than before. He knew that the blame lied in people like him.

A RAY OF HOPE IN THE FORM OF SWAMI LAKSHMANANDA SARASWATI

Shyam ji was wandering through Phulwani in search of a solution to the misery faced by the vanvasis. He had discovered the ailment, but the formula for the treatment was evading him. Yet, fate was on his side. He met Swami Lakshmanananda and he was filled with hope. He developed an urge to know more about Swami ji. Locals told Shyam ji that Swami ji was a popular saint in Odisha. Swami ji had spent a lot of time meditating in the Himalayas. While he was meditating, he was confronted with a question: what is the purpose of the meditation? Is it merely the attainment of salvation? Isn't it selfish? What have I done for the society where I have come from? The society is still downtrodden, uneducated, poor and helpless. He realised that true salvation lies in the service of society. The fervour to serve the society brought Swami ji from the Himalayas to Odisha. He established his ashram at Chakapad tehsil in Kandhamal district. This ashram was devoted to the welfare of the vanvasis.

Shyam ji was curious to visit Swami ji's ashram. He chose a day for this. He took some of his fellow volunteers and reached the ashram. (Those days, the ashram also ran a school and about 30-35 students were enrolled there.) It was winter. When Shyam ji and his colleagues reached the ashram, it was time for a meal. Shyam ji was surprised to learn that the meal time took four hours to be completed. When he inquired, he was told that the metal pot used for cooking food could only prepare meals for seven to eight people at a time. So, the food had to be cooked three to four times to cater to all eaters. There was no availability of a bigger pot that could prepare food for 25-30 people. Shyam ji's mind veered towards a solution to this problem. His younger brother ran a utensil factory in Kanpur. The factory manufactured all sorts of utensils—small, big and humongous sizes. Here, people were suffering because of the unavailability of a bigger pot. In fact, the people at the ashram were facing all sorts of problems. It was not how he had imagined the ashram to be. He spoke to people at the ashram and tried to understand the root of their problems and listened to their experiences. When evening fell, people started bracing for the evening tuition. The vanvasis would earn their livelihood in the day and would gather for study at night. Shyam ji was highly impressed by their devotion to education. However, he was shocked to see that only 10 people were studying and others were waiting for their turn patiently. When he probed once again, he was told that there was only one lantern and only 10 people could gather around it to study. Once they would finish their lessons, the second group of learners would sit in their place. Only one lantern for such enthusiastic learners! Shyam ji was heart-broken. He hadn't ever seen such poverty in life.

It was not over yet. After the shift-wise classroom ended, the shift-wise dinner ensued. After that, everybody dispersed to rest at night. Now, Shyam ji became curious about another thing: 'Let's find out how people sleep in the ashram hostel?' Shyam ji and his colleagues went on a tour of the hostel. They saw that students were sleeping on the floor of their rooms. There was no cot or mattress to sleep on. Moreover, the students merely had a loincloth to cover their private parts. Despite all this, no student seemed to be having any problems or was complaining. They were sleeping in peace. On the other hand, Shyam ji and his comrades had proper woollen clothes to protect them from cold. Shyam ji felt that the apathy of urban-dwellers towards these vanvasis was criminal. Vanvasis were enduring all types of hardships. Shyam ji thought that while these vanvasis were living without resources, people throng with offerings in dharamshalas in states like Uttar Pradesh. As the first step to help the vanvasis, he asked his brother in Kanpur to send the required utensils for the ashram kitchen. But it was certainly not enough. Shyam ji knew that the vanvasi society had an acute strength of patience. It only needed attention and care from those who could mould their lives for the better.

Thus, after knowing the vanvasi society from all angles, Shyam ji developed a deep-rooted love for it. He immersed himself in the love of vanvasis. The ashram of Swami ji became the first rendezvous of this passion. He had got a clear idea to work on the welfare of the vanvasis in the ashram. Now, the only thing that he had to do was to prepare a blueprint for this and devise ways to execute it. Shyam ji gradually became part of the night classes and other activities organised for the vanvasis. After years of working among the vanvasis, he realised that the pace of their development was not at par with their capabilities. There was so much to be done for this capable society of forest-dwellers.

VANVASIS ARE EDUCATING THEMSELVES FOR DHARMA

When Shyam ji, Swami Lakshmanananda ji and others were busy charting out ideas and implementing them for the welfare of the vanvasis, the government of the day also launched various programmes for them. The government was seriously planning to make every village in the forest areas literate. Every district was provided funds for the adult education scheme and district administrations actually worked for its success. Shyam ji was in Phulwani then. The District Magistrate there also took keen interest in the scheme and toured villages to see the results of its implementation. But he found that the adult education centres were non-functional. Only 'night classes' were being organised everywhere. He was stunned and curious to learn who was running the 'night classes'. He especially wanted to find out what was attracting the villagers to the 'night classes' and not the adult education centres. Do organisers of the night classes offer some enticements to the villagers? He asked an ordinary villager, 'Brother, who is running these night classes?' He replied, 'It's the Rashtriya Swayamsevak Sangh (RSS).' The DM asked, 'Who is their chief?' The villager replied, 'It's Shyam ji. He is a volunteer of the RSS.' The DM sent a message to Shyam ji, asking him for a meeting. Shyam ji agreed.

When the DM met Shyam ji, he asked, 'We are spending so much money on our adult education programme, but we are not able to attract villagers. How much money are you giving them that they are thronging your night classes?' Shyam ji replied, 'Sir, you will not be able to tolerate my answer. If you can bear to hear it, only then will I tell you.' The DM asked him to answer his query. Shyam ji told him, 'We are providing them money in the form of dharma (religion). You are incapable of communicating in the language of dharma. These people are not educating themselves for the sake of knowledge, but for dharma.' The DM was astonished and unable to fathom this response.

Shyam ji understood his discomfiture and explained, 'Imagine that your representative comes to the village and asks villagers to attend the adult education programme. The first thing the villagers will ask is "How will it benefit us?" That man will probably reply that the villagers will be educated and their and their children's future will be bright. They will become respectful people. On hearing this, the villagers will laugh and say that it's mostly the educated people who indulge in wrongdoings. We don't want to convert our kids into such educated people. Your representative agrees with them, yet he tells them that education will help them find jobs. The villagers will laugh more at this and say that there is a crowd of unemployed youths in the city. They ask your representative if their children study up to Class 10, will they work in the fields? The government representative says that such educated children will not work in the fields. They will start wearing pants and avoid going to the fields. So, the villagers tell him that the government education can neither make their children good men nor can it provide them jobs. They say that their only source of livelihood is agriculture and if the government education will keep their children away from agriculture, how will they feed their families? Why should villagers then send their children to the government education centres? On hearing this, your representative will be disappointed and turn towards some other village.'

The DM listened to Shyam ji with rapt attention and asked him, 'How do you convince villagers?' Shyam ji heaved a long sigh and then said, 'Listen, we had organised an ashtaprahri programme at Chakapad ashram some time back. In this programme, the statue of Lord Jagannath was brought from Jagannathpuri through transmigration of soul. Then, the Jagannath statue was taken from village to village on a chariot. As soon as the chariot would enter a village, all the villagers would descend to see it. Even those who had become Christians came to see the statue, felt blessed and proudly said that they were Hindus. Though it was not a re-conversion programme, thousands of people gathered for a glimpse of the statue. The fervour heightened so much that Swami ji began to blow the conch and it spelt magic on people. Whoever heard the sound of the conch became a Hindu. He also sprinkled water on people and whoever touched the water became a Hindu. After some time, this chariot had to stop, as it was economically unviable to take it to every village. Swami ji went to the rest of the villages himself. But as he entered the villages, people complained that why didn't Lord Jagannath come to their village? Swami ji cajoled the simple-hearted vanvasis that Lord Jagannath would soon visit their village and that he was tired after an arduous journey. 'He is resting now. But there is also a problem,' said Swami ji. The villagers asked him what was that? 'When we will bring Him, will you welcome Him?' asked Swami ji. The villagers replied, 'Why not? We will welcome him in a grand manner.' 'No, no. Lord Jagannath only wishes to hear Jagannath Bhagwat,' said Swami ji. The villagers then became downcast. They said that they were illiterate and could not recite the Jagannath Bhagwat. Swami ji told them that they should not lose heart. 'If you are not educated, you can at least educate your children,' he advised them. The villagers were now elated and said in a chorus: 'Yes, we will educate our children.' Shyam ji finished his story and looked at the DM who was immersed in his narration. He then addressed him, 'So now, you understand why these vanvasis are educating their children? It is because their children could read the Jagannath Bhagwat and welcome Lord Jagannath to their villages. They don't have the wherewithal to go to Puri and pay homage to Lord Jagannath there. They have developed a belief that if their children can recite the Jagannath Bhagwat, the Lord will be happy and grace their villages with His arrival.'

Shyam ji told the DM another soulful story of a village. 'See, how passion grips these villagers. I have also visited those villages where you have been. Once, I was visiting a night class in a village. I saw an old man sitting among the young students. One of his fingers was bandaged. He seemed injured, but he was attentively listening to the discourse of the teacher. I couldn't control my curiosity and asked the teacher why that old man was bandaged? My question unsettled that lady teacher. She looked somewhat perturbed. I thought I had communicated some abuse in my half-learnt Odia. One of my colleagues said that I should not ask any further questions. So, I said nothing more and retreated with my colleagues. However, my curiosity became more intense. As we exited the classroom, I asked my colleague, "Why should we not ask about that bandage? What's the matter?" He said that there was an emotional background story attached to it. When this village was told that Lord Jagannath would visit only those villages where people would recite the Jagannath Bhagwat, this old man was among those ultra-enthusiastic villagers who wished to learn to read to welcome Lord Jagannath. He was desperate to join night classes. Since he was very poor, he could not manage to buy slate and chalk to write. Even the class organisers couldn't manage to get these basic items. Hence, the teacher taught him to write on the floor using his finger. The continuous rubbing of the finger on the mud floor injured it and had to be bandaged.' Shyam ji then told the DM that they were not able to even buy a copy, slate and chalk for the villagers. Still, that fellow was hell bent on learning to read and write for the sake of Jagannath Katha. This is the appeal of dharma. This will turn vanvasis towards education.

This passion was the force behind Swami ji's endeavour to start the night classes for the vanvasis. Swami ji's efforts and Sangh's cooperation expanded this project. This formed the basis and a solid blueprint for the education of the vanvasi society. Now, Shyam ji's mind became busy in exploring other ways of vanvasi welfare.

In 1986 and 1987, two big vanvasi-centric conferences were organised in Odisha—in Chakpada and Mahendra Parvat. In 1989, on the proposal of Bhaurao ji, Madan Babu established the Ekal Vidyalaya. To expand this project, the name of Shyam ji was proposed and he finally became its charioteer. As a part of the plan to engage him in this task, Shyam ji was sent to Ranchi as the organisational secretary of the Vanvasi Kalyan Ashram. He was lodged in a room at Maheshwari Dharamshala. The family of Shree Gyan Prakash Jalan ji would send a tiffin of food for him. Shyam ji found it very difficult to plan ways to work for the welfare of the vanvasis as the Vanvasi Kalyan Ashram was in its primary stage then. He had once heard Bhaurao ji talking about a place called Lohardaga in 1971. Those days, Bhaurao ji would ask for Rs 1,000 to grace any marriage ceremony. It was his way of raising money for the activities of the Sangh. Even during the marriage of Shyam ji's younger brother, Bhaurao ji was offered Rs 2,000. Then, Shyam ji was puzzled: why did Bhaurao ji have to charge Rs 1,000 to gather money for his project in Lohardaga? He however left this question unanswered. Now, when he was in Ranchi, he was confronting the issue of collecting money for his work. To learn the basics of such a task, he learnt how to create a project at the office of Chartered Accountant and Sangh volunteer, Vinod Gaddhyan ji. But, the question of raising money was still troubling him.

He was dealing with all these issues, and then suddenly he met Sheshadri ji in a programme. When he was discussing this subject with Sheshadri ji, Madan Babu was also with him. After a session of brainstorming, they came to the conclusion that Kolkata-based Vanvasi Parishad must shoulder this responsibility.

One more interesting event took place during this time. A meeting of Sangh's full-timers was organised in Muzaffarpur, Bihar. Since there was nothing significant to do, all the workers decided to take part in the 'Let's Dream' competition. Everyone shared their dream. One dream caught everyone's fancy. It was about the budget of Vanavasi Kalyan Ashram, Jharkhand, being in crores of rupees. Everyone laughed at this dream. But Shyam ji took it very seriously and when a meeting of volunteers and citizens was organised in the evening, he said that he would raise crores of rupees for Kalyan Ashram in Jharkhand. After the meeting was over, everyone made fun of Shyam ji and said that dreams are not shared in public. But some unseen power was guiding Shyam ji and he was sure that one day, his dream would come true. However, those were very difficult days. The financial condition of almost all branches of the Sangh was in doldrums. Things had come to such a state that the meetings between the committee members and full-timers in Bengal would always end up in scuffles. The committee members would complain about collection of money and the regional secretary would demand honorariums to be distributed among members.

Despite these adverse circumstances, the project in Ranchi was launched. There was already a base there in the form of Vikas Bharti. When Shyam ji reached Ranchi, Vikas Bharti was in a crisis. But Bhaurao ji had given him the task to work in the midst of such crises. It was a tough test, but as workers from Kolkata started touring the vanvasi areas and Chitlangaya ji joined the project, things began to come on track. Chitlangaya ji's efforts brought focus to One Teacher School (OTS). The problem of money also improved with the Kolkata team working on this front. The Odisha model helped in increasing the number of volunteers for the project. This experiment was making a local vanvasi young man, Mahrang Oraon, the regional secretary of the organisation. Oraon's elevation encouraged other vanvasis to join the organisation and they came in hordes. Though the decision to make Oraon the regional secretary was met with sharp opposition within the organisation. Anyway, it's a separate story. Vinod Gaddhyan ji helped shift the ashram office in Old Commissionerate. Slowly, the project took wing. However, a bigger test was in the waiting.

□

3
Amazing Ekal

The Ekal Abhiyan has now completed 31 years. The age of 31 years is considered significant in any organisation's or individual's life. This is the age when family and society expect a young man to start earning after completing his education. The Ekal stands exactly at this point now. As a child turns into a grown up, his body takes a larger shape and his intellect finds new horizons. Shyam ji, the Ekal's charioteer, underwent a similar metamorphosis. When the Ekal schools were started, the only target was to make the vanvasi children literate. Gradually as the mission expanded, it was felt that an urban organisation must be formed to supervise this project and thus the Vanbandhu Parishad (Friends of Tribal Society) came into being. It took another 10 years to make this organisation effective and result-oriented. Its success was largely because of the active and colossal role played by Shyam ji and his team. This ensured that every plan or scheme would be tested in waters of rural hinterlands. No plan was formally launched unless it would be approved by the laboratory of rural experiments. This immensely effective working style was the strength of Shyam ji. He didn't let any plan be imposed from the top. Rather, he made it compulsory that workers from the bottom level should be engaged in the planning and execution. Hence, this project was slow and took many years to take proper shape. It however emerged as a grand success.

As this programme became national, it was thought that it must encompass adult education also. Only educating the children was not enough, it was also essential to educate their parents otherwise the education of children would remain incomplete. So, the education programme was altered to mould it in a way that could help both students and their parents gain sufficient education.

It developed new contours like Aarogya (Healing), Village Development and Jagran (Awakening). The awakening of rural folks was a Herculean task. Had working among villagers been an easy task, most of the government development programmes for villages would not have failed. Only one scheme like Aarogya Yojna (Healing Scheme) took four to five years for its experimentation alone. In 2005, the a Karyakarta Kumbh (a grand meeting of workers) was organised in Indore. In this meeting, the volunteers were taught the importance of swablamban (being self-sufficient). At this stage, Shyam ji was moving ahead with his mission but there was no clarity about the success of his mission. It was neither practical to expect the mission would be successful. The first step of this mission was that the team would have to win the hearts and confidence of villagers. And Shyam ji was sure that his team would be able to win over villagers after years of rigorous efforts. One interesting development took place in these crucial years. The government started taking keen interest in the education of rural children. Till now, only the Ekal team was educating rural/tribal children, but the government officials also became active on this front. In fact, the Ekal team started playing second fiddle to the government in certain areas where it was once leading. The number of children mandatorily enrolled in the Ekal schools dwindled and the number of voluntary students increased. Hence, the Ekal's role expanded from being only the educator of children to being educators of adults (named Gram Siksha) too. In simple terms, the Ekal became a leader not only in Bal Shiksha but also in Gram Shiksha. It was a very significant change in the life of rural people.

Now, with the panorama of the overall development of the villages visualised, the major hurdle was villagers' addiction to alcohol. Without finding a remedy for this problem, the whole education mission might prove to be futile. There was only one solution to this problem—Satsang or Sanskar Siksha (value-based education through religious gatherings). It was and is evident to the world now that the material education sans ethical education proves to be disastrous. The Ekal team turned to finding ways to amalgamate both of these educational methods in a balanced way so that they both could become complementary to each other.

THE IMPORTANCE OF ORGANISATIONAL STRUCTURE

Let's understand the background. The importance of structure in any organisation has as much significance as the veins and arteries in the human body. The way veins and arteries ensure the supply of blood to the heart and various other parts of the body, the structure of the organisation makes it functional. At the threshold of its beginning, the Ekal school had two aspects—first, the one started in Odisha as an experiment and named 'the night school'; and second, the one started by Madan Babu in Dhanbad, Jharkhand, aka the first experiment of the vanvasi vidyalaya. Later, they both merged to emerge as one Ekal Vidyalaya (One Teacher School). In Odisha, people were encouraged to revisit their religious roots and turn to education. There, the first school was established as a night classroom in Chakapad district. At that time, many villagers had questioned the very basis of being educated—why should we study? To address this query, Swami Lakshmanand ji suggested that Satsang (spiritual discourse or sacred gathering) should be organised to convince villagers about the importance of education. His logic was that since there had been a tradition of Satsang in those areas, they would be ready to listen to even educational discourse in such gatherings. Thus, villagers were told that if they wished to welcome Lord Jagannath in their villages, they would have to first learn to recite Jagannath Bhagwat. They were willing to learn to recite Jagannath Bhagwat for their love for Lord Jagannath. Therefore, villagers' faith in Lord Jagannath took them towards education. Here, the teachers didn't demand any remuneration, as faith was enough for both the teacher and students. But when the Ekal schools were opened in South Bihar (Jharkhand), religion did not provide sufficient inspiration and thus teachers had to be paid honoraria. It generated a need for regular funding.

Initially, Madan Babu took responsibility for collecting funds. Dr Rakesh Popli and Mahesh Sharma ji toured villages and shepherded youngsters to join the Ekal schools. They also trained these youths to run the Ekal schools. Since Madan Babu was a coal baron, he had a lot of influence in the area. So, even the children joined these schools along with youngsters. A huge amount was collected in the name of Madan Babu. The Ekal schools were officially established in 1989 with the formation of the Vanbandhu Parishad. Thereafter, the Ekal team worked on its organisational structure to run the mission successfully. It has been exactly 31 years since the Ekal began its journey. Then, its source of people was rural, while its source of money was urban. When Ekal stepped into the vanvasi villages, it focussed on generating empathy for vanvasis, educating them and taking care of their health. Ekal never wavered from its commitment and kept moving ahead. Its three pivots played their role in its journey—the urban organisation, rural organisation and associate workers. It was the joint efforts of these three pillars that earned Ekal international fame.

Today, Ekal has 7,000 fulltime workers and a vast network of its structural organisations. Though Ekal boasts of a mammoth organisational structure now, it didn't grow this big on its own. When its founders were contemplating ways to expand the organisation, they were puzzled with this question: how big should this organisation be? After long deliberations, it was decided that the organisation will be divided into two categories—first, a group of various workers to supervise the training of teachers and workers; second, the control and monitoring of the communication. At that time, senior members had marked those members as full-time workers who could spend a whole month travelling for the organisation's work. In this way, the worker could cover around 30 villages. So, a unit was formed for a group of 30 villages. This was the smallest unit of Ekal and its head was a full-time worker.

The unit head had to follow a rule that he would have to spend every night in a village. Step by step, Ekal made progress. Its area of influence broadened. The number of villages covered by Ekal began to increase. Now, the Ekal seniors felt that even units had to be put into groups so that there could be better coordination among them and all the units could be supervised. Three units were assembled into a consortium (sankul). As per this formula, the head of the consortium could monitor three units in a month. Then, the team discussed how many people could be trained by the training team in one exercise? After deliberating meticulously over this issue, the team found that a teacher should be trained for 10 days twice in a year. In this way, 18 training camps (varga) for nine units (sanch) were organised annually.

In the rainy season, it was impossible to work in the vanvasi areas. So, to ease things out, it was decided that a training team would handle

18 vargas. Hence, a group of nine sanch was called an anchal (zone). And then came divisions, sub-divisions, etc.

In the starting phase, most of the working system of the Ekal was only etched in the minds of its seniors. Only a few things were written down. When Ekal grew and its fame reached overseas shores like America, Indian-Americans became curious to know about its working methodology. Shyam ji took this responsibility on his shoulders and toured America to explain the working of Ekal to America-based Indians. He tried to answer every penetrating query of these people, but those oral explanations were not enough. It was now imperative to prepare a solid brochure and related literature for the introduction of the Ekal mission to people who were keen to know about it. Subsequently, Shyam ji compiled an English booklet titled *Ekal System* that explained all salient features about the organisation and its mission. Sometime later, he toured America. By then, the Ekal had acquired a full-fledged organisational form. So, the purpose of Shyam ji's tour was now to expand Ekal's wings in America. Shyam ji had also learnt that Americans seek to know everything in detail and once they understand the crux of things, they don't need to be explained anything further. On this tour, Shyam ji stayed in Bloomington near Chicago. There lived Chandak ji, who was the Sanghchalak of the Sangh. He invited Shyam ji to one of his programmes and asked him to broach the topic of the Ekal in front of the gathering. Shyam ji readily agreed, but Chandak ji shared with him that there was a hurdle. 'There is a gentleman here. He is very influential. He will not let the gathering take place unless he is convinced of its cause. He is very rational. He will throw his net of questions on you. Being a senior and regular member, his presence can't be denied either. So, you must be ready for an encounter with him. Are you ready?' Chandak ji forewarned Shyam ji. Shyam ji was perplexed. He didn't know whether Chandak ji was encouraging or intimidating him. Yet, he was determined. He told Chandak ji that he would come to the gathering and asked that he should give a copy of *Ekal System* to that gentleman.

Ultimately, the hour of the gathering arrived. Shyam ji gave a presentation about the Ekal. Then, the question-answer session ensued. The first person to raise his hand was the same gentleman. Chandak ji was terrified that he might mar the whole gathering by firing a salvo of 'unpleasant' questions. He was thinking about all of these things, when he suddenly heard the gentleman shooting his question at Shyam ji. His first question was: 'Are you Shyam ji?' 'Yes, I am,' Shyam ji replied. 'Are you the same Shyam Gupt whose name has been mentioned as a writer on *Ekal System*,' he asked. 'Yes, I am the same person,' Shyam ji politely replied. Then, that gentleman said very soulfully that whoever has generated the Ekal System is an extraordinary man. 'I have read this book several times and I have no question for that great man,' he said. Chandak ji heard this and started clapping like a child. The atmosphere of the gathering turned very friendly. Suddenly, that gentleman asked, 'Your system is wonderful, but please tell me how much is its practical workability?' Shyam ji replied without hesitation, 'It's 30%.' 'How did you achieve this 30%?' Shyam ji presented the complete framework before the audience. Shyam ji's sense of clarity and honesty about the practical success of the Ekal model impressed this gentleman and he announced in ecstasy: 'From now on, I will also work for the cause of the Ekal.' What impressed that gentleman the most was the plain honesty of Shyam ji about Ekal's practical success. Most fundraisers or missionaries boast about their projects and mix lies in their presentation. They claim that they have achieved their 100% target. But here was a missionary who accepted without any fear that his mission had tasted only 30% practical success. Such honesty won the hearts of everyone in the gathering and it heralded a new success for the Ekal.

The current organisational structure of the Ekal is registered as the Ekal Abhiyan Trust. It has three organs:

1. Nagar Sangathan (Urban Organisation)
2. Gram Sangathan (Rural Organisation)
3. Kendriya Karyakarini (Central Working Committee)

The board of the Ekal Abhiyan Trust formulates the policies for the functioning of the organisation. The representatives of all the registered organisations are the trustees of Ekal Abhiyan Trust. The Central Working Committee formulated by the Trust Board makes the action plans according to the policies. The Nagar Sangathan and Gram Sangathan are the two pillars of the Ekal and they are joined by one umbilical cord. If one is not functional, the other becomes inert automatically. If we analyse this relationship in simpler terms—the Gram Sangathan has united the villagers and has made them aware about their and their country's welfare; the Nagar Sangathan on the other hand has persuaded the bhadralok (elites) of cities to work for the welfare of the villages and thus contribute to the progress of the country. The Ekal mission has actually convinced people that the first ladder to the nation's development is the multi-faceted welfare of the vanvasi society—it's education, health and realisation of its full potential. This ambitious dream took shape in a tiny village in Jharkhand. Its initial and basic requirements were a teacher, space for a school, some basic stationery and other items. All these things required availability of funds. Therefore, the Ekal teams started fund-raising drives in cities by forming committees of urban elites.

THE ECONOMIC AND SOCIAL BASE OF THE ORGANISATION

In raising funds for Ekal, Shyam ji and Madan Babu were helped by their Sangh colleagues Mangilal Jain ji, Ashok Modi ji and Ramesh Saraogi. When Shyam ji approached people in Kolkata for funds, he was unable to make them believe that Ekal was running in faraway places like Vishnupur and Chakapad in Odisha. They in fact didn't believe that schools like Ekal were running in reality. Finally, Shyam ji proposed that some prosperous people from Kolkata must visit the vanvasi areas where the Ekal schools were established. So, a troupe of rich people like PD Chitlangaya ji, Ashok Modi ji, Ramesh Saraogi, Sajan Bansal, Sajjan Bhajanka and Manju Didi accompanied Shyam ji to vanvasi areas. Once they all themselves saw the functioning of the Ekal schools in extreme and adverse conditions in faraway vanvasi hinterlands, they readily agreed to donate towards the cause. Today, the same Ekal schools have travelled across borders to foreign lands. It had started as an idea in Kolkata long before.

The fund collection led to the establishment of the Nagar Sangathan in urban areas. This meant to organise the elites of cities to donate funds and inculcate discipline in the working of the Ekal. The urban people who are connected with Ekal are committed to provide all sorts of assistance to the mission. The Ekal team chose some influential and moneyed people from cities and made them a part of a committee that directed various economic and administrative activities. In big cities of each zone, chapters of the mission were opened to rope in rich and influential people. This method was and is called 'chapter working'. A renowned industrialist from Mumbai, Rameshwar Lal Kabra alias Bapu ji, played a key role in spreading these chapters in big cities of the country. The chapter works to collect funds for Ekal. The members of the chapter committee ensure that the collected funds are utilised for the functioning of Ekal properly. Each chapter has two wings—the first monitors the economic discipline; the second scans of the quality of the Ekal schools and Sanskar Kendra (meaning to verify that the collected funds are being used for the purpose they were collected for). To ensure transparency, each chapter works through a coordination committee formed for it in each zone. Presently, the Nagar Sangathan of the Ekal is active in 60 big cities of India. The Nagar Sangathan functions in eight forms (registered organisations). They are as following:

1. **Vanbandhu Parishad:** The Vanbandhu Parishad (Friends of the Tribal Society) runs the Ekal schools in all parts of the country, except North India.
2. **Bharat Lok Shiksha Parishad:** It operates Ekal schools in North India and oversees the Nagar Sangathan.
3. **Ekal Vidyalaya Foundation of India:** It manages the organisation of Ekal outside India.
4. **Shree Hari Satsang Samiti:** It focuses on the ethical side of the Ekal schools in villages and accordingly manages its own organisation in cities.
5. **Vanvasi Raksha Parivar Foundation:** It is one of the parts of the Shree Hari Satsang Samiti. It is headquartered in Delhi. The Nagar Sangathan of Delhi is known as the Vanvasi Raksha Parivar Foundation.
6. **Aarogya Foundation of India:** This foundation supervises the health projects in selected places of India and also runs its organisational structure.
7. **Ekal Gramotthan Foundation:** It directs projects undertaken as a part of the Gramotthan (village welfare) Yojna. It also operates various village resource centres. Its target is to help create conducive circumstances for the self-sustenance and welfare of villages.
8. **Ekal Sansthan:** The Ekal Institute connects mainstream Indian society with the Ekal mission. Besides, it works on research and innovations.

The second organ of the Ekal Abhiyan is the Gram Sangathan (rural organisation). This outfit creates a network of people in places where different languages are spoken. It connects them with the Ekal mission. It establishes a registered unit of the Ekal in rural areas so that villagers there can feel rooted to their religion and culture and be proud of them. It is ingrained in the functioning of the Ekal that it encourages local leadership and social participation. Anybody from India or abroad can donate for the Ekal but its rural committee consists of locals so that they can ensure the smooth and effective functioning of the Ekal schools. The rural committee selects even the teacher for the Ekal School. This committee also functions as the school's guardian council. Like parents, it watches over the students and teacher so that the teaching runs effectively. When a system works so meticulously, its success is guaranteed!

The Ekal system has converted the four-dimensional education into five-dimensional and the mission functions like a vast family, for it has made value-based and ethical education a mandatory part of its schools. The Shree Hari Satsang Samiti works in tandem with these schools to ensure that students and teachers are connected with their culture and values. This task was impossible without the support of the Satsang Samiti. For this purpose, the Ekal Abhiyan had to take the shape of Vanbandhu Abhiyan as well as many other organisations while working independently. The purpose of all of them was to ensure the achievement of the target set for the mission, despite their separate independent functioning. The interesting fact about these organisations is that their working style, economic dealings and the urban structure are completely independent, yet they complement each other. The synergy among them has reached a level that they celebrate the collective achievements of the mission and there is no sense of rivalry among them. Now, the Ekal doesn't merely focus on making villagers literate, it is also imparting skill training to them. The school children are taught skills of making organic fertilisers and clean water conservation. As the villagers' awareness has increased, Ekal has started to engage them with the Aarogya scheme and extra employment generation. Plus, Ekal also helps them understand schemes and programmes run by the government for their welfare and how to make them useful for their well-being. In simple words, Ekal has expanded from an education-centric mission to one that makes villages self-dependent. Now, the Ekal schools have become development centres that will help villages grow and walk into the future.

The quality of the Ekal schools is judged on two parameters:

1. **Regularity of the School:** There is only one way to ensure that the Ekal school runs regularly—the Gram Samiti (village committee) takes responsibility for its administration. This process is also called being swavlambi (being self-dependent). The gradual progress of this process is making the Ekal schools more self-dependent and ensuring they are being run regularly. As per the report of the Ekal Abhiyan office, around 85% Ekal schools are in category A and B. It means they are doing well. The Ekal believes that as the self-dependency increases, the Ekal schools will become more regular and successful.
2. **The Standard of Education:** The standard of education depends on the efficiency of the teacher. His/her efficiency is linked to the training at various levels—zonal, regional, unit and chapter wise. If the standard of the training is higher, the teacher will be equally efficient. Full-time Ekal workers are divided into two categories—first, the planning group and second, the training group. They have their separate tasks cut out for them. The planning group has to handle most of the administrative work and oversee the expansion of the mission. The training group is free of any administrative responsibility and it has to only adroitly impart training to teachers and make them completely skilled for their jobs. Even the workers at the central level have been divided according to their work. It has ensured that the standard of the training team directly affects the quality of teachers and finally the standard of education in Ekal schools. If trainers are effective, teachers will automatically be efficient. According to the Ekal Abhiyan office report, the trainers are 90% regular and dexterous in their job. So, this front is largely smooth-functioning. Since, there is a separation between the expansion team and the training team right from the unit level to central level, there is no possibility of overlapping of interests or any clash. In fact, like all successful coordinating teams, they assist one another.

The linking of the self-sufficiency of villages with expansion of the mission will only be fruitful and desired when the quality and regularity of the Ekal schools remain unaffected. When this equilibrium is maintained, then the mission naturally expands. Here, it should be made clear that the expansion of the Ekal is an external aspect of the mission, while the quality of its schools is its soul or internal aspect. They complement each other perfectly well. They both labour to achieve the same target—to keep the morale of the workers high. The expansion of the Ekal earned respect from a wide section of society and such recognition also keeps its workers motivated. It helps in improving the quality of schools. Thus, the expansion of the Ekal has so far only improved the quality of its schools.

In comparison to the Ekal, the government schemes for the villages have mostly flopped because even though they have requisite system and resources, they can't recruit motivated workforce that can understand the mentality of the rural society. Indian rural folks understand the language of devotion and faith. That is why the Satsang programmes were organised to gather them for moral education. When they started gathering and the Ekal began to expand, the villagers were taught the importance of discipline, as they would be deputed for various tasks of the Ekal. Thus, the Ekal, which started in the form of Satsang and rural education, is now a complete project of rural growth/development. As a part of this project, young men are encouraged to gather in groups and dedicatedly work for the welfare of the villages in their vicinity. Such groups of young men are called Ram Sadhak Toli and the social change they bring about is known as Ram Kaj (work of Sri Ram). The Ekal has overall formed eight sub-committees at village level for eight different tasks. Each sub-committee has seven workers. So, totally 56 young villagers are selected to run these eight sub-committees and commit themselves for the Ekal mission. The village sub-committee members also become associate members of the Gram Sangathan by donating some assistance money. The Gram Sangathan has to ensure that the villagers of every village have the onus of each village's development. The sub-committees of the village committee have been divided into eight categories according to the work assigned to each one of them. They are as following:

1. **Shiksha Samiti (Education Committee):** The foremost task of this panel is to supervise the teaching quality of teachers and the functioning of the Ekal schools. This committee also makes villagers aware of the Right to Information (RTI) Act and the rights it gives to

them so that they can seek any information about their schools and teachers. It proves to be a handy tool for smooth functioning of the school and monitoring of the teachers. This committee ensures that villages in the age group of 10-40 are properly educated.

2. **Aarogya Samiti (Healing Committee):** The speciality of this committee is that a woman heads it. She is called Aarogya Sevika (Health Worker) and she is efficiently trained by the Ekal team to take care of the health affairs of a village. She also makes sure that villagers observe health protocols. She carries a medicine box with her and distributes medicines to the needy. Besides, she has to gather women employed with various government schemes like Aasha, Aaganvadi and ANM for the weekly Satsang. In such gatherings, these women are encouraged to work towards making all government schemes successful.
3. **Vikas Samiti (Development Committee):** This committee draws the attention of villagers towards making and using organic fertilisers. They are also encouraged to devise ways for water conservation. This committee trains the students of the Ekal schools in making organic fertilisers from the very beginning.
4. **Jagran Samiti (Awareness Committee):** This committee is responsible for making the villagers aware of the RTI Act and its utility. Plus, the committee makes villagers aware of the various welfare schemes of the government like MNREGA, Old Age Pension, Public Distribution System and Mid-day meal. The committee also encourages villagers to plant more trees.
5. **Satsang Samiti (Satsang Committee):** This committee takes care of the weekly Satsang, the participation of people in it and the proper arrangement of training for the Satsang chief. This committee also has to ensure that people from all castes are taking part in the Satsang so that the harmony of the village is maintained.
6. **Mahila Samiti (Women Committee):** The committee has been basically formed to help villages become free of alcohol addiction.
7. **Yuva Samiti (Youth Committee):** The youth committee has been tasked with preventing external and internal exploitation of the villages.
8. **Sangathan Samiti (Organisation Committee):** The primary task of this committee is to keep a village united. In order to achieve this

target, three festivals—Ram Mahotsav, Krishna Janmashtami and the Annual Festival—are organised in the village. Besides, it has to inculcate habits of self-dependence among villagers and make them aware of their self-respect.

From 2005 onwards, Ekal had started focussing on self-dependence of villages. A target was set that four lakh villages should be ready with education, health, development, awareness and equipped with the values of the land so that they could become self-dependent. The day this target will be achieved, India will be a leading country of the world. This dream has filled full-time Ekal workers with renewed vigour and each one of them is taking care of five to seven Ekal schools so that villages become self-dependent as early as possible. This dream-filled task has been given the name of 'Gram Swabhiman Dayitva'. As a part of this pledged task, every committed worker will tour his/her adopted village and examine the functioning of the Ekal schools directly or indirectly. Then, they will go to every household in the village with members of the village committee to listen to villagers about the problems they are facing.

The third and most important part of Ekal is its Central Working Committee. It is itself divided into three parts.

1. Gram Sangathan Kendriya Samiti (Village Organisation Central Committee or GSKS)
2. Akhil Bharatiya Pratinidhi Mandal (All India Representative Board or ABPM)
3. Kendriya Yojna Kore (Central Yojna Core or CYC)

The Central Working Committee ensures that all rules and regulations of the mission are followed properly. This is the mind of the mission. It thinks and then makes decisions about the mission. The Central Yojna Core deals with workers and the programmes set for them. It assesses everything and then submits its proposals to the central committee of the village organisation. The village committee meticulously scans these proposals and then sends them back to the Central Working Committee that takes the final decision on them. Similarly, to assess and help with decisions to be made at the lower level of the organisation, a board of representatives is formed. The board has to ensure that the decisions taken by the Central Working Committee are implemented at all levels of the organisation. It also reviews these decisions on the implementation level and, if required, makes suitable improvements. In fact, such boards of representatives have been developed almost at all levels of the organisation. At the national level is Akhil Bhartiya Pratinidhi Mandal (All India Representative Board or ABPM), then come a number of Kendriya Karyakari Mandal (Central Working Board), Sambhag Karyakari Mandal (Divisional Officers Board), Bhaag Karyakari Mandal (Section Officers Board) and Anchal Karyakari Mandal (Zonal Working Board). All these boards have deserving office-bearers and volunteers. They merge into a group that supervises their working and ensures that the assigned project runs smoothly and is completed with success.

The top decision-making body in the Ekal organisation is the Central Working Committee. The lowest decision-making bodies are the Abhiyan Samitis (mission committees) that are formed by the CWC. These committees, hierarchically, are: Sambhag Abhiyan Samiti (Department Mission Committee), Bhag Abhiyan Samiti (Sub-Division Mission Committee), Anchal Abhiyan Samiti (Zonal Mission Committee) and Sanch Abhiyan Samiti (Cluster (or Unit) Mission Committee). The Abhiyan Samiti consists of volunteers from urban organisations, rural organisations as well as full-time volunteers. The coordination among these three types of committed workers helps in making concrete decisions and preparing a blueprint of their successful implementation. Each committee has the power to send its suggestions and proposals to its senior committee. Besides, the Abhiyan Samiti has following rights—they can take all decisions pertaining to the selection of workers, their promotion, laying out various tasks and ensuring that all decisions taken by the CWC are implemented. The senior members have granted decision-making powers to the committees so that volunteers on all levels feel empowered and trusted. The volunteers feel that the organisation believes in their capability to complete a project successfully.

In 2012, the working mechanism of the Ekal system was changed in an unprecedented way. Keeping in view the fact that Ekal might become a complex web of various committees, it was decided that there should be a single umbrella body that would oversee all organisations of the Ekal. Thus, a trust called Ekal Abhiyan Trust came into being. All the working Ekal units were linked to this trust. The CWC of this trust made various new Abhiyan Samitis and it was required that all the newly-formed committees will have to be reorganised every two years. It was also decided that these committees would have to shoulder the responsibility of controlling the working of the Ekal cadres who work under them. The Ekal has used words like Karyakarini and Samiti with a technical reason. Both words denote differences in the working of the committees. All the Ekal units at urban and rural level form their own working committees that aim to connect people from all strata of society with Ekal. Meanwhile, the committees formed by the Ekal Abhiyan Trust are limited in number and function as decision-making groups for various Ekal units. The committees formed at the zone, division and unit level basically perform following five functions:

1. To work as the communication bridge between the Centre and the village.
2. All the committees at all levels have to put in their signs at various projects assigned to them and the money allocated for them so that their responsibility is fixed.
3. To ensure the quality of the Ekal schools, the committee must have the requisite knowledge and arrange proper training for the teachers.
4. The committee has to itself follow economic discipline and make all units under it follow similar protocol. The committee will also ensure that the schoolteacher is paid on time and that units attached to the committee also keep checking the well-being of teacher's family in an amiable way. Besides, the committee has to encourage its workers to be self-dependent and create opportunities in the villages.
5. The key to upgrading the workability of a worker is his high morale. The best way to do this is to make any committee member Guardian (Abhibhavak) and seek his advice in the functioning of the committee.

Thus, the Ekal has the blessing of this land from the very beginning of its mission. The speciality of this mission is that it was not visualised and directed from the top. Rather, its style of functioning originated from the ground level. Whatever experiences were gathered while working in the villages went on to become the working mechanism of Ekal. The Ekal Abhiyan Trust formulates its policies and its Central Working Committee implements them through the rural organisation. The Ekal has an aura that automatically weaves magic, attracting students and villagers towards it. The government schemes for rural welfare lack such charisma. In 1990, the first booklet was written on the Ekal Abhiyan. This book had made it clear that the Ekal was devoted to provide genuine education to villagers/vanvasis and win their hearts by its efforts. It said that the Ekal would unite all the villagers to bring about change in their lives and uplift their standard of living. Once these villagers will be awakened in a true sense of the word, the country will be able to solve many of its problems that have been lingering only because of poor rural structure. The Ekal is exactly moving in this direction.

CHANGE THROUGH FIVE-FACED EDUCATION

The Ekal was conceived in 1989 in Tundi Block of Dhanbad district in Jharkhand. It was conceptualised by veteran Sangh leader Bhaurao Deoras ji. Deoras ji had discovered the pain of vanvasis after listening to their grievances: 'If you want to help us, save us from malaria and educate our vanvasi brethren.' The Ekal has made this grievance its guiding light and is walking on its path unwaveringly for the last 31 years as a 'five-faced mission'.

We are calling the Ekal 'five-faced' because it has five types of education:

1. Primary Education
2. Aarogya Shiksha (Healthcare education)
3. Vikas Shiksha (Development education)
4. Jagran Shiksha (Awareness program)
5. Sanskar Shiksha (Education of values and ethics)

The Ekal has reached around one-lakh villages with these programmes. Around 30 lakh vanvasi children have passed out of the Ekal schools and around 28 lakh students are currently enrolled in these schools. Around 35 lakh villagers are a part of various committees at rural level. Besides, around seven thousand vanvasi youth are working as fulltime volunteers.

Following are the results of the five-faced education being endowed by the Ekal Abhiyan.

1. Social Change Via Primary Education

The Ekal's educational programme has brought about meaningful change in society. Primary education has made entire villages literate. The ethical values taught in the Ekal schools have reformed the language and behaviour of the villagers. Now, even the animal-grazer child of a village can become a soldier in the Indian Army after attending the Ekal school. The Ekal school has in fact emerged as a model for rural development. Many of the Ekal pass-outs have either become part of rural committees or are working as teachers in the Ekal schools. Many of them have gone ahead and done various diploma programmes in colleges. Some of them have opted to pursue medical education. Some of them have earned fame as painters, while some of them have even become public representatives after taking part in elections. One of the Ekal students from Assam, Pinky Karmakar, has taken part in the Olympic torch relay. The most important aspect of the Ekal education is that all of its alumni carry a torch of patriotism within them. They love their country like fanatics. The Ekal alumni are also different from students of normal schools. They carry within them a special sense of identity.

Besides, the Ekal Schools also follow a self-dependence model and are connected to the local rural committee for their administration.

Completely Literate Village

There is a village called Bhadura in Aaklol Panchayat of Habibpur block in Malda district of West Bengal. This village is completely literate. This achievement can't be credited to any government scheme, but the Ekal Abhiyan. The Ekal opened its school here in 2001 when there were only two literate people in the village though the village boasted a population of around 300 people. The Ekal schools tried to make villagers aware of the benefits of being literate and counsel villagers very sympathetically. The Ekal's efforts fructified and now the whole village is literate and even old people in the village can read and write. Sushma Karmakar, the Ekal teacher, says that around 56 students of the Ekal school from the village have continued their studies further. Some of these notable students are Chandramohan Sarkar, Lalita Sarkar, Shyamlal Murmu and Vishwajit Burman who have successfully become graduates. Priya Karmakar, Pinki Rai, Sanjeev Kumar, Santosh Burman, Sukurti Adhikari, Ruby Burman and Nandita Rai have passed their high school exams. The villagers in Bhadura call their literacy as their new eyes. They say had they not become literate, they would remain blind. They say that now every family in the village has gained its eyesight.

2. Social Change via Healthcare Programme

The Healthcare Programme intends to make sure that no villagers fall ill. The health of the village is the foremost concern of the programme. The programme has run awareness drives to make every villager conscious of their health. Every household in the village has been encouraged to keep a 'nutrition nursery' (Poshan Vatika). The concept is to make villagers aware of what is dangerous and beneficial to their health. Every house has been encouraged to build a soak pit or leech pit in their lawns. Soak pit is a deep pit to retain the wastewater and is gradually soaked by the earth. Thus, they don't allow colonies of mosquitoes and bacteria to flourish. This method is very effective to prevent cases of malaria and diarrhoea in villages. Similarly, the Ekal team has run a drive to make villagers fight anaemia, which is mostly prevalent among women. The cases of anaemia have come down drastically after the efforts of Ekal. Not only anaemia, many other diseases have been treated by adopting home-developed methods in a similar fashion. Ekal has organised cleanliness drives and built public toilets to keep villages disease-free. Prabhavati Devi, an Aarogya Sevika (health worker) from Ramgarh district in Jharkhand, shares her experience of working with the drive for anaemia amelioration. She says that two such campaigns were organised in Gola block in Ramgarh district and Bhandara block in Lohardaga district. 'Initially, villagers were provided iron tablets and pesticides to help them fight anaemia. But this method can't run for long because of hazards attached to it. So, we thought of a plan to permanently fight this blood deficiency in villagers and for this, we started providing natural medicines and some domestic treatments. For this purpose, experienced doctors and natural medicine practitioners organised a two-day workshop titled Gram Aarogya Sanyojika for 60 villages in the vicinity of Ranchi. In this workshop, health workers were trained about various effective ways to help villagers stay healthy and combat diseases. They were taught to identify medicinal plants and prepare medicines with them. The trained health workers then returned to their respective villages and started making natural medicines and treating villagers with them. The Aarogya Initiative thus continued its various awareness and training programmes in other villages as well. As a result of this rigorous campaign, villagers were able to treat chronic diseases like haemorrhoids or piles, influenza, body ache, injuries and leucorrhoea. Villagers feel relieved after getting such diseases treated at home because the normal allopathic treatment is very costly for them,' Prabhavati Devi says, feeling extremely content. Today, she is working as a proud health worker in Ramgarh zone. When she takes a round of the village, villagers fondly call her 'domestic doctor'.

3. The Growth of Developmental Education at Its Peak

The developmental education endowed by the Ekal schools has made villagers become self-dependent. The branches of Shram Anand Shiksha Niketan (Centres of Joyful Labour Learning) in Jharkhand have trained village children in various labour works. Women of the villages have been taught to sew clothes and now they prepare their own clothes. The method has been developed to do organic farming even on barren land. One example of incredible village development is from village Jharmunda in Sundargarh district of Odisha. Here, a farmer, Ramlal Behla owned merely one acre of land. He could barely manage to grow grains sufficient for his family. Despite hard work every year, his family would suffer due to lack of grains and vegetables. But as the Ekal started its Gramotthan Yojna (Village Development Scheme), his fortunes overturned. Now, he is an entrepreneur farmer. In 2012, Ekal workers from the Jarangloi unit came to meet him. They advised him to start organic farming on his one acre of farming land. They helped with laying down an organic bed and gave him saplings of guava, mangoes, papaya and other fruits. These workers keep travelling to his village to keep his morale high and monitor how his field was flourishing with new plants. When fruits and vegetables were prepared, Ramlal sold them in the nearby mandi (bazaar). Not only his own family was able to consume organic food now, he himself became a successful organic farmer.

4. Jagran Shiksha Awakened Villagers

Eshwar Kishan Mohule is a poor young man from Nanded district of Vidharbha region in Maharashtra. The story of his struggle is quite surprising. He somehow managed to study till Class 12, but did not study further as the nearest college was 40 km away from his village. He came into contact with the Ekal mission in 2005. He became an Ekal teacher and taught in the Ekal schools for years. The Ekal trained him in RTI and general awareness for the masses. He shares his experience of prevailing corruption and his own awareness regarding it. 'In our village, the public distribution agent distributed only 25 kg ration instead of allotted 35 kg. When I objected, the distribution agent tried to get my name removed from the ration register. Besides, we villagers were forced to buy ration at the rate of Rs 20/kg even though it was officially earmarked Rs 2/kg. We had no other way but to endure this dishonesty as starvation stared everyone in the face. But, when I joined the Ekal and I was empowered to avail information benefits under RTI, I wrote an application in this regard to the tehsildar. However, it proved to be futile. Then, I filed an RTI with the Sub Divisional Officer (SDO). It worked and my ration supply was restored. Still, I was not given my ration card. So, I started a fast unto death and ended it only after the District Collector gave his assurance. Anyway, nothing happened in my favour. Ultimately, I registered my complaint with the Maharashtra Lokayukta (State Ombudsman) office and I was given back my ration card in 2013. This victory increased my confidence and I realised the power of the RTI. Then, I joined the Ekal team in making villagers aware of the RTI's benefits and we were able to help villagers sort out many of their problems this way. One such case was that of a villager who was struggling to get 7/12 part of his land allotted under his name. When we sought information regarding this from the related revenue officer, he accepted his fault and ordered the registration of 7/12 part land in that villager's name. Similarly, we managed to sort problems of many villagers by using the RTI,' he said, giving enough insight into the empowerment of the awakened villagers.

5. Sanskar Shiksha Restored Glory of Indian Culture

One of the most notable changes that the Ekal Abhiyan has brought in the society is sanskar or values to keep Indian culture free of blemishes. Its result can obviously be seen in society. Two major sources of this value-based education are the Satsangs (gatherings) and Rath Yatra (chariot procession). As part of these two events, trained village storytellers (kathakaars) share stories from religious epics to instil appreciation of ethics in the villagers. Satsangs are organised to encourage villagers to adopt sanskars in their lives and shun mal practices like addiction to alcohol. The Hari Mandir Rath Darshan Yojna organises chalchitra darshan (kaleidoscopic tour) of religious places. The Ekal-run Satsang Kendra has emerged as a classroom for villagers. These efforts are bringing constructive changes in villages. Villagers have freed themselves of alcohol addiction after attending Satsang moral classes. The value-based education has also made them socially responsible. Priti Ghimal Mansari, a Vyas storyteller, says about the complete alcohol de-addiction in her village that before the arrival of Ekal, every man and woman used to drink in her village. Whenever they would hear about Shree Hari Satsang Samiti, they would doubt them to be political workers. 'So, it was very difficult initially to convince villagers about the evils of drinking. Then, one of the village youths, Tulsibhai, was sent for Satsang training. After getting proper training, he returned to the village and started Satsang assemblies. However, not many villagers turned up for his gatherings. So, as an alternative, a Satsang Sanskar Kendra was started for children. Slowly, around 40 children became regular visitors at this centre. Seeing the interest of people, Ekal started its Satsang programme in the village. The Hari Katha Satsang cast such a spell on villagers that all of them stopped drinking liquor. Masari village was now a changed place. It had acquired culture. It even started attracting villagers from nearby villages and soon various kinds of constructive social changes were witnessed in the region,' she narrates her experience of the impact of Ekal in Sikkim. Similarly, one more Vyas storyteller, Sri Ram Aasre Das, shares his experience of change in villagers' attitude after listening to moral stories in the Satsang. 'Villagers in Dharampur Retia village came to tears often whenever they heard the story of Ram and Kevat. I was stunned to see their emotions. They got so overwhelmed after hearing the story that they started calling themselves children of Ram and Kevat,' says Das.

One of the most pivotal aspects of the Ekal Abhiyan is that it has given roots to constructive social change in Indian society, especially in its rural hinterlands. The pain of the old vanvasi who had encountered Bhaurao Deoras ji has found its purposeful remedy in the form of education, health, village development, government facilities, protection and enhancement of cultural and religious values. Such a fruitful culmination is the result of Deoras ji's divine insight that manifested itself in the form of Ekal schools.

□

4
Expansion Through Self-dependence

Ekal is functioning in such a way that only complete dedication on the part of its volunteers can deliver desired results. So, the Ekal seniors have carefully thought about how an ideal Ekal volunteer should be. They have come to the conclusion that an Ekal volunteer should be like a soldier, alert and disciplined. Only then will he understand the demands of the mission and will be able to work on war footing. Then, they ruminated over the formation of the society that they wanted to construct. Now, the question before them was: What sort of society will be able to effect the desired changes? For building such a society, its basic unit—a man—has to be self-respecting. Only a self-respecting man, self-respecting caste and self-respecting society may dare to dream about social change and work towards realising this dream. The source of self-respect is self-dependence or self-sufficiency. If someone is not self-sufficient, he or she can't be self-respecting. And if someone is not self-respecting, he or she can't bring about epochal social change. Therefore, social change is the prerogative of a man who nurtures self-respect and has the willpower to shake the status quo.

SELF-SUFFICIENT FULL-TIME VOLUNTEER

To introduce self-sufficiency among its cadres, the Ekal decided to make its full-time volunteers self-sufficient as an experiment. Generating self-sufficiency in volunteers was imperative to prepare them to mould the society into a self-sufficient unit. For this purpose, Ekal launched a movement called Anudaan Parv (Donors' Cultivation). It ran for about three years. Then, the Udyoga Parv (Celebration of Efforts) took place for another three years. Both of them then merged to turn into another phase called Aashirvaad Parv (Blessing of Supporters). Some prosperous families of Delhi, Mumbai and Kolkata helped in organising finance-gathering events but Ekal ensured that such assistance should be within limits so that it doesn't lead to continuous dependence on outside sources for existence. The easily available money could nip the efforts for self-sufficiency in the bud and mar the substantive brilliance of the Ekal mission. Keeping these fears in mind, Ekal announced that it would become self-reliant in every sense of the word. None of its units would depend on outside support and the mission to complete self-dependence would be achieved as soon as possible.

Here, it is also noteworthy that only those Ekal volunteers who demonstrated genuine dedication for their mission were trusted and supported by the society. And this rule will continue to apply in future as well. This is also the mantra for the self-sufficiency movement. It was also found that only those Ekal teachers and volunteers who were genuinely devoted to the mission could carry forward the mantle. Others, who only dabbled with the mission as if it was a part-time enterprise, slowly parted ways with the mission. Even the society didn't lend any support to such non-serious volunteers. Actually, the swablamban sangrah (exercise to become self-sufficient) is a test of Ekal before society, which is another form of Parmatma (God). Only a rare and devoted taskmaster can come through this test with flying colours.

What is self-sufficiency or self-dependence? How is it achieved? This picture should be crystal clear before any Ekal volunteer who wants to be a part of this endeavour. In simple terms, self-dependence indicates that a village should muster all resources on its own for every entrepreneurship it wishes to perform. The village should formulate a budget for the planned task and then collect resources for its execution. All the fulltime volunteers deputed in the village must be able to bear expenses of their budget from their own efforts. The budget of an Ekal unit must be borne by the Ekal committee. This scheme has three easy parts. First is the budget of the Ekal School in the village. What is it and how much does it run into? It is the remuneration for the teacher, study material and necessary items for the school. It overall becomes Rs 12,000 per year. This money has to be raised through donations from the village itself. Three ways were invented for this collection. First, donations will be collected from the family of the student enrolled in the Ekal School. There was a purpose behind this collection. The Ekal detests charitable donations. It considers them sweet poison. Such donation generates the evil practice of bhiksha (begging) in our society. Even a mother suckles her child for only a certain period of time and then she teaches him to walk on his own. No mother wants her child to get addicted to her lap. Similarly, the Ekal survived on outside help for some initial years, but it didn't allow itself to become a government school that thrives on government crumbs. The government is a heartless system. The government school merely teaches children (whichever actually does so). On the other hand, the Ekal school shapes the personalities of its students. It teaches them values along with education. Thus, Ekal sought the participation of the children's parents in the Ekal mission so that they could also be aware of and avail the facility of education.

Ekal wants every parent to realise that the way they make efforts to feed their children, they must educate them in the same way. No self-respecting parent wishes to beg for feeding his or her child. So, when they are not ready to beg for food, why should they allow their children to study on begged money?

Ekal floundered in coming up with a self-reliance model for its schools. It had sowed some confusion in the minds of villagers how the school would run. It took more than required time to make its schools donation-free and convince parents for this to become active participants. It should have been Ekal's foremost goal as this is the link to the world of education and teachers. In fact, the Ekal in itself is a true teacher.

FROM EKAL SCHOOL TO A SCHOOL FOR THE ENTIRE VILLAGE

The second stage of self-dependence is the mushti bhiksha (fistful of begging). This step was designed to make every household realise that they were contributing for the education of their children. So, parents were encouraged to separate a fistful of food grain or its worth of money before every meal for the education of their children. Such contributions were intended to allocate ownership of the Ekal school throughout the village. The Ekal school would become a school run by the village itself.

The third and last stage of self-dependence is anna sangrah (collection of food grains). It was decided that whenever it would be harvest time in the village, the students would accompany their teacher and beg at every doorstep in the village. They would tell every villager that the school belonged to them and that they had to take care of its economy. Once, someone told Shyam ji that the villagers or tribals were too poor to contribute to the cause of the school. He took a grave offence and retorted, 'I have been working among the tribals for the past 30 years. I feel pity on those who call them poor. Only those who shirk their duties towards them would call them poor. I have met some teachers who would utter, "Arrey, these people are so poor. How can they manage to donate even a small sum? They won't be able to cough up even Rs 5." I immediately realised that the man speaking these words is dishonest with his work and has no dedication for the mission. The tribal society may be poor materially, but their hearts will outsize even those of tycoons living in big cities. It is true that they will not be able to donate Rs 1,000-2,000. But to assume that they will not give even Rs 5 is an insult. You only have to approach them and make them understand your mission and the advantage of education for their children. They will at once open their hearts and shell out whatever they can. They in fact donate for every activity organised in the village. You only have to win their confidence.'

The Aarogya Yojna (Health Scheme) run by the Ekal is based on self-dependence. The Ekal charges a nominal fee for the medicines distributed to the villagers. It is called registration fee. There is a psychology behind this experiment. It has been observed that when patients pay for their medicine, only then they feel cured. If they do not have to pay for the medicine, they feel they are not being treated properly. So, we have seen that some doctors only sell water in the name of medicines, yet their patients get well. Ekal is not in favour of distributing water or fake medicine, it only wants patients to pay something, even if it is a nominal amount so that patients feel responsible and relieved. That is why it started charging registration fees at its rural clinics.

SELF-DEPENDENCE IN SHREE HARI KATHA (LISTENING TO HARI'S STORY)

Organising Shree Hari Katha generates self-dependence in three ways. In every katha and satsang, the money is to be collected with the ritual of aarti. In every block, a mangal anusthan (a special ritual) is organised in a family and the money collected in this programme is deposited in the coffers of the Ekal to make it self-dependent. Another important factor of this self-dependence are the fulltime volunteers of Ekal. The more the Ekal volunteers have self-confidence, the more they will have self-respect. Ekal decided that the full-time worker would contact urban families for collection on three days in a month. Every worker will make a city his centre and visit families there for 10 hours a day. He has to perform three fundamental tasks—to select a family and explain to them the Ekal mission in detail; second, he has to show them the video presentation about the Ekal mission; and third, he has to request them to cooperate in making the Ekal mission self-dependent.

There is an anecdote in the Upanishada (Hindu sacred text written in Sanskrit). A devotee is praying to his Lord, 'Oh Lord, you have given me this life. Make me capable enough so that I can return to this world more than what you have endowed me with.' What a wonderful devotee he is! He does not want to depart this world being indebted to God. He seeks to return back to this world in whichever way he can. The Ekal wants and inculcates this spirit in its workers. The full-time workers get a limited remuneration for their travel, lodging and food during their tours to various cities and they wish to return with numerous times more for their organisation. This is the resolve of the full-time volunteers of the Ekal. This process is yet to get its desired results as some weak-resolved volunteers have joined the Ekal and are slowing down its progress. Unless a full-time volunteer will undergo this process of collecting resources for the Ekal's self-reliance, they will not turn into its time-tested pillars.

On the process of self-dependence, Shyam ji says, 'Volunteers must zero in on their centres (cities) from today itself. Their sole target should be that they would collect more than their travel expenses. This test will determine who is a true full-time volunteer.' Full-time volunteers are not allowed to raise funds directly. They, however, can invigorate the local committees in their zones and raise money through them.

COMMITTEES SHOULD ALSO BE SELF-DEPENDENT

The Ekal believes that it is not enough that only full-time volunteers should take initiatives for self-dependence, the various committees of the organisation must also share this responsibility. The Ekal volunteers must work with such zeal that they should contact every household and convince them to assist their mission. Every household must contribute something for their self-dependence. Their contacts should include even children and women. The Ekal today spends around two rupees on a child every day in various ways—the Ekal school, health clinics and village development. Thus, the Ekal volunteers have to convince donating families that every child in their household must receive a donation of two rupees daily or twice in the donation box. It means he or she will donate 500-700 rupees in a year. For this purpose, the Ekal volunteers have to keep donation boxes in every household. This is a guaranteed way of ensuring self-dependence for the Ekal.

The volunteer has to decide how much will be donated and how the committee members will collect the donations at the unit and block level. It was decided for the Aarogya Yojna that every doctor would charge a registration fee for the medicines he would provide to the village patients. The committee members screen the functioning of the volunteers who collect donations at the city or town level. They have to ensure that the collection programme is run error-free and the workers are encouraged to redeem their lapses.

Similarly, the Ekal decided on the following steps for the kathakaar yojna (preaching scheme):

1. Organising a ritual for the welfare of the family
2. Organising a ritual for the welfare of the village
3. Aarti Sangrah (ritualistic collection of offerings)
4. Organising a gathering of preaching (Satsang)
5. Welfare of the family of the preacher (Kathakaar)

It is a comprehensive exercise for self-dependence. As a part of this, regular satsang (gathering) is organised. The volunteer would have to select a family to organise a special gathering at their place once a week. They are properly trained to manage this task. The preacher organises a religious festival for the welfare of the village and collect donations for the Ekal's self-dependence. Likewise, the offerings of every satsang and preaching session will go to the Ekal's funds.

Every village will be encouraged to make a family 'bhagwat parivaar'. This family will connect all the households for dissemination of religious teachings. Both men and women preachers will be invited for this purpose. Groups will be formed to collect money in such gatherings. So, the way the Ekal school has its seva parivaar (serving family), the kathakaar samuh (preachers' group) has its serving family. The preacher is adopted by a family as its son or daughter at the Anchal Samiti level. And this family will have to invite the preacher once or twice a year for the Bhagwat Katha (religious preaching via story-telling). This Katha session will last three or seven days. The said family will have to invite its relatives and friends as per its capacity to this Bhagwat Katha and collect offerings from them for the Ekal's self-dependence.

When all these steps were counted and the estimated collection was measured, it was found that every preacher could collect around 20,000-25,000 rupees in a year. One preacher is connected to almost 20 satsangs. If we count the collection of all these satsangs, the Kathakaar Yojna (Preaching Scheme) of the Ekal becomes fully self-dependent.

Some of these preachers should be trained in an advance course and sent to mega cities like Delhi, Mumbai, Kolkata, etc. The Ekal seniors know that people mostly hear stories of Ram and Krishna from those who have never experienced life of forests like Ram did and who have never traversed the length and width of forests as Krishna did. Now, those people should be selected as preachers who have toiled in forests and lived among forest-dwellers. The Ekal has to tell Indians that they are not renowned preachers of the country, but they come directly from those lands where Lord Ram and Krishna lived and performed many of their divine antics. These preachers are rooted to the land. In this way, the stories narrated by these preachers will sound more realistic and powerful. Besides, it will generate collections for the Ekal's self-dependence project. Plus, we know that famous sants and mahatmas (saints and great souls) will demur touring far-flung villages as they are used to luxurious city settings. Only these working, toiling and trained preachers will go to the interiors of villages and so, we must popularise them as modern religious preachers (Real Kathakaars).

Once Shyam ji went to the house of a worker and met his 80-year-old grandmother. He sought her blessings and asked her permission to allow her grandson to devote his life for the Ekal and the service of Hinduism. She didn't flinch a bit and pleasantly said to Shyam ji, 'Beta, what can be more satisfying to me than this? I will pray to the Lord that my grandson devotes all his life for this noble mission.' While other members of the family were making preparations for this young man's marriage, his old grandmother was asking him to devote life in the service of the religion. How blessed the Hindu society is! It is its good fortune that it didn't allow the whole of its mass to study in the modern schools and colleges. While the modern-educated people of Hindu society are serving only their self-interests, its old women are sacrificing their young ones at the altar of religion. This is the strength of this country! We only need to promote and establish the prestige of such devoted young men and women.

Recently, the area of development has caught everyone's fancy. This is the development of villages or Gram Vikas. As a civilisation, we call our land our mother and believe that it showers its blessings on us. In fact, we revere three mothers—Dharti Maa, Gau Ma and Ganga Ma (Mother Land, Mother Cow and Mother Ganga). The progeny of Dharti Maa are earthworms. The fecal matter of Gau Maa is its gobar. Both are used in making bio-fertilisers. The village development has rubbed off some of its colour on the Ekal as well and has shown it a new way of making its schools self-dependent. Every fulltime member and his family have been trained in making bio-fertilisers. This training will also be imparted to the Ekal school teachers, helpers and common villagers. This way, those who will be part of the village development committee will increase their income through village development programmes like making bio-fertilisers. They will have to submit 10% of their income to the village fund. Besides, a cow will be made available for every household. If they already have Gau Ma, then well and good. Gau Ma will help every family generate income by producing gobar, mutra (urine) and milk. Only gobar and mutra can help a family earn around Rs 5,000 per month. The Ekal found this out after a successful experiment. Even the Ekal students, who are in the age group of 10-12, can take out some time to make bio-fertiliser and cow urine syrup. It will help them earn some easy bucks to support their future education. This way, we will be able to generate our own treasury in villages. Why should then we need financial support from outside? Both the Ekal's school and dispensary will run on its own-generated money. This is the desired swablamban (self-dependence or self-sufficiency or self-reliance). It will make Indian villages self-dependent.

SWAVLAMBAN SE SWABHIMAAN

Unless the Ekal schools are made self-dependent, the self-respect of the brave castes associated with them will remain dormant. Their cumulative strength will remain unused. Hence, Ekal has kickstarted a movement through its schools to energise such castes that are born to become the Lord's army. However, their self-respect will rejuvenate only after they become self-dependent. Just imagine a village school. It has 30 students. Now, imagine a father who feeds his son but begs for his education. Can this father walk with self-respect? Even when the school, its students, teachers will be funded by donations collected from overseas shores, will this set-up produce self-respect? Therefore, Ekal launched a mission to convince villagers that their purpose was not to merely establish and run a school for their children. Rather, to enable villagers to run this school from their own collected resources. The parents of the school children have to understand the importance of the education and treat the school as a holy place that demands their complete attention. It is a temple for village development. Its Lord is education.

Earlier, whenever the villagers would hear the name of a school, the prototype of a government village school would emerge in their mind. The Ekal changed their mental landscape. It successfully instilled in their minds that the Ekal is not merely a school, it is in fact an institution for multi-faceted development of the village and villagers. Now, when villagers are asked to name a school that imparts one education to a child and four educations to his parents, the villagers promptly name the Ekal school. The Ekal provides primary education to its enrolled student, but for his parents, the Ekal organises health education, development education, awareness education and value education. So, this is not a mere school, it's the abode of the goddess of learning. It's a temple. When all the villagers realise that a temple of education exists among them and they are supporting a religious cause, they will not accept a single penny from outside to run this temple.

THE PATH TO MULTI-DIMENSIONAL DEVELOPMENT OF A VILLAGE

The Ekal Abhiyan envisages the multi-dimensional development of a village. It imparts two types of education—one is imparted to the students and the other to the villagers. There are four dimensions of education for villagers. A three-hour weekly satsang and classroom are organised for them. The satsang in-charge takes care of the satsang. Any properly educated person of the village takes command of the weekly classroom. He is tasked to explain the working of the Ekal school and its benefits for the village. This person also functions as Gram Pramukh (in-charge of the village). One woman of the village is made Aarogya Pramukh (health in-charge). She discusses issues related to the health of villagers and provides easy tips to them to stay healthy. One young farmer of the village is made Vikas Pramukh (in-charge of farmers). He delineates topics related to the development of villages and various agricultural issues. One young man of the village is given the responsibility of an awareness campaign in the village. He makes villages aware of various general topics whose knowledge is essential to them. All these in-charges for various tasks are members of the Ekal's village committee. All of them are trained by schoolteachers as they themselves undergo rigorous training for such tasks at their training stage. Like the head of the Ekal school is its teacher, the head of weekly satsang and classroom is the head of the village committee.

STUDY MATERIAL

The quality of the study material is proportionately equal to the quality of the school. The Ekal school has three types of study material—compulsory material, extra material and local material. The compulsory material is itself of three types—school material, teacher material and student material. All these materials are of four types individually. Thus, they make up 12 types of materials collectively.

1. School Material: Nameplate, blackboard, picture of goddess Saraswati, number and alphabet charts
2. Teacher Material: Teacher's diary, his prospectus, students' attendance register and material for extra-curricular activities
3. Student Material: Slate, copy, language book and maths book

RESPONSIBILITY OF VILLAGE SELF-RESPECT

To maintain and enhance the quality of the Ekal schools, a new plan was devised in Nadiad city of Gujarat. This plan was named—Gram Swabhiman Dayitva (Responsibility of Village's Self-respect). To implement this scheme, a full-time worker was made in-charge of five village schools and it was mandatory for him to spend a day and a night every month in all of these five villages. This responsibility of five villages was additional to other duties of every full-time worker. So, they toured villages, taught in Ekal schools or helped in teaching exercises, organised a meeting of the village committee and they themselves prepared the health box of the schoolteacher. They also ensured the regular organisation of weekly satsang and classroom. They also enquired whether every village has four organisational committees and four service committees. Besides, the most important task of these full-time workers was to knock at every door of the village with the schoolteacher and collect donations for self-dependence mission of the Ekal. This full-time volunteer has thus had to enliven a sense of self-respect in every villager. The Ekal believes that the planning and ideas of the Central Team should reach every village. Now, who will be the carrier for this? Till now, the schoolteacher used to shoulder this responsibility, but given the possibility of his sudden transfer to other places, the onus shifted to the full-time volunteer. An Ekal anchal has 270 schools and 54 full-time volunteers (52 of them are connected with Ekal and value education; 2 are appointed as part of the regional group). These volunteers have to attend monthly and weekly meetings. They receive direct instructions from the top body of the Ekal. Then, they transmit these instructions to members at the village level. This mechanism has worked and now the Ekal has started talking about 'results' because of its success. However, the 'results' can't be achieved by Ekal teachers alone. These workers have to pitch in to achieve that target. The biggest 'result' of the teachers working in tandem with these volunteers is swablamban (self-dependence).

It was earlier believed that a unit, group or collection committee would fill the coffers of the Ekal more. Later, it was found that the collection would be more in villages. This is because villagers are more emotionally attached to village schools and want to educate their children with more passion. The allocated or required amount for a village school is Rs 22,000. Its 60% is 13,200 and this amount is set as the target for self-dependence of the village. Around Rs 12,000 are collected from the villagers. Remaining Rs 1,200 come from the unit, group and the collection committee or village committee. From experience, it has been found that the target is easy to achieve in a village, while the collection committee struggles to amass the required amount in urban areas. Since children of villagers attend the Ekal schools, they donate generously for the cause. The similar attachment is missing in the urban folks. But the question was when should the collection in the villages be held? It was decided that when a full-time volunteer would visit the village, the collection exercise would be launched.

How does the material reach from the Ekal Anudan Kendra (Handout Centre) to the village? The process is that the material and money is sent to the regional centre from the Anudan Kendra. From there, it reaches the unit centre and ultimately the designated village school. Two Ekal volunteers oversee this process—regional representative and the in-charge for the working area.

ECONOMIC SYSTEM OF THE EKAL

According to the economic system of the Ekal, no financial transaction should be conducted by the full-time volunteer. No fulltime volunteer will debit money from the bank. He will not be part of the distribution of money. In short, a fulltime volunteer will not indulge in any sort of money transaction at all. If a committee is found to be employing its evaluation in-charge or Abhiyaan Pramukh to conduct its financial business, it will be considered as a disciplinary crime. This is not permissible at all. The committee office-bearers will issue a cheque to a full-time volunteer only after he will submit a written request to such an effect through anchal, group or collection committee. Thus, a cheque will be issued after thorough verification and any withdrawal more than the required amount will be treated as a disciplinary crime. Besides, all these volunteers will be required to open their bank accounts at anchal, sankul and sanch level. There will even be similar accounts in the name of the schools. Without opening an account, no school will be established. These bank accounts could be in the name of an institution or joint accounts. There are rules for institutional accounts and joint accounts. At the anchal level, the bank account will be in the name of the institution and below this, for sankul and sanch, only joint accounts can be opened. The financial system will run through these accounts. The Ekal focuses on such minute details because it has to build up a powerful society not merely set up schools. Where there is no discipline, there can't be any powerful structure.

The purpose of the Ekal was not merely to provide education to villagers, as it was and is also being provided by the government through its schools. Almost every village has a government school. The Ekal neither has ambition to form a government nor it wants to compete with the government. The Ekal has to orient its workers in a particular sense of discipline by employing their energies in the mission of the Ekal school so that a powerful structure may be erected to serve the country.

When the Ekal formed its organisation at unit, regional and zonal levels, it had made it clear that wherever people would not show enthusiasm for its mission, it would not open its branch. It was also learnt that the people who were actively assisting Ekal were doing so after being fully convinced of the veracity of the Ekal mission and knowing its background. Whatever the Ekal decides, it becomes a firm guiding principle for its workers, supporters and followers. Those who are unable to observe the code set by the Ekal can't be its true associates. They are in fact betraying their pledge to the Ekal. If any fulltime worker insists that he will take care of the collection and distribution of the Ekal funds, he doesn't deserve to be in the Ekal family. All workers have to follow 'Ten Golden Rules' of the Ekal discipline. These rules test the resolve of a devoted volunteer and fill him with self-respect, which plays a key role in the generation of self-dependence.

SARVA SHIKSHA ABHIYAN (UNIVERSAL ELEMENTARY EDUCATION PROGRAMME OF THE GOVERNMENT) AND THE EKAL ABHIYAN

Since the Parliament of India passed the Right to Education Act, it has been debated what is the purpose of running the Ekal schools now? The government has allocated thousands of crores of rupees for its much-touted Sarva Shiksha Abhiyan (SSA). Primary education has reached every village in the form of government schools. The children are also encouraged to join schools through schemes like Mid-day Meal. Then why should they come to the Ekal schools? Shyam ji tackles this query and explains: 'First, we have to understand that there is a fundamental difference between the society and government. This difference also influences people's perception about the SSA and the Ekal Abhiyan. A system like that of the government could be huge and flush with cash and other resources, but the termites like corruption, inept bureaucracy and politics will make it hollow and it will crumble on its own. Its productivity will be limited. On the other hand, we are imparting value-based education. How can vices prevalent in the government system compete with the values of the Ekal? The SSA only teaches three subjects (Language, Maths and General Knowledge). The Ekal teaches four additional subjects (Moral Education, Health, Handicraft and Yoga-Sports). Thus, the Ekal maintains its edge and utility. Yes, we have noted a difference. When we started the Ekal 30 years ago, we used to attract compulsory students in bulk, but now we get more extra students in every region instead of the compulsory ones. In the government schools, students enrol themselves for the sake of the mid-day meal, but most of them don't study there. In small provinces, yes, the government is doing a fine job and students are getting good education at the government schools. But, even in these provinces, parents take keen interest in the Ekal schools as the moral education of the Ekal school impresses them a lot.'

When a child gets up in the morning, he or she touches his or her parents' feet. He or she recites mantras before touching food. He or she respects elders and avoids abusive language and unworthy sports activities. He or she tries to become an ideal boy or girl. Which parents would not like such children? The example of Himachal Pradesh comes to mind here. It is a small state and thus government schools are doing fine here. Nevertheless, the demand for the Ekal schools has been increasing here for the past 10 years. Himachalis show unparalleled zeal in tasks of self-dependence for the Ekal. Today, Himachal is at the first position as far as the collection of self-dependence funds for the Ekal are concerned. Plus, all the Ekal activities for self-dependence like touring to cities and villages, organising of satsang and the annual festivals are managed by Himachalis themselves. Now, a question may arise in any curious mind: when the government schools are running properly in this state, why do parents send their children to the Ekal schools? Moreover, why do they contribute to the self-sufficiency of such schools?

We may accept the fact that our country has progressed quickly in the last 20-30 years. Earlier, we only had Ekal schools in villages, now even government schools have arrived in every village. So, now the Ekal has taken the role of the supporter of the village education. The Ekal has a significant role in making the government effort more effective and competitive. However, one very important aspect remains invisible to everyone. Children study in primary and elementary government schools, but the rate of dropout during or after completing school is very high there. In such a desperate situation, who will motivate children to prepare themselves for further education? The government system has its sharp limitations. It will be unreasonable or impractical to expect emotional efforts from the government system. Here comes the responsibility of the society to educate the children who somehow remain deprived of proper and complete education. The Ekal has this responsibility. It has generated matchless social harmony in villages and filled the parents with full confidence to push their children towards education. This effort of the Ekal has no parallel. One more thing distinguishes the Ekal from the government system: the Ekal plans overall all-round development of the village through education. Its definition of education is different from that of the government. Originally, the syllabus of the Ekal had four-dimensional education for its students (Elementary Education, Health Education, Village Development and Developing Self-respect), yet it also organises weekly classes for the parents and guardians of the students (meaning common villagers). The government education is limited to classroom education; the Ekal emphasises on functional education that provides life skills. The SSA's vision is only limited to its schools and their functioning, but the Ekal's target is to develop the whole village. The SSA is admittedly doing fine, yet the Ekal has maintained its uniqueness and utility.

The Ekal has made its mission clear from the very beginning—to educate and empower the tribal or forest-dweller community to make India stronger. So, the Ekal school is functioning as the bridge between residents of cities and rural tribals. Can the government's SSA perform this task? When urban and affluent families consider educating tribal children as their responsibility and the tribal families see in urban dwellers their sympathisers, we can only imagine the power of this enormous psychological connection. It will produce wonders for our country. More than 1,00,000 Ekal schools have woven an unprecedented relationship between urban India and tribal India and this horizon will only further widen in the future. The enormity of this task and its importance in the progress of rural India can't be imagined. It can't have any other better alternative. Its contribution towards nation building is mammoth. Hence, SSA schools may perform at a scale of excellence, the Ekal schools will continue to serve the society and nation in their quintessential way.

The flip side of the SSA is also that children educated in government schools drop interest in traditional work like agriculture. They only dream of government and private jobs. Consequently, the villages are being uprooted and jhuggi-type settlements are increasing in cities. The agricultural lands and gardens are lying unattended and are slowly decaying. The rapid rate of industrialisation and smoke from factories are destroying our climate. What could be a remedy to this crisis? A society that only looks up to its government for solutions can never solve its problems and become great. The Ekal has also ruminated on such remedies and has included certain steps for this purpose in its charter of plans. It is planning to establish Swablamban Prashikshan Kendra (Self-reliance Training Centre) in each zone. It means village youth will be trained to generate employment in their villages itself. They will study in their village and open their start-up in the same village. Now, people may ask: 'Where will a student who passes out from the Ekal school go?' Shyam ji answers this, 'Today, we have the same answer that the government has, but it is of no use for the villagers and the country. We have to find the answer to this very relevant question in a very comprehensive way. In future, the Ekal will invest its mental faculties to find a practical and workable answer to this question. We will do our best in our endeavour. But we must keep in mind that the government can never replace society, so the answer has to come from the society itself. Both the society and the government have their separate roles in solving the problems of the country. If the government has dhan (money), the society has dharma (conviction). The base of the government's efforts is money, while the society functions through links of affection. The government efforts are vulnerable to malignant things like corruption and reliance on government machinery, but the society works via goodwill that creates a sense of self-reliance and love for values. The government education is giving rise to demand for government and private jobs. Social efforts are leading to the generation of self-employment, which is the basis of a life full of self-respect. Hence, let the government do its work, and the society will shoulder its share of responsibility.'

□

5
A Powerful Movement for Social Change

Nahi Daridra Kau Dukhi Na Deena
Nahi Koi Abudh Na Lakshan Heena
(No one is oppressed, neither suffering, nor poor
No one is illiterate and bereft of qualities either)

This *chaupai* (quatrain) extracted from Goswami Tulsidas' Ramcharitmanas summarises the whole story of the epic. In Ramrajya (the ideal rule of Lord Ram), no one was oppressed. The Ramrajya doesn't depict life of any specific religious community or class, its ideals are universal. Ramrajya means that no one should be poor, devoid of opportunities and illiterate. Literacy was the primary concern and priority of Ramrajya. The Ekal Abhiyan takes inspiration from Ramrajya and is determined to achieve its target of universal literacy in India. The Ekal is committed to an equal and just society and that's why it has said in its manifesto: 'We will build a society that Dr Ambedkar imagined.' To make this imagination a reality, the Ekal is trying to make the powerful and affluent people of the society stand with the weaker sections. It is making them become the patrons and well-wishers of the weak of the society. This has worked. Hundreds of resourceful families of India and the world are supporting the Ekal. They are not only donating money, but they are also spending time among the tribal people in distant lands. The Ekal has almost achieved its target of creating an equal society in thousands of villages of India. The Ekal's pledge to bring Ramrajya in India is coming true as its one-lakh schools are making Indians literate all across the geography of the country. The Ekal members are devising innovative ways to make rural folk understand the value of education. It has run an aggressive awareness campaign in villages and it has resulted in villagers working for equal society and bringing education for all.

The Ekal members are working like the army of Lord Ram to turn this country into a land of Swami Vivekananda's dreams, India ruled through its villages as envisioned by Mahatma Gandhi, a society of equals as imagined by Dr Ambedkar and a grand and powerful India of Dr Hedgewar's determination. When a man is blessed with a sense of being an army man, a sense of duty automatically develops in him. For this ideal situation to emerge, a sense of harmony must prevail in the society and the Ekal is making efforts in this direction by reviving the ideals of the Ramrajya.

The Ekal's dream of making villages powerful and self-reliant will only be possible when villagers have the determination to make themselves educated and healthy. As an effective method for this purpose, the Ekal has invented 'value-based education'. Shree Hari Katha and Shree Hari Mandir Rath schemes will be tools of the 'value-based education'. These two tools can easily convey their messages to the villagers that they have to shun mal-addictions like alcoholism and turn to values like cooperation with one another and educating themselves. The satsang (gathering) activities aim to make villagers grasp the power of being united and organised. Overall, the Ekal wants to bring villagers into the mainstream of Indian society. As we have already discussed that the magic of the Ekal schools is such that despite a government school in every village, the parents send their children to the Ekal schools. Not only this, they go a step ahead and helps make these schools self-sufficient by donating money to the village committee according to their capabilities. Their trust has a solid basis: they know that the Ekal schools are not only about education; they are preserving the values of Indian culture and morals of the society.

When the Ekal planned to start primary education, health clinics and awareness campaigns in villages, it had to first think about ways to convince and gather villagers for this purpose. But, how will they gather? It wasn't an easy question. After brainstorming over this, the Ekal seniors decided that the satsang would play this role successfully. Initially, the satsang was effective in limited circles and it needed to be properly advertised to make it popular among villagers. As a result, Shree Hari Katha or Kathakaar Yojna was conceptualised.

THE BIRTH OF KATHAKAAR YOJNA IN ANDAMAN AND NICOBAR ISLANDS

The idea for a Kathakaar Yojna didn't strike Shyam ji all of a sudden. It has its own story. It was 1992 and he was in Andaman and Nicobar Islands. These are about 500 tiny islands that have been grouped as one Union Territory. Neta ji Subhash Chandra Bose had formed his Azad Hind Fauj here in 1943. During the British Raj, Japanese had conquered it and handed it over to Neta ji. Veer Savarkar was also kept here at the infamous Cellular Jail by the British when he was serving his Kala Paani sentence. The life for the tribals here was notoriously gruesome. Seeing their circumstances, Shyam ji decided to work for their upliftment. The British had brought a large number of tribals to the Islands to work as labourers from provinces like Jharkhand, Bengal, Andhra Pradesh, Tamil Nadu, etc., as all these areas were in the vicinity of the sea route. When Shyam ji toured the Islands, he was the general secretary of the Vanvasi Kalyan Ashram. He was sent to the Islands to study the conditions of the tribal society. The responsibility of taking care of his Andaman tour and making sure that he successfully undertook his study was with the organisation secretary of the Ashram, Swami Aseemanand ji.

Aseemanand ji had a problem in hosting Shyam ji. It was not difficult for him to organise a tour for a colleague, but he could neither read nor write Hindi and it could create a lot of trouble in communicating with Shyam ji. He was very worried about this. However, he was reminded of Madhvendra Singh ji, who was the principal of the Saraswati Shishu Mandir run by the RSS' Vidya Bharti Trust and it brought him relief. Singh ji was from Lucknow and fluent in Hindi. He had contributed a lot in establishing the Kalyan Ashram in Port Blair. Aseemanand ji knew him. When Basant Rao Bhatt ji, the regional organisation secretary of the Ashram, Kolkata, had come with a blue print for Ashram's work in Port Blair, Singh ji was acquainted with the Ashram while meeting him. In a very short span of time, Singh ji gained sufficient foothold in Port Blair. He grew close to the powerful families there. So, he had introduced Bhatt ji to the affluent people of Port Blair. Within a short time, all these efforts fructified and the Ashram successfully established its registered branch in Port Blair.

For the regional registration, this institute was first established as the Akhil Bharatiya Vanvasi Adivasi Kalyan Ashram but Singh ji objected and suggested two corrections—first, the word 'Akhil Bharatiya' must be removed as the unit was being opened for a specific region; second, one of two words, 'Vanvasi and Adivasi', should be deleted as both were synonyms. Thus, the unit was registered as 'Vanvasi Kalyan Ashram, Port Blair'. This episode earned Singh ji enormous respect as a Hindi scholar and his service to the Sangh and Ashram cemented his place in the annals of the Sangh. This episode had also introduced Singh ji to Aseemanand ji. Swami ji was highly impressed with his Hindi diction and writing. Hence, he handed over the job of writing down Shyam ji's tour to Singh ji.

Those days, doted sky colour printing papers of the Dot Matrix Printer were used. Singh ji hand-wrote the whole plan of Shyam ji on the sky colour paper with a black ink pen in a beautiful handwriting. Now, Shyam ji arrived in Port Blair. Being a tough disciplinarian, he first enquired about the tour plan. Swami ji swiftly presented him the paper written by Singh ji. Shyam ji knew it was not a Hindi-speaking region, so he was perplexed and curiously asked, 'Who has typed this paper?' Swami ji said it was not typed. Shyam ji asked again, 'Has it been typed in Kolkata?' Swami ji said it was not typed but hand-written. Shyam ji was mesmerised on seeing such a beautiful handwriting. It was as if words were themselves speaking. He asked, 'Who has written it?' Swami ji indicated towards a gentleman sitting on one side. 'He is the principal of the Saraswati Shishu Mandir School in Port Blair. This is his handwriting,' Swami ji said. Shyam ji looked at Singh ji with affection and admiration and thus they both were introduced to each other in a very cordial manner.

Not only did Shyam ji have a magnetic personality, his organisational skills were matchless. Whoever would meet him, he would make sure that he would remember him and try to engage him with his mission. Naturally, he developed fondness for Singh ji and remained in touch with him. In return, Singh ji ensured that Shyam ji's tour of Islands got every support from the local unit and it amassed as much information about the tribals as possible. As a result, the first batch of Satsang Kathaakar (preachers) was produced jointly by Singh ji and Ganesh Shenoy of the Vivekananda Kendra. Shyam ji's tour included a series of visits to temples, as the Hindu society would gather in these temples. Shyam ji had to hold talks with the tribals in these temples. In a temple meeting, a huge number of tribals came. These people would see India as their mainland. When they got to know that Shyam ji had come from the mainland, they descended in hordes. Shyam ji was ecstatic to see such a huge gathering and greeted them with utmost respect. 'I have brought the message of love for you from the mainland. You are our brothers. You yourself tell me what we can do for you? I have come here to know this,' he told them. A middle-aged man stood up and began to address Shyam ji. 'Bhai Saab, we have a grave issue. There is a church in our locality. It is visited by Christian priests. Besides, there is not much difference between Hindus and Christians in our society. We also visit the church. Christian priests tell us a lot about Jesus Christ. They also ask us whom we revere as our Lord? We say that we worship Ram ji. Then, they ask us to tell them about Ram ji. At this question, we become speechless. We hang our head down with shame. Can you send some Kathaakar for us so that we know all the details about the life of Ram ji?' he pleaded.

Shyam ji heard that tribal with rapt attention. Those tribals had heard about famous Kathakaar Murari Bapu and were eager to hear Bapu's katha. Shyam ji knew Bapu very well. He bluntly said, 'Please excuse me as I can't bring Murari Bapu. His katha means a grandiose management that neither we nor you can afford.' It disappointed the tribals and they became silent. Now, Shyam ji was in a fix: Which kathakaar could he bring for them? All the renowned kathakaars would only grace events organised in big cities. Their events meant collection of a lot of money. He folded his hands and said to the tribals, 'Brothers, please pardon me. I can't bring any famous kathakaar.' Suddenly, an old man emerged from the gathering and suggested a solution. 'You can take our kids to be trained as kathakaars. They would return and tell us the story of Lord Ram,' he said. Shyam ji felt extremely relieved at this suggestion and an idea germinated in his fertile mind. He said, 'Yes, it is possible. It's a novel idea. Give me some time. I will go the mainland and discuss this with kathakaar trainer saints and then will inform you.' When the tribals heard this, they were over-joyous. This opened the route to the heart of the tribal society. This episode also made Shyam ji and his colleagues realise that the tribal society was extremely eager to know about their gods.

AYODHYA, THE GUIDE

When Shyam ji returned from Andaman, one question was haunting him—how to arrange for kathakaar training for the tribal children. It was only this question that occupied his mind. He was being reminded again and again about the curious and hopeful eyes of the tribals. Their faces came in front of his eyes and he was getting impatient. He was struggling with these thoughts when he had to suddenly leave for Ayodhya on a tour. He was unknown to everyone in Ayodhya. As a Sangh pracharak, he had only worked in Agra and Varanasi. It is said that when someone works for Lord Ram, the gates miraculously open for him. Shyam ji experienced this in Ayodhya. Out of nowhere emerged Sri Champat Rai ji, who was Shyam ji's friend and a senior member of Vishwa Hindu Parsihad. Shyam ji met many religious figures with Sri Champat ji, but nothing worked for him. No one agreed to train the tribal children. The reason was the caste system of India. The saints said, 'Oh you will train tribals… you will bring untouchables here. They will sit beside us… what will you train them? No, no, it is not possible.' It hurt Shyam ji a lot but he controlled his emotions and said to the saints, 'As you wish. I could only request you for this.'

Now, both Shyam ji and Sri Champat ji were discussing this issue, when suddenly Sri Champat ji said, 'Shyam, you don't lose heart. There is one more saint in Ayodhya. His name is Swami Paramhans Ramchandra Das. We will go to meet him. He is a top category saint in Ayodhya.' So, the next day, Shyam ji and Sri Champat ji arrived at Sant Das ji's residence. Shyam ji was still hopeless and the reminder of his promise to the tribals was pinching him from inside. Yet, he and Rai ji put their case clearly before Sant Das ji. Before Shyam ji could finish, Sant Das ji chastised him, 'Have you come to snatch the living of saints? If you will train those tribals, who would invite us?' Shyam ji got terrified and tears rolled down his eyes. He said timidly, 'Maharaj, please pardon me.' And he began to stand up to leave. Now, Sant Das ji again scolded him, 'Where are you going? Sit here.' Shyam ji was now dumbfounded. He didn't know whether he should leave or sit there. Anyway, the atmosphere became calm and cordial.

Then, Swami ji addressed Shyam ji, 'Shyam ji, you have come with this proposal. Actually, we should have gone to you with this idea. You are in fact doing us a favour. The tribals who made Ram ji the Lord are now curious to know about Him. It's their devotion. We even didn't know about this. And when we actually came to know of this, we didn't have guts to go there. You please bring those tribal children here.' Swami ji's assurance made Shyam ji feel like he had won a war. He asked Swami ji to name a saint who would train the children. Swami ji discussed something with Sri Champat ji and dialled the number of some saint. No one could say 'no' to Swami ji in Ayodhya and thus he fixed a meeting of Shyam ji and Sri Champat ji with a saint. Swami ji also advised Shyam ji to meet Swami Nritya Gopal Das ji and seek his blessings. 'He is a very open-hearted saint and would definitely meet you,' said Swami ji. Sri Champat ji agreed with Swami ji.

Shyam ji was satisfied that he had crossed one big hurdle and now he must meet Nritya Gopal Das ji. They both arrived at his ashram and were welcomed warmly. Sri Champat ji first introduced Shyam ji and then explained about his scheme. He also asked, 'What do you expect from me? I am ready for whatever you expect me to do.' Perhaps Ram ji guided Shyam ji at this moment and he requested Sant Das ji, 'If you agree to train those who would come to learn katha, they would be indebted to you forever.' Gopal Das ji paused for a moment and was lost in thoughts. Then, he said that if he had to take care of the training, he would also have to manage food for all the trainees himself. 'All the stuff would be used from my ashram,' he said. Shyam ji was now overwhelmed with pleasant emotions and thanked Lord Ram. Sri Champat ji was also joyful and agreed to contribute from his side.

Now, the ball was in the court of Shyam ji. When will the first batch of training kick in? There should be a committee to decide this. Rai ji suggested a way out and he took Shyam ji to the kshetra karyakarta (area in-charge) of the Sangh. He felt blessed to have welcomed Sri Champat ji at his office, as Rai ji was the right-hand man of Ashok Singhal ji, the man behind the Ayodhya Movement. He thought that some new movement would start. But, when Rai ji introduced Shyam ji and explained his proposal, he took a sigh of relief. They all discussed some names for the proposed committee and the karyakarta agreed to talk to everyone. Now, Shyam ji felt that he had won another war.

The first season of the katha training was charted out. For this season, girls came from Andaman and both girls and boys arrived from Jharkhand. Ultimately, their training started in Ayodhya. Rai ji also roped in other saints who made the training multi-dimensional. The first session of the training was held in Karsevakpuram of Ayodhya. Pramhans ji himself graced the occasion to share his experience and bless the children. Andaman was under the influence of Christianity. So, the girls from there had no hesitation in talking to boys, share light moments and intermingle with them. As a precaution, Shyam ji had appointed two senior men from Jharkhand for the protection of the trainees so that it could be conducted free of any hassle. However, these two guards were conservative and old-fashioned. They didn't like the girls and boys intermingling and being free with each other. So, whenever they saw boys and girls interacting, they would chastise them. After some days, people began to feel that the girls should not be brought for this training. If they would be brought there, some 'immorality' might occur. This problem was also put before the saint community in Ayodhya. At this time, Shyam ji was preparing the trainees for the second session and the girls were showing more enthusiasm for the katha than the boys.

Shyam ji returned to Ayodhya, elated and satisfied. But he was shocked to hear the proposal that girls should not be brought for the next session. He was very disappointed, as he had promised the girls that their training would continue. Shyam ji also didn't share any intimacy with the saint community in Ayodhya so that he could convince them. Hence, he sent out a message to Jharkhand that girls should not be sent for the session. But the girls who had attended the first session were adamant to complete their training. 'We will not return home until we learn the art of katha. What will we do after returning to home? Our parents will enquire about it,' they said. Shyam ji was in a deep dilemma. Ayodhya was not ready to welcome these girls and the girls were not ready to go back. Shyam ji tried to go into the root of the problem so that some solution might emerge. He sought help from the members of the local committee and took them to meet saints who were imparting training to the trainees. Shyam ji opened his heart before them and tried to convey to them the necessity of training girls. The saints were very receptive to Shyam ji's explanation. They said the problem is only because of the mindset. 'The old guards whom you have appointed for their protection are seeing them from the prism of their mindset. But we think that our sisters and daughters are fit to be trained as kathakaar because the satsang is largely attended by women. If a girl will narrate the katha, they would feel more engrossed. Besides, if boys and girls are chatting in groups, it should be seen as a healthy sign. These are our future kathakaar. If we bind them unnecessarily, we will limit their capabilities and it would be dangerous for the future. So, you should not worry at all and be certain of our cooperation. Have faith in us. We also study the body language of the boys and girls. Therefore, it should be our concern, not yours. This is a matter of prestige as all of them will ultimately represent us as kathakaars in villages. It's a matter of pride for us,' they said. Shyam ji successfully presented the case of girls before the saints and removed all their doubts. At last, the girls were brought for the second session of training with the intervention of Paramhans ji and the kathakaar training continued unabated.

You see, it's easy to talk about the katha training at a distant place for girls, but it proves to be a Herculean task in reality. These girls face uncountable hurdles. The biggest hurdle is our own people. They even face eve-teasers and other unsocial elements. But once they underwent katha training, they themselves underwent a personality change. Now, they were very confident and ready to take on any hurdle head-on. They would feel like they had become Ram's troopers and were full of as much energy as a soldier. Now, who would dare to challenge them?

The second round of session ensued in Ayodhya. Shyam ji also managed to get a very suitable place. It was an old temple of Lord Ram. It needed some repair that was carried out by workers from Kolkata. It became a very pleasant site. Shyam ji would tour this place every month. The trainees would look up to him as a father figure. He would also treat them as his sons and daughters. When he would embrace the boys, it would be a very emotional and jovial moment. The girls would see them gleefully from a distance.

Once, a girl asked Shyam ji, 'Are you the father of boys only?' Shyam ji asked mildly, 'Why do you say so, daughter?' She replied, 'We see that you chat and interact with boys for hours. We girls keep waiting that someone will share our joys and sorrows as well.' She then walked away from there. Shyam ji was shocked to hear this and turned pensive. Her words kept haunting him. It also meant that girls had some complaints. Something was troubling them and Shyam ji was in the dark about it. Coincidentally, there was a meeting of the local committee the same evening. Everybody came to attend the meeting. But Shyam ji looked downcast and it was visible on his face. He was lost in the memory of that complaining girl and was thinking what could be the possible solution. Suddenly, he saw the local Sangh karyakarta. He had gone for a meal at his residence a day before. He had chatted well with his wife and had fun with his children.

An idea struck Shyam ji. He asked the karyakarta to bring his wife. The karyakarta and others were stunned what emergency had risen? But Shyam ji was adamant. He said, 'I will tell you about the crisis later. First, please bring your wife.' That gentleman obeyed and brought his wife. Then, Shyam ji shared with everyone what was troubling his mind. He asked the karyakarta's wife, 'You please go and sit with the girls. Try to know what their problems are.' She went to see the girls and the meeting started as usual. Before the meeting was about to fold up after an hour, she came back, furious and seething in anger. She even did not mind the presence of the committee members and burst out at her husband. 'You people have brought girls here for training and don't care for their personal and practical problems,' she said in extreme anger. Then, she called her husband aside and discussed something with him. She then left for the market and bought some articles for the girls. She handed them to the girls and returned to the meeting venue. She told everyone that if girls have to be made part of the training programme, then a woman had to be roped in. All present agreed with her suggestion and Shyam ji pleaded with her that she herself could become part of the committee. This episode was like a lesson of life for Shyam ji.

THE EMERGENCE OF SHREE HARI SATSANG SAMITI

The training for Shree Hari Katha started as planned, but the problem was who would fund this? If the trained kathakaar would visit different areas, then who would take care of their remuneration and expenses of their tour? So, it was decided that the Shree Hari Katha programme should be popularised in the affluent society of Kolkata and the fund should be collected from them. But again, a question was puzzling—who would manage and afford any famous kathakaar? As a solution, Shyam ji decided to call a little known but expert kathakaar. He was Vijay Kaushal ji Maharaj. He had been a Sangh pracharak and a friend of Shyam ji. Shyam ji spoke to him and he agreed. However, he was a complete stranger to people in Kolkata. Shyam ji had to make serious efforts to convince the Kolkata team about his abilities. The Kolkata team also had no other option and after some hesitation, they accepted Kaushal ji Maharaj.

Kaushal ji started his katha in Kolkata. Local organisers arranged a small tent for the programme, but as the katha progressed, the size of the tent increased day after day. On the last day, the crowd became so huge that a large number of listeners had to sit outside the tent. Seeing this, the Kolkata team was on seventh heaven. They felt grateful to Shyam ji. Kaushal ji Maharaj melded the story of Lord Ram in the Shree Hari Kaha so artistically that the listeners were spellbound and many influential families readily agreed to join the Katha project immediately. After the Katha was over, the local organising committee set up a meeting of Kaushal ji Maharaj with people who had come forward to join the project. Here, Kaushal ji himself proposed formation of another committee. After some suggestions, the Shree Hari Satsang Samiti (SHSS) came into being. Shyam ji proposed the name of Kaushal ji as its patron and thus a new organisation became part of the Ekal family.

KANTI, THE PIONEER OF SOCIAL CHANGE

Among the girls who were enthusiastic to become a kathakaar was a girl named Kanti. The story after she became a kathakaar is heart wrenching and inspirational. Completing her training in Ayodhya, she returned to her village and made Shree Hari Katha popular even in nearby areas. Then, she was married off and came to Chhattisgarh. Her in-laws were not as interested in the story of Lord Ram as she was. They even didn't like her reciting the katha and touring other areas for this purpose. They were actually totally against her passion. Years passed in this way and Kanti served her in-laws to the best of her ability and with pure dedication. She gave birth to a son. When her son grew up a bit, her passion for reciting katha reignited. Her in-laws again objected, but the story of Lord Ram flew in her veins. She defied her in-laws and took her son on her shoulders and came to meet the Ekal volunteers. She was helped to tour various rural areas to recite Ram katha in front of the villagers. She toured umpteen villages and popularised Ram everywhere. One day, Lord Ram miraculously changed the heart of her husband. And gradually, her in-laws also bowed before her.

THE TRIBALS BECAME NOT ONLY KATHAKAARS BUT ALSO ADVOCATED THEIR WOES

During the training of the kathakaars, the president of Vanvandhu Parishad, Sri Chitlangaya ji, also toured Ayodhya with his family. He had no clue about the new initiative of Shyam ji for the tribals. It was in Ayodhya that he came to know what Shyam ji was up to. At that time, the Ekal was not very popular. People only knew Shyam ji by his name. The training session was being conducted. When Chitlangaya ji heard about this, he couldn't control his curiosity and reached the training venue. He was very impressed with the training. It was an entirely a new experience for him. He was aware of schools being run by the Ekal, but it was beyond his imagination that it could run katha training programme for tribals as well. In his excitement, he wrote to Shyam ji, 'Whenever you come to Kolkata, please do meet me.' When Shyam ji went to Kolkata, he met Chitlangaya ji. Chitlangaya ji was very humorous person. He quipped, 'Arrey Shyam ji, your theft has been found out.' Shyam ji was aghast. 'Have I committed any theft?' he innocently asked. 'You haven't even told us and are doing such a great work secretly. How did this idea strike your mind?' Chitlangaya ji said. In reply, Shyam ji narrated the whole story of what happened in Andaman.

Chitlangaya ji said to Shyam ji, 'I have invited you for a proposal. Can you bring four to five trained tribal children to Kolkata after they complete their training in Ayodhya? It will show to people in Kolkata what these children have learnt.' Shyam ji agreed for that.

So, when the tribal children completed their training, their first programme was scheduled in Kolkata. Chitlangaya ji wielded enormous influence in Kolkata circles. Therefore, the Vanvasi Katha Karyakram (Tribal Preaching Programme) was organised in the prestigious galaxy auditorium. Around 200-300 people gathered for this programme and majority of them were elites of Kolkata. Four tribal children were given four different stories to narrate. First was given the Kevat story, second the

Shabri story, third the Nishad story and the fourth the Jatayu story. Each one was given 15 minutes to complete his/her narration. As the katha programme progressed, the whole auditorium became devotional. A big industrialist of Kolkata was chairing this programme. He was requested by the organisers to say few words about the katha and kathakaars. He came to the dais and started weeping like a child. Shyam ji was sitting right in front of the dais. He was shocked and thought that something untoward happened. Ironically, no one could ask why that gentleman was weeping, as he was alone on the stage. After some time, he himself calmed down. Meanwhile, the whole auditorium had turned extremely serious. The first sentence he uttered was: 'I am weeping, but why are you people crying as well?' Then Shyam ji turned back and saw that most of the eyes were actually moist. That industrialist gentleman proceeded to say, 'Look, I have organised a number of katha programmes. Perhaps, there is no renowned kathakaar who has not been invited to Kolkata. They all would narrate the story of Shabri. But, today, Shabri herself came to tell her story.' These words moved every soul present in the auditorium. Now, the katha had turned magical. The tribals were not merely working as kathakaars, they were intervening as agents of change. This programme became so successful that the satsang became a household name in Kolkata.

RASHTRA JAGRAN KE SAADHAK GAN (PERFORMERS OF NATIONAL AWARENESS)

Now, the Ekal was making progress. The residence of Kolkata's renowned personality, Ashok Modi ji, had become a pilgrimage site for the Ekal. People would only discuss Ekal here. Once, all prominent members were discussing some matter here. At that time, Ashok ji's elder brother, Sanvar Bhaiya, was also present. He was the patriarch of the affluent family. His original residence was in Dibrugarh, Assam, and he was a pillar of the Sangh. It was his farsightedness that had taken the family business to new heights. He listened to all the Ekal workers very carefully. Then, Ashok ji introduced Shyam ji to him. Ashok ji by nature speaks high of people. After he finished Shyam ji's introduction, Sanvar Bhaiya asked Shyam ji, 'Have you ever been to the North Eastern states?' Shyam ji had by then only heard about the North East and had never been there. Sanvar ji shot his second question, 'How much do you know about the state of affairs in the North East?' Shyam ji mustered this much in answer: 'I have heard that Hindi-speaking people had to flee from there and settle in other states.' Hearing this, Sanvar ji shot his next question like an arrow: 'After knowing all this, what are you doing in the North East? What is the Sangh doing about it? I am hearing from you for such a long time and the only thing you people are discussing is one school and its expansion. Who will care about the country? Who will accept this challenge? However, I think the path you are treading on will lead to the solutions of country's grave problems. You will prepare yourselves for this. I will support you by all means.'

This worked like a lightening on Shyam ji. He foresaw a new direction and a new challenge. Shyam ji assured Sanvar ji that his next destination would be the North East. But, now the first question before him was who would apprise him of the exact status of affairs in the North East? Who would prepare the strategy for the North East project? This task will not be possible without support of the Sangh. Who would convince the Sangh office-bearers? It is said that Lord Ram first tests the determination in your heart. If you pass His test, he illuminates your path and opens the doors that ultimately lead you to your destination. It happened exactly like that. The Sangh seniors somehow came to know of the problems in North East, Shyam ji's determination and his Ekal vision. Actually, the Sangh was itself worried about the situation in the North East. So, a Sangh senior Sheshadri ji prepared a detailed plan to tour the North East to take stock of the situation there. He sent a message to Shyam ji that he would accompany him in that tour. Shyam ji had experienced such miraculous blessing of Lord Ram many times in his life. A blind person only seeks two eyes! So, Shyam ji agreed to accompany Sheshadri ji to tour the North East.

First, a meeting was called in Assam. Some tea-growers were invited to this meeting. In this meeting, Sheshadri ji asked the questions and Shyam ji made notes of the gist of their answers. Some of the conclusions that emerged from this meeting were:

1. Majority of labourers in tea gardens were brought by the British from the nearby regions like Jharkhand, Odisha and Madhya Pradesh. Most of them were from Jharkhand.

2. These labourers still had faint memories of their lost culture and it could be revived.
3. Tea-garden workers are getting influenced by the Church and Maoism.
4. Tea-garden workers of Assam come from tribal areas and still they have not been added in the Scheduled Tribe category.
5. There is no proper arrangement for the education of their children.
6. Many militant outfits are active in the region and the youth easily fall prey to them. They are brainwashed into hating mainland India.
7. Tea gardens play a pivotal role in the politics of Assam.
8. People employed in tea gardens on the border with Bangladesh face brutalities of Muslims.
9. The working of the Sangh in these areas is in a primitive stage. There is hardly any effective Sangh branch in these areas.
10. If the education of the children is made the target, then the Sangh can easily make inroads into the hearts of these people.

After this rigorous meeting, it was decided that the Vidya Bharti and Ekal must play active role in these areas. From Assam, the team proceeded towards Arunachal Pradesh. A similar meeting was organised there and its key points were:

1. Arunachal borders China that considers it its own territory. China has its own arguments for this claim.
2. Vivekananda Kendra Vidyalaya has established itself well in Arunachal. But it has failed to check the growing influence of the church there.
3. The local society is peace-loving and culturally very active.
4. They worship the Sun and Moon, but they are not very aware of the Hindu religion.
5. Earlier, the Church couldn't enter Arunachal, but they have been able to intrude into society because of their political approach.
6. The population of Christians is increasing very fast and they constitute around 30% of the total population.
7. The standard of education here is higher to than that of other provinces due to Christian schools and the Vivekananda School.

8. But the health facilities are scarce and locals are also not very aware about it. The region being in the hilly areas also makes it difficult to arrange such facilities.
9. The defeat of India in 1962 War with China has dampened the morale of the locals. They suffer from defeatist mentality.
10. Arunachal borders Nagaland in the north. In Nagaland, separatist forces are very active.

Therefore, it was decided that a Sangh branch will be opened in Arunachal and the Aarogya Yojna will also start there. Arunachal became the focus in the beginning and the other parts of the North East were not covered, as the situation there was not conducive enough. It was not practically possible to launch any programme there. So, now some prominent workers had to be taken into confidence for Arunachal project.

Ultimately, the North East was divided into three colours. The first was red zone where the entry was not possible. The second was green zone where the Sangh could start its enterprise. The third was yellow zone where any project could be launched after the success of the green zone start-up. Now, even beginning in the green zone was only in the planning stage and nobody had any clue how to make a start. Finally, the area that Sanvar Bhaiya had suggested was selected—Teensukhia and Dibrugarh. Dibrugarh was the home of the Modi family and all sort of assistance was possible. Even in nearby Teensukhia, Modi family had sound connections and it was not difficult to work there. Both these areas have a number of tea gardens where Shyam ji had to start Ekal schools for the children of tea-garden workers. Fortunately, the Sangh was also active in these areas and thus there was no dearth of cooperation. The Vivekananda Kendra was also active in this area. It was an ideal location for the Sangh-oriented outfits. So, it was decided that Teensukhia would serve as the headquarters of the project. Now, Shyam ji had to find someone from the Ekal family who would shoulder this responsibility. Luckily, an old and experienced Ekal worker agreed to shift there with his family. It was a huge favour for the Ekal Abhiyan. This family first visited the place where they had to settle and then selected a place from where an Ekal unit could start. Then, they started befriending the youths of the area. However, there was a roadblock in this endeavour as most of the youths of the area were already members of some separatist outfit. Hence, there could only be a discussion with them on education.

One day, when a group of youths came to meet the Ekal team, Shyam ji was called to explain the Ekal Abhiyan to them. Shyam ji was forewarned that he would have to talk about only education and nothing else. He had to avoid any mention about the Sangh, Vishwa Hindu Parishad, Vanvasi Kalyan Ashram, Hindu, Marwadis or India. The slogan 'Bharat Mata Ki Jai' should not crop up in the conversation at all, as most of those youths belonged to militant groups where they were taught to detest such slogans. Shyam ji was in a fix. So many restrictions? How would he then effectively put forth the case of the Ekal before them? Yet, he prepared his detailed presentation and practiced it couple of times. He ultimately met those youths and started unearthing the Ekal Abhiyan before them with all prescribed cautions.

Shyam ji was tense and agitated from within. It was because he had to deliberate things by suppressing a lot of things inside. His discourse was on the right track, and then suddenly he slipped and blurted out 'We all are Bharat Mata Ki Santaan.' As soon as the youths heard this, they stood up to leave. The local Ekal worker sensed the trouble and tried to salvage the situation. He said something to the youths in their local language. The youths calmed down and sat down again. Meanwhile, Shyam ji was sweating profusely as he knew that he had committed a grave mistake. He swiftly changed his topic and started praising the local workers. He quickly finished his deliberation and urged the local worker to take charge of the conversation thence. The local worker was adept in the local language. He spoke to the youths in local idioms and very clearly explained everything. The youths were impressed and they clapped as he finished. Thus, the meeting was over on an encouraging note. Shyam ji was curious to know how did the local volunteer assuage the agitated youths after his 'Bharat Mata…' remark? He replied, 'I explained to them in the local language what you said in a different way. I said the speaker meant by "Bharat Mata…" that some people consider themselves as sons of mainland India, but we are not among them.' Shyam ji was flabbergasted and he wondered that there were still some Indians in India who were not ready to call themselves as sons of this soil. But the local worker consoled him: 'You don't need to worry, Shyam ji. One day, these very youths will proclaim 'Bharat Mata Ki Jai' in New Delhi.'

Slowly, a small group was formed. The Sangh was ready with its full support, so it was finalised where the first unit would be established. But how would the workers be gathered for this uphill task? Till now, the Sangh would pool resources and cadres for the North East from other provinces. Thus, this small group had no other option but to do the same. However, Lord Ram had His own plan. He hadn't depended on forming its army (Ekal team) on other regions, why would He then raise the workforce from those regions for this unit? In fact, a local full-time volunteer who had shifted from the Sangh to the Ekal raised this question and insisted that the workforce for the unit formation should entirely be local. His logic was that if the Ekal only wished to open a school, then he could call outsiders to help run it, but if its ultimate aim was to raise an army for Lord Ram, then locals would be given the leading role. This also suited Shyam ji. He considered it as blessing of Lord Ram, as he knew that even the Sangh could not help given the situation in the North East in those days. So, Shyam ji welcomed that worker's proposal and started the project.

One more important requirement of this project was the economic side. It was also to be taken care of by a committee of locals. But this proved be an easy task as the influential Modi family headed by Sanvar Bhaiya was there. He provided very appropriate members for the committee. Finally, the army of Lord Ram set out on its mission to win hearts of the North Eastern people and change the society there.

RECOGNITION OF THE EKAL BY WEST BENGAL GOVERNMENT

With the passage of time, the Jagran Shiksha (Awareness Campaign) of the Ekal was also progressing by leaps and bounds. The awareness was showing its results and the villagers were becoming enthusiastic about education and development of their villages. Meanwhile, a new challenge came up before the Ekal. It was 2017. The Ekal had deepened its roots in Bengal and Kolkata was linked to its umbilical cord. The Panchmukhi Shiksha (Five-faceted education) of the Ekal was making Bengal villages literate and aware. When the ruling party of Bengal took appreciative note of the Ekal, it was deemed that the mission had tasted real success. As the results of various level elections came out, the Bengal government took serious note of the fact that there was an engine behind the change in the attitude of villagers. It searched for answers to the question what is making the tribals literate, aware and powerful? Who is making tribals, forest-dwellers and villagers so aware of the government schemes run for them? Who is making villagers politically educated that they had begun to understand basic nuances of the politics and could even talk about it like city-dwellers? The ever-increasing influence and success of Ekal was no longer a secret. Thus, the Ekal schools became sore of the eyes of the government officials. The reign of the Ekal schools was in the hand of the Vanvandhu Parishad in Bengal. One day, it received a government communiqué that it would have to shut down the Ekal schools. All the members of the Parsihad were utterly shocked and clueless about what to do. The Parishad consulted its attorney. He told the Parishad members that a petition was filed in the court and in its response, the District Inspector (Education) of South Dinajpur submitted that some private schools were running in his area without the No Objection Certificate (NOC) issued as per the Right to Education Act, 2009, and the West Bengal Right of Children to Free and Compulsory Education Rules, 2012. So, the Inspector said that all those private schools had to be shut down immediately. The Ekal knocked at the doors of the court for the first time in its history to respond to the submission of the Education Inspector through Vanvandhu Parishad. The Parishad lawyer argued that the RTE and West Bengal Rule for Compulsory Education applies on formal schools and informal schools are not bound by such obligation. The whole structure of the Ekal school is informal. So, it is exempt from government rules. They don't need to seek NOC from the concerned government department. Ultimately, the court ruled in favour of the Ekal schools. This victory entrenched the reputation and importance of the Ekal schools in the government circles.

THE WAVE OF HINDUTVA IN TAMIL NADU

There was a time when we heard the name of Tamil Nadu, the pictures of Hindi and Hindu-hating 'Madrasis' would flash past our eyes. There, people would go to such an extent that they would worship Ravana in opposition to Lord Ram. Ravana was their ideal. However, now the tribal and rural society of Tamil Nadu has developed affinity and love for Lord Ram. This is all due to the efforts of the Ekal Abhiyan. They now feel proud to be followers of Lord Ram. A wave of Hindutva can be perceived in Tamil Nadu. In this context, Shyam ji's tour to the state to establish and spread the network of the Ekal there is a story in itself. Once Shyam ji and the regional secretary of the organisation, Vishwanath ji, were travelling to Chennai from Nagercoil. As soon as the train halted at the Trippur station, around 10 Ekal schoolteachers were present there to receive them. After formal introduction, a teacher proceeded to present Shyam ji a gift. Shyam ji hesitated. He thought, 'They earn a meagre salary. How could they save as much as to present a wall clock? Have they all contributed for this? Besides, this clock has the name of the village inscribed on it? How come this rural woman teacher wants to present such an expensive gift?'

Shyam ji was lost in these thoughts. His reverie was disturbed by a pleasant voice. 'Shyam ji, you can't imagine that these teachers were waiting for your arrival ever since they heard that you would come here. They were waiting for you hysterically. Who could be God for them other than a person who is even touring foreign lands to collect funds for the education of their children? We could be poor resources wise, but our hearts are not poor. For what you have done and are doing for our future generations, please accept this small gift,' said a local volunteer. Shyam ji and all others were overwhelmed by this love of sister teachers and they bowed before them. Shyam ji took the gift in his hand and touched it on his forehead. In the stupor of emotions, he said to those teachers, 'As long as you tribal people have this passion and genuine conviction for your mission, no one can harm the Hindu religion.' In the middle of this emotional meeting, the train whistled to leave. Everyone invited Shyam ji to visit his or her village. It seemed that those five minutes generated bonds of five centuries. Shyam ji shared with Vishwanath ji, 'Vishwanath ji, today's experience was unique. They were unable to comprehend my language and neither did I understand theirs. It was love exchanged through translation and yet it was so powerful. It was no less than a miracle.'

They were having this conversation that the train reached its destination, Kodaikanal. Kodaikanal hill areas are also considered a pilgrimage site. In the evening, Shyam ji visited an Ekal school in some village. The whole village wore a festive look. Every family of this tiny village was there to greet and see Shyam ji. He was welcomed with pomp and show. The villagers were competing with one another to garland and touch the feet of Shyam ji. Amid this festivity, a man and woman went into trance. The pitch of the drumbeat peaked. All the villagers (tribals) turned towards them, tried to calm them down by touching their feet, yet they all themselves were dancing like maniacs. The local unit chief took Shyam ji to that man. Shyam ji took out all his garlands and respectfully offered them to that drummer. Slowly, the festivity ebbed and the atmosphere became normal. Shyam ji and the local Ekal volunteers wondered why such a heightened emotionalism was demonstrated by the villagers. What was new that day? They guessed something. The villagers only knew one thing about Shyam ji that he had come from Uttar Pradesh, the land of Lord Ram and thus they went berserk to welcome Shyam ji as he was a representative of Lord Ram for them.

In this heightened festivity, children of the Ekal schools also presented their programmes. Around 40 children, most of them being girls, were present there. When the time came for Shyam ji to address the gathering, he thought that he must address them in Hindi, as it would be finally translated. Nevertheless, he asked the children, 'How should I address you, in Hindi or English?' A little girl said, 'In English.' But Shyam ji requested the children that when his address would be translated into Tamil, he must be allowed to speak in Hindi. Everyone was surprised that an all India-level official was requesting so humbly to the kids and they were not ready to entertain his request. When that girl was asked the reason why were children insisting on an address in English? She replied, 'Some educated people of our village talk to the government officials in English and thus we have some familiarity with English words. But our knowledge of Hindi is nil.'

So, Shyam ji surrendered before the children and spoke in English. The key takeaway from this episode was that the students of the Ekal school had developed this much confidence that they could persuade a senior Ekal official to address a very important speech in the language they wanted to listen to. Finally, the meeting ended with the chants of Lord Ram. Suddenly, it struck Shyam ji that how come did the children learn chants of Lord Ram? He was told that children are taught these chants every day in the Ekal school. Seeing such enthusiasm of the children, Shyam ji offered a challenge before them. He picked up the flower garland from the statue of Lord Ram and said whoever would recite hymns of Lord Ram maximum number of times at his/her home, that garland would be gifted to him/her. It let the cat loose among the kids. Everyone claimed to outdo one another. The bid started from 10 and reached 100. The maximum bid came from a little girl. Everyone was startled how could such a small girl complete this challenge? People asked her whether she had understood the challenge properly and when she confidently said she had, Shyam ji put that garland around her neck. But, now one question perturbed Shyam ji. He said that some moments back, those same kids were unable to listen to his address in Hindi and then suddenly that girl was ready to recite hymns of Lord Ram 'Shri Ram Jai, Jai Ram, Jai Ram'. How was that possible? Then, he and others realised that the name and hymns of Lord Ram are not bound by the language. This is how Lord Ram must have won hearts of tribals, forest-dwellers and villagers that they still chant His name and love everything attached to Him even after ages.

Then, Shyam ji left for his night stay. With him was also Uma ji, the vice-chief of the local unit. She was a graduate and could converse with Shyam ji in broken English. She told about herself that she was the eldest sibling in her family. 'I have a younger brother and sister. Whatever our father earns, he spends on his liquor addiction. Most of the time, he remains ill and confined to bed. Even our mother rarely gets any work, as she is very weak physically. I had to discontinue my education and return to the village to support my family. My meagre earning somehow manages to keep us all alive. As the Ekal school became established and popular among villagers in our area, a church-run NGO tried to open a similar school. They offered enticements to our teachers and other workers to switch to their side. They also offered me a higher salary of Rs 2,000 per month. When I didn't show interest, they came to meet my mother. They tried to cajole her that her daughter was merely getting Rs 600 per month from the Ekal school and she also had to roam in the entire village for that. They said that they would give me Rs 2,000 for the work limited to the office. But my mother displayed exemplary wisdom and courage. She plainly told them that Uma was not a child and that she knew what was best for her and that whatever she would choose, it would please her,' she opened her heart to Shyam ji. He asked Uma, 'Why didn't you accept their offer?' Uma replied, 'Why are you even asking this, Shyam ji? We are Hindus. Will we betray our faith just for few more rupees? The day the Ekal school started here and I joined it, I have felt inner peace and satisfaction. The affection for this school is natural. I feel free of any pull towards money. Yes, it's true that some villagers had fallen for the greed, but that is also not possible now. Now, no teacher from the Ekal school will get trapped in the net of the church.'

She was speaking in a flow and her emotions overwhelmed Shyam ji. He got lost in his thoughts: 'Is she the woman from the same Indian society where educated and respected men get involved in all sorts of corruptions and compromise their ideals and commitments? For them, the money is God. She barely manages meals for her family two times a day. But her moral courage that emanates from her love for Lord Ram has given her so much strength that she refuses the offer of a hefty amount.' Giving example of Uma, Shyam ji said to other villagers, 'See, this is the only and pivotal strength of our Hindu society. This is the root of our society. So, if other parts of this tree like leaves, fruits and stems that have grown in the urban societies and have turned disappointingly maligned, we don't need to feel disheartened. We will gradually make our rural society so educated and powerful that it will be able to decide what is good and bad for it. Then, it will prepare a bedrock upon which a gigantic tree of Hindu culture will grow and all its leaves, fruits and stems will be pure. It will grow not only to give rise to similar other trees in cities but in foreign lands as well. Then, the Hinduism will pave the way for the welfare of the world.' The villagers had heard such words only from the organisation's seniors and office bearers thus far, but Shyam ji's words touched the core of their hearts and soul.

THE LAP OF HIMALAYAS

When Shyam ji arrived in Udhampur, Jammu, on 6 August 2015, he heard about an incident that took place around 11 kilometres away. He was informed in the early morning of 7 August that a village on the border of India-Pakistan had created history. Showing exemplary courage, the villagers had nabbed a terrorist. This village had an Ekal school and its villagers had been keenly taking interest in the functioning of this school and other activities of the Ekal. However, the news made Shyam ji happy and gloomy at the same time. He was happy because the villagers had become aware enough to discharge their duties as active citizens of the country and capture a terrorist. He was sad as two soldiers had to lay down their lives and he thought it was because of the fact that other villages didn't have Ekal schools. Had other villages had Ekal schools and been equally aware, the two soldiers would not have to die.

From Udhampur, he travelled to Himachal. He was now moving right in the lap of the Himalayas. As he entered Himachal, he came to know that a whole village was washed away because of a cloudburst. Shyam ji wondered: 'What message are the Himalayas emitting?' It was as if the Kailash sent him a message: 'Be careful. Now, you are in the Himalayas. The whole range of the hills has been seriously damaged by tempering with the ecology and by the infiltration of foreigners. Only Himachal is safe. It has to save the whole of Himalayas. You have to raise an army of Shiv ji and show them how much strength Shiv ji bestows on His true devotees! This message only has to convey this to you. Take it as a warning call.'

In this observatory tour of Shyam ji, the first day was devoted to the meeting of the local committee. The next day, the Ekal volunteers discussed the message conveyed from Dhanbad. Before this journey, Shyam ji had gone for around 10 tours to various places in India. But they were all in plains. He was experiencing the difficulties of life in the hills, and that too in the Himalayas, for the first time.

One member of the local committee arrived on the meeting venue a little earlier. He began to discuss in an informal way and spoke highly of the local volunteers. Shyam ji said to him in a lighter vein, 'You are praising them, but most of the organisation members are disappointed with them.' That member felt as if he had been electrocuted. He said, 'Shyam ji, I don't know what had been happening in the past. But I have seen all of them working with full devotion and vigour since I joined here. If anyone has any complaint, please ask him to discuss that with me. I have worked as an accountant in a government job for 30 years and thus I am quite adept in keeping record of even small details. I have kept a record of every penny spent here. I have toured a number of Ekal villages and have attended numerous meetings. So, I am responsible for the honour of Himachal as far as working of the Ekal here is concerned.'

After hearing all this, Shyam ji said to him, 'You will have to go to Delhi once in a month and face the examining committee.' Now, he roared in a higher volume, 'I am ready to go to Delhi twice not once.' Then, the meeting started. But turmoil was rising within Shyam ji. He felt that if that gentleman was speaking the truth, it must reflect in meeting his family members. Meeting families of the workers was already part of his itinerary. Shyam ji and others boarded a car to meet that gentleman's family. His son was driving the car. And the car also belonged to that volunteer. The young driver was driving as most of the young men do. He would turn the car even on dangerous turns of 120 and 180 degrees with nonchalance. Shyam ji would shiver with fear whenever the car would take such a turn. Though the roads were well constructed, yet there were hiccups in some places. Sometimes, the car would enter a road, which was full of pebbles, and the car would move on it as if it was a toy. Its tyres would slip hither and thither. Shyam ji would convulse to this and that side. But he was unable to complain. On the other hand, both father and son were enjoying the ride because Shyam ji was going to their house. Then, suddenly the car screeched to a halt. Father and son asked everyone to get down. 'We have arrived,' they said. Shyam ji looked in all directions, but no house was visible. Then, he was told that they were still to climb some height of the Himalayas and then the houses would be seen. Shyam ji had undergone a knee operation and though he was okay, yet climbing a steep hill could be problematic. He put his hand on a volunteer's shoulder and kept climbing. He soon became breathless. Finally, they reached the house of that gentleman. His whole family was on the door to welcome Shyam ji. But Shyam ji was not in a state to care for any hospitality at that time. He only wanted to sit for a while and normalise his breath. When he regained his breadth, he felt that he must ask that gentleman his life story in the presence of his family members.

That gentleman started baring his heart: 'I am the only son of my parents and I had seven sisters. I joined the school at the age of five on the insistence of a friend of my father who was the principal of a school. My age was advanced by two years in school to fulfil the formality of the minimum school-joining age. By the time I reached 10th Standard, my father passed away. My mother had already left for her heavenly abode. Four of my sisters had been married while my father was alive. After my father's death, the family began to face hardships. I was unable to find any employment. One day, I heard that a project was underway to pave a road 14-kilometre uphill. There was a chance to get a job in this project. I had no other option but to join this tough job. I used to get up at 4 am in the morning and would set out for my work at 4.30 am. My wife would wrap breads in a bundle. At 8.30 am, I would have my meal and then would work hard from 9 am to 5 am. I would then travel four hours to return home at 9 pm. After dinner, I would go to bed to rise up again at 4 in the morning. It continued for about two and half years. When my employers noticed my hard work, they promoted me. I was merely a labourer earlier and was then promoted to be a supervisor. Slowly, I was made in-charge of around 500 workers. Then one day, I got a job in the government roadways. I became a bus conductor. You know, there are always incidents of cloudburst or falling of boulders or landslides in Himachal and it leads to blockage of roads. One day, even my bus met an accident after hitting some rock on the road. It was about to fall into a gorge. It somehow stuck against a stone for some time. All the passengers were being evacuated from the emergency door. Suddenly, a child slipped from his mother's hand. At the same time, the bus also started slipping towards the gorge. The life of the child was in grave danger. The mother and others were making fervent appeals to save the child. I was a young man. I jumped towards the child and tossed him towards his mother. She successfully caught the child. Then, while I was trying to come out of the bus, my foot stuck and as the bus fell, it split into two. Somehow, people must have taken me to the hospital. It took me six months to stand on my feet again. My seniors were satisfied with my work, so all the expenses for my treatment were borne by the government. When I was able to walk, I was assigned the work of an accountant. Later, I came to know that because of my school record, officially I was two years elder than my real age. The issue was about my retirement age. The whole government department was in my favour. Thus, a search operation was launched to find the records of my birth. Now, you may deem it the wish of the Lord or a coincidence, even the records before my birth were found, yet there was no record of the year when I was born. Finally, I had to retire at the age of 56 being of the age of 58 in government records. I had decided to work in Hindi since the very first day of my job and continued it for

30 years. The chief minister of the state publicly honoured all my family for my service to Hindi language. That was a memorable day of my life. During my government job, I married off three of my sisters. Later, my own three sons were married. All of them are doing fine and happily living their lives. Luckily, my daughters-in-laws are also educated and cultured. I had retired from the government service, but I was not ready to sit at home. My sons also said that I was free to do whatever pleased me. They said that they would take care of the family. Some politicians invited me to join politics, but my heart was not ready for it. Those days, I heard that a young man of our village had joined the Ekal as volunteer. Once, he asked me to join an Ekal programme. I was so impressed that I attended all the Ekal events then onwards. My heart became full of contentment. And now, I am before you today.'

As he finished his story, Shyam ji was feeling a storm within himself. His head was spinning. The next day, this gentleman came a little late for the meeting. Shyam ji, who was strict disciplinarian, asked him the reason. He said that he had to walk to the road from his village. Then, he caught a bus, then another bus to reach the meeting point. It took three hours. Shyam ji said to himself, 'For me, the volunteers arranged everything suitable so that I reached the meeting place on time and with ease. And this man took so much trouble to come here. Do I have any moral right to say anything to him after seeing his *tapasya* (devotion)?' Shyam ji felt ashamed of himself and now he truly became conscious of hardships in the Himalayas.

AND THE DEVOTION FOR THE EKAL DEEPENED

Now, there is another story of another Ekal worker. Shyam ji used to wonder about him. He was himself a physician; his wife was a full-time volunteer and stayed away from home. Then who would take care of their children? His home was here and his clinic was there, poles apart from each other. How did this gentleman coordinate all his affairs? On one side, there were these upheavals of questions in the mind of Shyam ji, and on the other side, there were the bumpy roads of Himachal, with deep valleys along them. There was a sharp turn in every five-minutes. The roads were not only narrow, but they were difficult as well. It would sometime go upward, sometimes down. Anyhow, Shyam ji reached the home of that doctor saheb. It was a lonely house, surrounded by hills and jungles. It was actually a beautiful and serene sight. Shyam ji thought for a moment that he must take a break of few minutes and only view that beautiful scenery. But the family of the doctor saheb was eagerly and warmly waiting for him. He was overwhelmed and accepted their invitation into the house. Doctor saheb and his Mrs had already met Shyam ji, but his mother, adult son and daughter were meeting him for the first time with their granddaughter. As Shyam ji touched feet of Mata ji and asked her well-being, her face glowed with happiness. She said, 'I have told my son and daughter-in-law that you devote yourself in the service of our nation and leave your kids to me. I am both their father and mother.'

Shyam ji was now convinced of the genuine devotion of the family for the Ekal and for the service of the nation, but he wanted answer to another question. He was eager to know that how did doctor saheb's mother draw inspiration for this devotion? He replied, 'I was a small child when my father passed away. My taya ji (elder brother of my father) raised me and educated me. My father was in the army and was martyred in some operation. Taya ji's wife had also died quite early after his marriage. Family members pressurised him to remarry, but he refused, as he wanted to take care of us. I was raised in the shadow of his love. I completed my medical course. I was meanwhile introduced to the Sangh. I also took part in the student politics and then I was on the course of becoming a politician. We were also landed people and had a lot of property. I was also the only son of both my father and taya ji. Then, an Ekal school opened in our village. My wife became its teacher. It would actually run in our own house. I was pleased that my wife was running this school, but I was eager to carve a political career. Once, on the insistence of my wife, I had to accompany her to the school and also happened to listen to the discourse there. It was entirely a new experience for me. I felt eager to know more about Ekal. As I knew more about Ekal, my interest in it increased further. Now, I felt that reptile roads of politics were no more attractive for me. They in fact started repulsing me. Suddenly, I got a big political offer, but I had decided to devote myself to the Ekal by then and thus rejected that offer. My wife by that time had become a full-time Ekal volunteer. An unusual thing happened with me. The less I attended my clinic, the more lucrative became my practice. More patients came when I was at the clinic. Perhaps, it was a miracle from the Lord. I had become a renowned medical practitioner. My wife was an official full-timer, while I was an unofficial full-timer. My mother had already made both of us free from raising our children. Most of the time, we were away from home, working for the Ekal. Our devotion for the Ekal has only been rising. Now, whatever responsibility you will hand me, I am ready for it. Wherever you will order me to tour, I will be ready with my luggage.'

When he stopped, Shyam ji got lost in the admiration of Lord Ram that how He showers His blessing on His lovers! How He performs miracles in mysterious ways! As he came to his senses, he saw that the table he was sitting beside had books like *Prerna Pushp* (Inspirational Flowers), *Kranti Ram Ki* (Revolution of Ram), *Ekal Prakashan Ke Prerna Prasang* (Inspiration Guides of the Ekal Prakashan), etc. As Shyam ji admiringly glanced at those books, doctor saheb said, 'Whenever I have free time, I read these books and my devotion for the Ekal deepens all the more.'

□

6

An Inspiration to Becoming Sanjivani (Panacea)

The tribal society of our country is very simple and deeply attached to its original culture. This society has protected Hinduism for ages. Remember the vanvas (exile to jungle) of Lord Ram! These tribals had shown Him the way out of His troubles. They had even become His army to face the demonic threat to India—Ravana. Ironically, in the age of Kalyug (the age of darkness), the same tribal society was mocked and they were deprived of their love for Hinduism in several cunning ways. It was a plot to weaken the Hindus of India. This began with the arrival of four Christian priests in India in 1845. Their mission was to establish a local mission of Christians to coordinate propagation of Christianity and convert locals to their faith. It was the time of the mighty British Raj. Yet, these priests had to struggle for 25 years to actualise their dreams. They established the Lutheran Mission in 1869. It means that the tribals must have resisted to their full potential. Thereafter, the Christians opened their first college in Hazaribagh. It also took 25 years. Then, the Christian Students Sangh was founded in 1910. After some time, this Sangh evolved into Chota Nagpur Society. In 1928, when the Simon Commission visited India, this society handed it a charter saying that the tribals were not Hindus. Their argument was that the tribals have their own culture which is distinct from Hindu culture and thus, there should be a separate state unit to safeguard their culture and identity. Subsequently, the tribals were scheduled in a separate category in the 1931 census. By 1938, the Lutheran Mission had established Unnati Samaj. The Anglic Mission had formed Kisan Sabha and the Roman Catholic Church had founded Chota Nagpur Catholic Sabha. They all merged into the Chota Nagpur Adivasi Mahasabha. In 1938 itself, then famous Hockey player, Jaypal Singh returned from England after being educated and converted to Christianity. He was made the head of the Chota Nagpur Adivasi Mahasabha. In 1950, during the Jamshedpur Conference, the Mahasabha turned into the Jharkhand Party.

In 1948, after the Independence of India, Prime Minister Nehru was welcomed with flowers everywhere he would go. One such welcome ceremony was organised at the Jharkhand-Chhattisgarh border. It was a huge gathering. Suddenly, some people started showing black flags to the Prime Minister. Nehru was a person who could easily be provoked. He got angry and the meeting had to be halted. The agitating people were called to the dais and asked why they were protesting. They said, 'As India was partitioned, Hindus got Hindustan, Muslims got Pakistan, and now we Christians want Englishtan.' It was shocking for Nehru. Later, the Bharatiya Jana Sangh (which later emerged as the Bharatiya Janata Party) led a counter-protest movement, 'The Anti-Foreign Missionary Week'. The Nehru government felt the heat and constituted a commission under Supreme Court judge Justice Niyogi. The Madhya Pradesh government published the Niyogi Commission report about the activities of the Christian missionaries in 1956. This report is available in two volumes of three parts each. This commission had proposed to enact a law to prevent religious conversion. However, the recommendations of the commissions were dumped in cold storage. The commission had also found that the Church activities were a part of an international conspiracy. The fundamental purpose of the Church, according to the report, was to establish a Christian state after sufficient conversions. And it could be dangerous to the unity and security of India. The Church used, according to the report, deceit, falsehood, enticement and fear to convert simple-hearted tribals. The report went on to say that the Church even sought to divide the country on the basis of religion. The report proved to be explosive and became the talk of the town in the entire country. It exposed the Church before the country. The Niyogi Commission wished to exterminate the demand of the Church for a separate state. However, it didn't happen. Some embers were still burning. The Christian priests were slowly spreading their network. Their target was innocent tribals living in the forests. The appeasement policies of the post-Independence

Nehru government provided the Church missionaries encouragement and they spread their tentacles throughout the tribal belt.

The tribal society was already living in complete isolation from mainstream Indian society. Moreover, being illiterate, they were unaware of the government schemes being run for them. Then, there was their own inefficiency to learn about the outside world. Several afflictions like addictions to liquor were a part of their life. Thus, they were easy prey to the Church's inducements.

The tribals were also dreaming of a better life in independent India. But, as time passed, they only got the neglect from both the society and government. Their anger kept accumulating and it finally turned into an inferno. The rift between them and the government was increasing. As a result, a flood of conversions swept across tribal areas within 20 years of Independence. The conversions that took place during this period were more than the overall conversions that had occurred during the British Raj of 200 years. It led to the Church planning a combined Christian state comprising tribal areas of Assam, Bihar, Odisha and Madhya Pradesh. But divisions appeared in the divisive forces themselves during the parliamentary elections of 1957 and 1962. Since they couldn't get electoral success, the enthusiasm for their movement ebbed and finally, the Jharkhand Party led by England-returned Jaipal Singh merged into the Congress. By 1970, the tribal movement had completely disillusioned. A proposal in this regard was presented before Janata Party's Prime Minister Morarji Desai around 1979. Even Mother Teresa had supported this proposal. Desai had rejected this proposal and it had led to serious violence in the Kolhan area of Jharkhand.

On the other hand, a staunch Hindu nationalist organisation, the Rashtriya Swayamsevak Sangh (RSS), was active since Independence to create awareness for their identity among Hindus. The Sangh had started various programmes for tribals to save them from falling into the trap of Christian missionaries. The Niyogi Commission report provided background information for charting out development schemes for tribals and to safeguard their dignity. Then RSS sarsanghchalak (chief), Honourable Guru ji, sent a lawyer from Nagpur, Balasaheb Deshpande ji to Jaspur, Chhattisgarh, to find solutions for the problems of conversion. The Sangh knew long before the Niyogi Commission made it clear that the Church had suspected designs and might shake the foundations of independent India. So, taking inspiration from Gandhian leader Thakkar Baapa, Ramakant Keshav Deshpande ji (who later came to be known as Vanyogi Balasaheb Deshpande) founded Vanvasi Kalyan Ashram on 26 December 1952.

The Vanvasi Kalyan Ashram was originally a hostel for children of the tribals. As a part of this project, the first hostel was opened with 13 students in Jaspur area of Madhya Pradesh (which is now in Chhattisgarh). At that time, it was the best possible remedy suggested by Guru ji Golwalkar to counter the activities of the Church. A pracharak was appointed to take care of the hostel.

When the Sangh workers studied the methods of how the Church worked, they found that its strength was not their services to the people, rather their regular contact with them. They had made the services to the people 'the face of their work'. They would devote only 10% of their workforce and finances in the service of the people. The rest 90% was invested in making contacts with the masses. They would go door-to-door. In order to prevent the Church's growing influence and make inroads into households, the Vanvasi Kalyan Ashram started organising various Shradha Jagran programmes. Satsang kendras were opened in villages. Then, primary schools were opened in villages as a part of its primary education programmes. This expanded the reach of the satsang people and they realised the true reason behind the success of the Church's efforts. It was because of the health facilities provided to people by the Church. They were converting people by helping them improve their health. Those days, it was common for people to die because of malaria and diarrhoea. The Church would use, and still does, such opportunities to convert people. They would offer conversion in exchange for treatment of these prevalent diseases. The Ashram did set up their own aarogya kendras (health centres) to help people. And, thus these aarogya kendras emerged as a successful working model to make tribals disease-free and counter the Church's designs.

Now, let's move to the 60s. The Bhartiya Jana Sangh had been established to link Indian politics with the main national stream. After the blessing of Honourable Guru ji, Syama Prasad Mukherjee was appointed its first chief. Syama Babu was earlier a Minister in the first Cabinet of India under Prime Ministership of Pandit Jawaharlal Nehru. He resigned from his ministry following differences over the Nehru-Liaquat Pact.

It was at the insistence of Syama ji that Honourable Guru ji had handed over Pandit Deendayal Upadhyay to the Jan Sangh. He was appointed its secretary. At that time, he was the first line pracharak of the Sangh. He invested himself completely for the cause of the Sangh. While touring various regions for the work of the Sangh, he came to know about South Bihar (Jharkhand). It was the time of assembly polls in the region. The Church was so influential at that time that no candidate was finalised without the blessings of the Church. Pandit ji chose some Hindu candidates for the Jan Sangh and hired a jeep to run their campaign. The jeep had the party flag on its bonnet. He took one or two colleagues with him and the Jan Sangh jeep toured almost all the villages of the state. And when the results were announced, around 10-15 (unsure of the numbers) candidates won. This was the first experiment to win the hearts of the tribal society by the Sangh and it was a great success.

Now, other Hindu organisations were also showing success in their own ways through the various activities that they were conducting for the people. These organisations were sowing the seeds of Hinduism in the tribal society with passion. As a result, the Church began to feel threatened and felt that its dream of creating a Christian state would perish. Therefore, the issues of India were raised in the meeting of Urban Rural Mission at the Christian Conference of Asia. The delegates were of the opinion that 'Hindu hard-line forces' had become active to interfere in religious conversions and as a consequence, the influence of the Church was shrinking quickly. So, the religious conversion was sidestepped and the Liberation Theology was proposed. As a part of this resolution, the following points were discussed.

1. The vanvasi samaj (tribal society) has its own distinct identity and the continuous influence of Hinduism has corroded it.
2. The state of Jharkhand has its own nationalist identity. It should become a separate state.
3. A liberation movement should start to free the tribal society from the servitude of the majority Hindu community.

As a part of this plan, it was propagated in the tribal community that 'your religion, Sarna, is different from Hinduism. You are not Hindus. Let's bring Sarna and Christians together and start a liberation movement.' This plan further moved towards its political end and Shibu Shoren, who was till then leading a reformist movement in Santhal Pargana area, was instigated to agitate for a separate state. Thus, a political movement known as the Jharkhand Mukti Morcha (JMM) came into being in 1975, with the help of the Church.

In 1975, the Emergency was also imposed on 25 June, midnight. Then President Fakhruddin Ali Ahmed declared the State of Emergency at the request of Prime Minister Indira Gandhi using powers under Article 52 of the Indian Constitution. The next day, on 26 June, the whole country heard the voice of Indira Gandhi detailing the imposition of the Emergency. The sudden decision to impose the Emergency was due to the judgement of the Allahabad High Court against Mrs Gandhi. In its judgement of 12 June 1975, the High Court had found Mrs Gandhi guilty of using government machinery in her parliamentary victory from Rae Bareli constituency in 1975 elections and forbade her from contesting elections for six years and also from holding any government office. The Supreme Court didn't change the High Court order, but allowed Mrs Gandhi to hold the office of the prime minister. Meanwhile, Jayprakash Narayan, principal opposition leader against Mrs Gandhi, had asked his supporters to protest from 12 June onwards.

After the Emergency, the country had descended into chaos. There were strikes throughout the country. A strong wave of protests had emerged in the leadership of Jayprakash Narayan and Morarji Desai. The opposition was mounting pressure day after day for lifting the Emergency and freedom of the political prisoners. The Emergency was imposed in such a manner that the fundamental rights of citizens were suspended. Right from the night of the Emergency, the political leaders were arrested. All big leaders of the time like Jayprakash Narayan, Lal Krishna Advani, Atal Bihari Vajpayee, George Fernandez and Morarji Desai were arrested. The RSS opposed the Emergency and a large number of its members were jailed. Ultimately, Indira Gandhi had to give in to the pressure from the opposition and she announced general elections. All political prisoners were freed and the opposition parties merged to form the Janata Party under the leadership of Morarji Desai. The general elections were held in 1977. The Congress was trounced in the election and the Janata Party won with a landslide majority. Morarji Bhai Desai was sworn in as the first non-Congress Prime Minister of the country. The ban on RSS was lifted but internal fissures in the government didn't allow the movement that had started against the Emergency to take firm social and political roots. Anti-national forces capitalised on this scenario of political instability. The Janata government finally crumbled under its own weight. Another general election was held in 1980 and Indira Gandhi returned to power. Unfortunately, the political upheavals returned, now in sharper intensity. She was finally killed because of her own political misjudgements and operational errors.

Now, it was 1986. Rajiv Gandhi was the Prime Minister of the country. He had married Sonia Gandhi with Christian rituals and thus his whole family had become Christian. His government invited the Pope, the highest spiritual authority of Christians, to India. When he was asked the purpose of his visit before his departure to India, he clearly said, 'In India, there are crores of people whose souls are roaming in the dark.' Everyone understood the 'meaning' of his words and purposefully, his first programme was convened in Ranchi. Even a target of converting around one lakh people was set during his visit. It made all Hindu organisations furious. A huge movement was built up. Hundreds of RSS volunteers left their homes. They toured from village to village and created awareness. The Christian community opposed it. As a result of this, the opposition movement turned tense and violent. Congress was in power both in Bihar (Ranchi was in Bihar then) and the Centre. Both the governments were building pressure on the commissioner of Ranchi but he was adamant to not let the Pope enter the city.

Now, can you imagine how much a sense of elation and courage it would have generated in the Hindu society? In the meantime, Rajiv Gandhi, who was hailed as the youth Prime Minister of India, got a bill passed in the Parliament, which was to ensure literacy in the whole country. But it failed to bring desired results.

In 1990, the new Prime Minister of India, VP Singh, constituted the Acharya Ramamurti Commission for evaluating the progress of the National Policy on Education of 1986 launched by the Rajiv government. Acharya ji was a Gandhian and renowned for his immense contribution in the field of education. Inspired by this commission's findings, Anil Bordia ji, a former civil servant and educationist, started a scheme in Rajasthan. It was called Shikshakarmi (One Teacher, One

School) that later came to be known as the Ekal Vidyalayas (Ekal schools).

INSPIRATION BEHIND THE FORMATION OF VANVANDHU PARISHAD AND ITS BACKGROUND

An organisation has natural strength and if it works formally, its strength shows its effect in society and earns the respect of the people. The Ekal schools are also moving in the same direction. The Vanvasi education that started from Dhanbad as a formal tribal education programme is now widening its wings in various dimensions and has proven to be quite effective. When Vanyatras (visit to tribal villages) were organised, the Ekal volunteers came across myriad kinds of experiences and all of them taught something innovative that could be tried for the betterment of the Ekal programme. It made the future road smooth for the movement. Impressed by the Vanyatras 'tribal tours', Smt. Prema Pandurang shared her tour experience with her close friend, Sri PR Krishna Kumar Varier (a renowned Ayurvedacharya, owner of the famous Ayurveda College of Coimbatore). He was greatly impressed by listening to the experiences of Prema ji and he himself desired to go on such tours. People in the Vanvasi Kalyan Ashram felt heartened and proud that a person like Varier ji was ready to join their welfare work for the tribals. Therefore, even the president of Vishwa Hindu Parishad (VHP) showed not only keen interest in this tour programme, but he himself decided to join the people for this programme. Shyam ji was in-charge of this important tour.

It was not an easy task to introduce such important people to the tribal society. So, Shyam ji carefully selected a village in Odisha to welcome these guests. Those days, the Church wielded a lot of influence in these villages. Still, the villagers waited for the arrival of the guests like eager kids. They felt no fear. Shyam ji explained the whole arrangement of the welcome programme to the tribals, provided all necessary things and then he left for Cuttack to take Varier ji. It was to be a grand programme and thus it was not possible to keep it a secret. The news spread to all surrounding villages. When the local Church came to know about this programme, it became active to get it aborted. They spread fake news in the villages that the 'Hindus' they were waiting for would not ultimately come and that only Christian priests were their real sympathisers and would rush to help them every time. The innocent villagers believed them and did not make any preparations to welcome their Hindu guests.

Shyam ji arrived with the guests from Cuttack. The caravan had to stop at a distance from the village, as there was no pucca road to the village. As per the welcome plan, the villagers had to be on this spot to welcome the guests and then take them to the welcome ceremony spot. Shyam ji alighted from the car and saw that there was a crowd of villagers at one end of the village. But there was no sign of any welcome programme. Sensing something Varier ji came out of the car. He looked like a Church priest in white clothes with a fair complexion. When the villagers saw him, they believed that he was a Church priest. Before Shyam ji could understand anything, there started a bustle among the villagers. Shyam ji became terrified and went to the villagers. The villagers told him what they thought. The villagers were actually discussing that what the Church priest had foretold them was coming true and only a Church priest had come to meet them. 'A white Church priest had come in a white car,' they thought. Shyam ji at first didn't believe them. Later, when Shyam ji heard them out properly, he tried to convince them. He got help from some village elders and ultimately the villagers were ready to listen to him and were finally convinced. Some of them rushed to arrange a stage and welcome the Hindu guests. Ultimately, the welcome programme kicked in. When the introduction of Varier ji was given, they were exulting that such a 'big personality' had come to meet them. When Varier ji was apprised of this development, he was very disheartened that our tribal society was still living with such innocence that some Christian priests were able to brainwash them so easily. He saw the similar situation in whichever village he travelled to. And on this note, this van yatra (tribal tour) concluded.

On the way back, all the members stayed at a dharamshala to rest. Shyam ji was curious to learn the impressions of all the team members of this tour. The purpose of the journey was clear from the very beginning. Varier ji and other senior members of the delegation, most of them from cities, observed the vanvasi compassion, simplicity, emotionality and poverty at every stage of this tour. Every heart had felt the pain of the vanvasis. At the end of this tour, a review meeting was organised to study the findings of this tour. Shyam ji asked everybody to share their views. They all insisted on one point: 'There is utter poverty. We should take steps to eradicate it.' So, all the city-dwellers decided to devise a plan for the poverty alleviation of the tribal society. Varier ji had also attended the meeting. He was grateful to Shyam ji for showing him and others the real face of the tribal society. 'We have been living in the cities and have only heard about tribal societies till now. But now, you have shown us the reality and we are feeling very disturbed. You are working like a mercenary to create awareness among these tribals. We think that this movement must widen. You tell us what we can do for this?' said Kumar ji. Shyam ji was just about to say something, but Kumar ji himself said that the requirements of the vanvasis are enormous, they have enough workers as well, but their resources are zero. So, you need to make a body that could collect money from the prosperous families in the city for the welfare of these societies. And as a starting point, you can establish Odisha Vanvandhu Parishad.

Thus, a new intellectual body to collect money and other resources came into being. Soon, the active volunteers of Kolkata were informed about this. They called a meeting to discuss how this body would function. One of the volunteers raised a very relevant doubt in this meeting: 'Shyam ji, we are residents of Kolkata. If we will collect money for the Odisha Vanvandhu Parishad, they might hesitate to donate with an open heart. So, it should be renamed as Vanvandhu Parishad.' This suggestion was unanimously accepted.

Now, Shree Mangilal Jain ji had to get a go-ahead from the Sangh and Vanvasi Kalyan Ashram for the formation of the Vanvandhu Parishad. The Ashram headquarter was in Jaspur. The Ashram would hold meetings once in three months. Jain ji also attended its meeting, but he couldn't muster the courage to present his proposal. He was so doubtful of his proposal that he felt that if he broached that topic in the meeting, it would be outrightly rejected. He was waiting for the right moment. At that time, Shree Balasaheb Deshpande ji was also in the Ashram. His residence was near the campus of the Ashram. He was a lawyer and this residence would also function as an office. Jain ji went to see him at night. He was doubtful whether Deshpande ji would understand his proposal and its importance? But he was very confident of his own and Deshpande ji's patriotism and the passion to serve their country.

Jain ji explained to Deshpande ji that all of his dedicated colleagues were desperate to work for the welfare of the tribals but they had neither the resources nor any skilled workers to set out on this mission. 'Thus, our progress on this front is very slow. If we will continue to suffer from this resourcelessness and paucity of committed workers, we would not be able to achieve our target. As a solution, we have decided that we must form an all-India organisation in the name of Vanvandhu Parishad and through this body, we have collected money for our project,' he said. Deshpande ji reacted, 'Why should we form a new body when we already have the Kalyan Ashram for this job?' At this, Jain ji said that his colleagues wished to bring some changes within the Ashram. 'And for this purpose, we will have to make one renowned industrialist the chairman of such a body. It will help connect prosperous families to the mission and thus the collection of the money will be easy,' he said. Deshpande ji nodded but expressed his anxiety: 'Who will control this money?' Jain ji replied impulsively, 'I will declare myself the treasurer. No transfer of money will be possible without my signature. I am one of your co-volunteers. I hope you trust me? You are our guide. In the end, whatever you will say, we'll do.' Deshpande ji was overwhelmed at this response and accepted Jain ji's proposal immediately. In this way, the Vanvasi Kalyan Ashram permitted the establishment of the Vanvandhu Parishad.

Jain ji shared this news with Shyam ji. Shyam ji was elated but he was also worried about whether the Sangh would agree to this or not? Jain ji assured him that he would talk to the Sangh and would hopefully get the permission.

After consulting many of his close colleagues, Jain ji went to meet Sangh volunteer Shree Vimal Lath ji at his office. There were also other Sangh members present at his residence. Jain ji explained his proposal in detail before all of them. He said that it was a big project and demanded proportionate resources. Therefore, he said, he needed money collected from the society. 'And that's why we felt that we felt the need to establish Vanvandhu Parishad to attract people living in the cities,' he said. The Sangh officials immediately sniffed that it was Shyam ji's plan. They were full of doubts. But they said, 'Oh, this seems like Shyam ji's scheme. Okay, work on it.' Hearing this, Jain ji was extremely glad. He dialled Shyam ji and told him about this. And now after the Vanvasi Kalyan

Ashram, even the Sangh cleared the path for establishing the Vanvandhu Parishad. It actually became an all-India organ of the Sangh and started working under the supervision of the Vanvasi Kalyan Ashram.

PROGRESS THROUGH MATRUSHAKTI (WOMEN EMPOWERMENT)

It was 1971. Shyam ji had become the bhibhag pracharak (Zonal In-charge of RSS). In one of the meetings of the pracharaks, a pracharak from Indore put a very thought-provoking question before Guru Golwalkar ji. He said, 'One day, a student went to appear in an exam. On his return, his father asked him, "How did the exam go?" The child responded, "It went superbly. I am hopeful of 100 out of 100 marks." The father was exalted. He said, "It means you have solved all 10 questions." The son replied, "No, I have attempted only five." The father was perplexed, "How come you will secure 100 marks? How is it possible?"' The pracharak finished his story and tried to explain that the Sangh was working to unite the whole Hindu society in a similar fashion. 'We don't have participation of 50% of our women in the shakhas. How can we claim to unite the whole society?' he continued. This question dug deep into Shyam ji's mind. Shree Guru ji tried to assuage pracharaks that women might not have entry in the shakhas, but they could join the Sangh anyway. However, the reality was that the Sangh was unable to connect to women of all sections of society. One major reason was that only individuals were a part of the Sangh, not their families. The planning to connect individuals and their families took a lot of time. In 1989, the Sangh celebrated the centenary celebration of Sangh's founder, Dr Keshav Baliram Hedgewar. In the meeting at Nagpur, it was discussed whether the Sangh was able to build India of Doctor ji's dream? And how much of this target had been achieved? When the meeting concluded, there was nothing significant to celebrate on this front. Then, the Sangh members tried to find out the key areas where they had erred. They came to a significant conclusion about this: 'Any change in society starts from the family. And a mother plays the pivotal role in shaping the family. And the role of mothers was almost negligible in expanding the horizons of the Sangh in society. So, how could we expect any significant societal change? As a resolution to this burning question, Shyam ji decided to connect Matrushakti (Women Empowerment) with the Ekal Abhiyan.

When Shyam ji was a pracharak in Banaras (Varanasi), he met a Swayamsevak family. He was a Lecturer at the Jaunpur Degree College. He would attend the Sangh activities with his family. Shyam ji met his daughter, Manju Srivastava, at a Sangh programme. She was then merely a Class 9 student. Shyam ji was familiar with the family and would keep visiting their home because of some Sangh-related work. After some time, Shyam ji was transferred to Agra. Thus, though the connection was snapped, there was a link of communication through the channel of Sangh. After some years, Manju was married and shifted to Delhi. Her husband's job was transferrable. So, she first went to Lucknow and then to Kolkata. She had studied Psychology and Education. She had taught at various colleges. She was teaching Psychology at Anglo Indian College, Kolkata. She had not communicated with Shyam ji all these years. It was around 1986 that Shyam ji contacted her and went to see her with industrialist Ramesh Saraogi. By that time, the Vanvandhu Parishad had not come into being. After his meeting with Manju ji, Shyam ji would always visit her whenever he was in Kolkata. Her husband and children had grown very close to Shyam ji. As they met often, the discussion about the tribal society also cropped up. Manju ji developed an interest to know the tribal society more closely.

Meanwhile, Shyam ji and his colleagues planned another tour to the tribal areas around 1986-87. The intention behind this tour was to establish a connection between the tribals and people living in the cities. Shyam ji sent an invitation to Manju ji to join this tour. Many affluent people from Kolkata were a part of the Vanyatra team. For most of them, it was the first opportunity to see the tribal society. This tribal area was in Jharkhand (then South Bihar). That touring team visited many areas in Ranchi, Gumla and beyond. This journey proved to be a life-changing experience for Manju ji. She had so far only heard about the tribals and their lives and now, she had seen everything first-hand. It is said the experienced truth is always life-altering. Manju ji saw the tribal women and children struggling for survival. She was completely stunned to see the hardships tribals face in their lives. It was eye-opening for her. She and others felt that there also existed a world so near yet hitherto hidden from them. For the first time, she felt so moved by seeing the conditions of a social group. Those tribal faces kept haunting her long after she returned from that tour.

After a while, Shyam ji happened to visit Manju ji's house. Now, he asked her straightforwardly: 'Would you be part of the efforts for the welfare of the tribals?' She didn't blink even for a second and nodded her head in agreement. It was as if she was waiting for this question. She seemed to have found the purpose of her life. She shared with Shyam ji that she was always concerned with the problems faced by women in every society. 'Wherever I went, I saw only men dominating in all spheres. I once even asked Sangh office-bearers, "Why don't women have a role in the organisation?"' she said. She continued that she would always get a one-line answer: 'We have Rashtra Sevika Samiti.' But it was not an answer to any women-related problem, she said, as most of the Samiti women remained limited within its circle and contributed towards nothing significant. 'Some women spent their lives as pracharak and contributed to the Sangh. But many such volunteers preferred to marry and thus escaped their duties towards society,' she added.

Shyam ji heard Manju ji out with patience and after some deliberation gave her the task to form a women committee. Since Shyam ji and his colleagues were initially related to the Vanvasi Kalyan Ashram, Manju ji also formed a committee linked to the Ashram. This committee was actually a training ground for women working for the Ashram in Kolkata. Manju ji moulded this committee for the maximum benefit and developed its own working mechanism. In 1989, on the day of Makar Sankranti, the Vanvandhu Parishad was formed. This introduced Manju ji to women from elite families of Kolkata. After meeting many such women, she came to know that a number of capable women were sitting idle at home and could be employed in a productive project. All these women, found Manju ji, were not only capable, they also had ample resources, money and power. They were also independent to choose any path in their lives. 'If there is no purpose in their lives, let's seed one. It will put their energies to some constructive use,' thought Manju ji. So, under the initiative of Manju ji, the Vanvandhu Mahila Samiti was founded in 1992. All the members of this Samiti were women from the families of Vanvandhu Parishad's city-based volunteers. Manju ji began to be called 'Manju Didi' among the Ekal family members. It was not an easy task for Manju ji to convince the women to come out from the confines of their houses and dedicate themselves for the welfare of tribals whom they had never seen or heard before. But Manju ji was a woman of steely resolve. She not only forced ordinary women to join her welfare project, but she also started contacting a wide network of influential women. Sometimes she used to call around 30 women for a meeting, but merely five would turn up. But every effort deserves a promised fruit. Slowly, the Samiti (committee) started spreading its wings at the city, zone, unit and then village level. The committee gained numerous types of experiences and compiled an array of thoughts from various quarters. Now, wherever Manju ji went, she ensured that she would spread word about tribal welfare among the women and would plan something concrete on this front. She would try to explain how important tribal welfare was to the women who had never visited the tribal areas. With the women who somehow had connections with the Ekal and knew something about tribals, she would discuss ways to ensure their participation in the project. She would cite various examples like progress of the country through its villages and the various challenges posed to our rural life if welfare work was not carried out in the villages. Delineating the condition of tribals, she would cite an example of Yashoda Maa. 'A tribal kid is like Lord Krishna. He was born from the womb of Devaki, but she was chained to poverty and illiteracy and thus unable to raise her kid properly. Had Yashoda Maa not adopted Lord Krishna, He would not be a pivotal character (Chkradhari Karmayogi) of Mahabharata. Sisters, you have become like Yashoda Maa. I know many of you can't go to the jungles. But you can contribute for the jungle-residing tribals right from your own households,' she would explain. Her words would cast magic on women and they would readily agree to be part of the Ekal. Then, these women were engaged in different tasks of the Ekal.

In order to make the Vanvandhu Mahila Samiti a properly ordered organisation, its chapters were opened in big cities in the beginning. Then came the turn of districts, zones, blocks, and sanchs (units). In this way, Ekal became an amalgam of women from all walks of life. These women would be entrusted responsibilities as per their capabilities and time. Women members from the cities were rich, resourceful and modern. They were quite adept at effective communication and hence they were given the responsibility of collecting money for the Ekal. They were allowed to organise programmes for this purpose. They were provided total independence on this front. They could fund the education of rural tribal children and could also organise exhibitions of paintings of such children in cities. The rural members of the samiti were taught sewing, embroidery, pickle preparation and making papads (poppadom) so that they could become experts. The rural women would also help in the exhibition of paintings by preparing various items needed for such an exhibition. This exhibition has become so successful that it is now known as the Ekal Carnival.

On the day of Makar Sankranti, the samiti members collect special donations and present gifts to the full-time volunteers and village teachers. This gesture aims to impart the feeling in the women members that 'You are mothers and these young workers are like your children.' The volunteers work with complete diligence and devotion. They never waver from their commitment however hard the circumstances become for them. And for such faithfulness for their mission, they naturally expect something in return. That's why women members are encouraged to become guardians for such volunteers for one day. This exercise is part of the Abhibhabak Yojna (Guardianship Programme). As part of this programme, workers are divided into groups based on chapter, region, zone and unit level teams. A woman member becomes the mother of a worker as per the programme. She has to communicate with her son/daughter once a month. This communication is always informal and the real purpose of this interaction is to find out about the conditions of the family of the worker—how the family is pulling through, what are conditions of their children and whether they are studying or not, etc.? This exercise directly touches the hearts of the volunteers as they feel that there is someone motherly who cares for them while being in the city. This motherhood fills the volunteer with more vigour and the whole exercise becomes a great source of inspiration for the Ekal family. Similarly, a programme runs for the teachers in village schools and a mother is appointed to communicate with them on a regular basis.

Manju ji and her colleagues have also run a scheme to organise marriages of needy girls. As a unique part of this programme, a gift box is prepared for bride's clothes and other necessary items. In addition to it, the samiti also gives a small amount to the volunteer as a shagun (good omen). Such efforts have built up the women's organisation of the Parishad, or

The Gandhi Peace Prize, 2017

to

Ekal Abhiyan Trust

from

The President of India,

Shri Ram Nath Kovind

In 2017, Ekal's founder member, Shree Mangilal Jainji, accepted the Gandhi Peace Prize from President Ram Nath Kovindji and Prime Minister Narendra Modiji.

Former Sarsanghachalak Prof. Rajju Bhaiyya, Shree Madanlal Aggrawal, Shyam Guptji and other members discussing the Ekal Abhiyan in then Jharkhand.

In the annual function of the Vanvandhu Parishad, former Sarsanghachalak Prof. Rajju Bhaiya, Mr P.D. Chitlangaya, Madan Babu, Vimal Lath, Kalidasji (Regional Sanghchalak, Kolkata)

The Ekal Parinaam Kumbh, Dhanbad, 2015. Shree Ashok Singhal, Sadhvi Ritambhara, Shyamji Gupt and others.

The inaugural session of the Ekal Kumbh organised in Delhi in 2009. Shree Ashok Singhal, Sarsanghachalak Shree Mohan Rao Bhagwat, Shree Satyanarayan Vandhu and other guests.

Yoga Guru Baba Ramdev inaugurates Ekal Kumbh exhibition in Delhi, 2009.

The concluding session of Ekal Abhiyan Parivartan Kumbh on 18 February 2020. Present on the occasion are Sangh's Sah-karyavah Shree Dr Krishna Gopal, Defence Minister Rajnath Singh, Kathavachak Shree Rameshbhai Ojha. Also present are two Ekal School's former students, who are currently serving in the Indian Army.

Former Rajya Sabha member and then global president of the Ekal, Subhash Chandra, is with Ashok Modi and others during a tour of Odisha.

Dr. Rakesh Popli is giving Sidhartha puruskar to Ekal students.

Manjudidi welcomed by village pramukh in 'Singbay' gaon in Assam.

In Chota Nagpur (Bihar), then Lok Sabha Speaker Shree kariya Munda tries his hands on dholak and mesmerised vanvasis (tribals) and members of Vanvandhu Parishad dance on the music.

Villagers are making biofertilizers in Gram Resource Centre in Karanjo village

Scene of an Ekal School being run in Uttar Pradesh.

An Ekal Abhiyan procession led by Nashik Shehar Mahila Sangathan in Nashik

The inaugural function of Jamshedpur Van Yatra (Forest Tour)

Free Health Camp organised by Aarogya Foundation of India in Leh, Ladakh

Vanvasi kathakaar in a ShreeHari Katha programme organised by the ShreeHari Katha Satsang Samiti.

the Ekal. Today, if we take examples of Uttarakhand and Himachal, we will find that there are 100% women in various committees of the Ekal and related organisations. Many of them hold key official posts and these women officials regularly tour the villages in their working zones once in two months. She inspects the school and holds the meeting of the village committee. She speaks to the women teachers. Such meetings serve many purposes. One of them is that the families of these teachers are assured that their girls are working with a secure and prestigious organisation. (Excerpt from the book, *Ekal Abhiyan: Janm Se Jan Aandolan Tak*).

A CHILDHOOD ASPIRATION SHOWS A NEW PATH

We know that the Vanvandhu Parishad was born in Kolkata. Two Vanyatras (tribal tours) from Kolkata proved to be historic. An elite family of the city started touring tribal areas to connect the urban people with the tribal lands. They first chose Phulwani district and sent a team to visit the tribal areas in the district. They stopped at a designated place for the satsang. Everyone got so engrossed in the satsang that they forgot what was the next item in their itinerary. As they got ready to board the bus, the elite family that was leading this team, realised that their youngest child was missing. It had become dark. All the village tribals had already returned to their villages. Now, everyone was worried. Several types of doubts crossed the minds of the family members. Fortunately, some local workers, who came to see off the team, were yet to depart. Shyam ji instructed them in Odia language and they ran in various directions. Shyam ji also went to a village with them. The tour members began chanting the name of Lord Ram in the bus. It was a very sensational moment for everyone. Some extremely tense moments later, a worker came to Shyam ji and said, 'A kid has been seen with a family, but we don't recognise him and he neither seems to be understanding our language.' Shyam ji rushed to the house of that family and what he saw there was unbelievable. He didn't know whether he must cry or exult in joy. It was the same lost child. He was playing in the lap of an old woman. She was cuddling him and also feeding him something. They both were happy and laughing together. Shyam ji approached them and apprised the old lady of the whole episode. She started weeping. She said, 'I was under the impression that the visiting team would stay in the village and this child followed me from the satsang.' That innocent child was oblivious of what was happening and he reached the bus with that old woman. Finally, he was united with his mother, but the old lady was inconsolable at the separation. She was also filled with a 'guilty conscience' as everyone was greatly troubled because the child was with her. Her condition disturbed everyone in the touring team. The local workers had to somehow convince her that it was not her fault at all and that it all happened naturally. Ultimately, her heart felt relieved and she went back home. All these scenes created a tableau of tribal life before the visiting Kolkatans who now had a fair idea how delicate-hearted tribal people are. It would prove very beneficial for the welfare of the tribals and the Ekal Abhiyan in the future.

Another tribal tour of the Kolkata team became historic. Once, a renowned industrialist of Kolkata led a team visit to the tribal areas. When they were returning, he asked Shyam ji at the railway station, 'Shyam ji, you have shown us a hospital. How much is its annual budget?' Shyam ji replied, 'You are our guest right now. It will not be proper to discuss the budget with you. I will visit Kolkata soon and then we will discuss the budget.' After some time, Shyam ji visited Kolkata and met the industrialist at his office. After some discussion, that gentleman took out a cheque and tried to hand it over to Shyam ji. Shyam ji forbade him and said, 'This is your office. We can only discuss business-related things here. Charity must be discussed and distributed at home with family and parents. When I visit your home, I will accept it from the hands of your mother.'

Later, Shyam ji visited that businessman's home and spoke about charity and his mission in the presence of his mother. His mother heard everything with patience and got slightly angry with her son. She asked him to increase the amount he was offering as charity. It was increased to be multiple times more than decided. When Mata ji moved that cheque towards Shyam ji, he folded his hands and politely said, 'Mataji, charity is best done at a pilgrimage site. I would be grateful to receive this cheque at the hospital for the rural poor.' A mother is ultimately a mother. She is the embodiment of love and compassion. She agreed. And thus, another tribal vanyatra under the aegis of this family was planned. After a few days, the whole family was in the hospital of Lohardaga, Jharkhand. Mata ji was full of enthusiasm and feelings for those being treated. She carefully inspected the entire hospital. She enquired what were the available facilities and what was missing? Her peering eyes found that there was no generator at the hospital. How could a hospital run without an arrangement of emergency electricity supply? She asked her son whether he had examined everything at the hospital. She scolded her son for not spotting that there was no generator in the hospital. She ordered him to prepare a cheque for the generator immediately.

Then, the time came for the handover of the cheque to Shyam ji and his team. Almost all the prominent citizens of Lohardaga were present. Now, the question was: Who should accept the cheque from the Kolkata family? The first obvious name was the head of the regional committee. However, a noble idea struck Shyam ji's mind. There was a very old servant at the Lohardaga campus. He would cook food for everyone and was called 'mama' (maternal uncle). He was everyone's favourite. Shyam ji said that 'mama ji' would accept the cheque on behalf of the organisation. Everybody was puzzled by this surprise but everyone was elated on hearing the announcement. When workers called mama, he was working in the kitchen as usual. He was busy preparing refreshments for the gathering. Since he was called in an urgent manner, he rushed towards the stage in the same clothes that he was wearing in the kitchen. He was unable to fathom why he was called this way. When Shyam ji asked him to come forward, he was stunned. He moved ahead and stood before Mata ji. When Mata ji handed him a cheque amid a round of applause, he was overwhelmed with surprise and emotions. He fell on the feet of Mata ji. Mata ji asked him to get up and hugged him with the affection of a mother. It was a rare and wonderful sight for everyone. Later, when Mata ji enquired about mama ji's family, she was livid with her son and said, 'Why didn't you people think about this fellow and his family?' The obedient son immediately cut a cheque for mama ji. Now, the atmosphere of the whole gathering turned emotional. With the inspirational initiative of Mata ji, the foundation of such donations for the Ekal was laid. Since then, her family became one the largest donors for the mission. The more this family donates for the Ekal, the more their income is increasing. It's all the blessing of the Lord! Mata ji started taking so much interest in tribal welfare that she kept making enquiries about the hospital regularly.

It was 1989. Shyam ji was sent to Kalyan Ashram in Bengal. He was made the in-charge of Bengal, Bihar, Jharkhand, Odisha and Andaman. He had to attend an introductory meeting in Kolkata. But this meeting turned out to be very disturbing. A scuffle broke out between a senior office-bearer of the regional committee and the secretary (of the organisation) of the region. The secretary was asking for money for the payment of the full-time volunteers, but the committee member was showing his inability to do so. He was insisting that the arrangement of the money was also the responsibility of the organisation and not the committee. Nothing constructive was achieved in this meeting. Shyam ji was very disheartened. He also took this up as a challenge.

When he asked the secretary how he collected money. He said that he would go from shop to shop asking for donations. 'Sometimes, shopkeepers agree to shell out some bucks, sometimes they simply say "no",' he said. This secretary was older than Shyam ji and has been working as a pracharak of the Sangh. His words pierced Shyam ji's heart. He didn't sleep that night. He never had to collect money in such a long association with the Sangh as its pracharak. His whole night was spent thinking about possible ways out of this wriggle of money collection. He was lost in thoughts and suddenly he was reminded of a meeting between Dr Hedgewar ji and Pandit Madan Mohan Malviya ji and the lightning of an idea struck his mind. Malviya ji was very happy with Doctor ji that at least someone had taken up the challenge of the Hindu cause. However, once Malviya ji noticed that Doctor ji's shoes didn't even have soles. It moved him so much that he himself proposed to raise funds or resources for the Sangh. He asked Doctor ji to choose between two M's—money or man. Doctor ji chose man or manpower over money. Malviya ji was shocked, but he was extremely pleased as well. It was under this impression that Malviya ji handed the most talented teachers at his university (Banaras Hindu Vishwavidyalaya)—honourable Guru Golwaklkar ji—for the service of the Sangh. It was the victory of the strength of heart (mann) over money (dhan). It became a permanent teaching of the Sangh that first the heart of a man has to be won over; the money will automatically follow. This became the remedy that was divinely suggested to Shyam ji that night. He decided that he would have to first win the hearts of people and the money would naturally come to the coffers. He decided that he would not broach the subject of money in front of the people at all and that he had to make inroads into their hearts. Now, it was to be seen whether the Sangh's teaching would bring practical results for the Ashram or not?

A list of 30 children from 20 families in Kolkata was prepared. When Shyam ji conducted the orientation about the tribal lands for them and told them story after story, the children began to call him mama ji. He chalked out a plan to take these children to tribal areas. When Shyam ji went to seek permission from their families, the ladies would ask him, 'Where will our children stay?' He would say that they would stay with a village family. Then, the ladies would ask, 'But there would be no AC there?' Shyam ji would stay silent on this question. But the children would themselves try to convince their families, 'We will manage… we will manage somehow.' Then, the ladies would come with another urban motherly query, 'Will they get cold drinks there? Do those houses have a fridge? How is the arrangement for the toilet?' Shyam ji had no answer for these questions. He could only utter this: 'Let the children go for the sake of their own interest and experience of rural life. If they feel uncomfortable there, we would send them back immediately.' Hearing this and surrendering before the insistence of their children, their families finally agreed. Now, a team of 30 children from Kolkata had to leave for Ranchi. Their stay was arranged in a school of Khunti unit near Ranchi. When these children returned to Kolkata, Shyam ji started visiting their homes in Kolkata. After formal conversations and refreshments, the only subject on which he would talk to the families was the experiences of the children in the tribal areas. He came to know that most of those families didn't know what creature a tribal was before he shared with them his own lively experiences of Odisha. These conversations also provided Shyam ji a valuable insight that children are the most receptive members of a family. He noticed that whenever he spoke, the children would listen with rapt attention as if he was telling them their favourite night time story. With these children, the ladies of the households would also show keen interests in those tales. Menfolk would either show little interest or they would remain occupied with their businesses. Such conversations turned the minds of families curious day by day. They would now want to experience tribal life first-hand. Thus, the idea of children's tour to tribal areas took birth. It was also quite a coincidence that the children's tour happened to be during their school vacations. It was summer time.

The children were themselves planning to go to some place during their holidays. Therefore, a seven-day tribal tour in Ranchi for these young Kolkatans was planned.

As these children landed among tribals, they intermixed with them within two days. They didn't feel like strangers at all. Village children had never seen urban kids. When beautiful Kolkatan kids would be seen playing and happily roaming in villages, the whole village would turn up to see them having fun. The tribal mothers would take them to their homes and would show so much affection that they would not even have received at their own homes. In Kolkata, their parents for some reason would always upbraid them, but here, they were fully free and on their own. These urban kids had never seen agricultural fields. When they entered such fields, they asked so many innocently curious questions about farming that village children had fun listening to their queries. These touring kids neither had any idea how the hills looked from close vicinity. They didn't even know how kids could climb high trees. How can someone swim and enjoy in ponds for hours? Rural and urban kids would together play kabaddi. However, there also came some moments when urban kids would feel so sad that tears would roll down their eyes. It was when they would ask tribal children whether they attended schools and knew how to read and write? The tribal kids would answer in the negative. The urban children would attend the Ekal schools daily and it would fill them with both hope and sadness. They would feel hopeful that there was a teaching arrangement for tribal kids and that the pedagogy was very impressive, but they would feel sad as there was no other school to cater to all the tribal kids.

When these children returned to Kolkata, their families and other friendly families planned to organise a programme where these kids would share their experiences of the tribal tour. When the children narrated their experiences, the whole gathering felt the motherly warmth shown by the tribals, especially their ladies, towards the children. All the children also looked overwhelmed with the love they had received. It was evident from their body language. After the children, their mothers were called to share their side of the story. They had also gone to the tribal areas for one day. Their narration was magical. Some listeners had taken the stories of the children as kiddish, but the accounts of the mothers filled them with a 'guilty conscience' as they must have felt that they were doing little for their tribal brethren. Now, it was the turn of fathers. Instead of praising Shyam ji, they unleashed their fury on him. Why? 'Shyam ji had been visiting our homes for such a long time. He kept narrating tales to our children, but he never told us that he was working in such unliveable circumstances. Our eyes opened when we experienced the lives of the tribals ourselves. Now, Shyam ji must tell us what we should do.' they said. Shyam ji stood up from his position and first apologised to all of them. Then he requested them, 'This is not the right occasion to put any demand before you. You all decide among yourselves and call a meeting. Our office-bearers will come and allay all your doubts. You first get fully convinced and then whatever you will decide, we will together follow that blueprint.'

Now came the festival of Deepavali. The children invited Shyam ji to celebrate the festival with them. As soon as he arrived among them, they started singing, '*Mama ji aaye hain, kuch tohfe laye hain* (Mama ji has come with some gifts).' He became sad, as he hadn't brought any gift. Suddenly, the children changed their song, '*Mama ji aaye hain, kuch tohfa payenge* (Mama ji has come, he will get a gift).' Shyam ji was startled. Then, a mother came to his rescue and explained everything. 'These children want to gift you something,' she said. A child came forward and said, 'Mama ji, you have done a great favour on us. You have opened our eyes. We never knew that children like us were leading such miserable lives in our own villages. Hence, we have decided that we will not spend a penny on crackers this Deepavali and save that money for the tribal children.' When Shyam ji was told of that saved amount, he was shocked that children spent so much money merely bursting crackers.

Shyam ji thought of an idea. But he first hugged every child. Then, he addressed them, 'Children, this one hug to each of you is my gift for you. You have written a new chapter in the service of tribal welfare.' Then, suddenly he also thought of another plan. He asked the children, 'Whatever I ask you, will you do?' Those children were ready to do anything Shyam ji would say. They said in a loud chorus, 'Yes.' Then, Shyam ji asked them whether they would convince their mothers to do something for the villages and villagers? They said, 'We have already told them.' And to your fathers? They were overenthusiastic and said, 'Yes, we have told our fathers as well.' Then, Shyam ji explained to them, 'We have to now form a mohalla samiti (colony committee) of the Vanvasi Kalyan Ashram. As part of this, you and your parents will have to organise meetings every month. Are you ready for this?' All of them agreed and a plan for formation of at least 10 colony committees was promulgated right on the spot. Then came the turn of family elders. They had assembled in large numbers as most of them had also brought their friends with them. These friends had heard about the children's tribal tours while talking to their own children and thus, they had developed curiosity to know more about tribal welfare and meet Shyam ji. A senior member of the Kalyan Ashram was present at the meeting. He presented the functioning of the Ashram to the audience in a very effective way. His presentation was followed by a question-and-answer session. Interestingly, everyone asked the same question—how does such a vast organisation manage its expenses? They were told that there was no regular resource availability and that whatever people like them donated was spent to run the Ashram.

It surprised everyone, for they had in their minds that some government scheme or big corporate funding was behind such a venture. The second most asked question was: 'What is your budget?' When people were told about the payment or remunerations of the full-time workers, they refused to believe it. They looked at each other. It was unbelievable for them how could a young man work for such a paltry payment? The last question was: 'What is your current economic condition?' The Ashram office-bearer told them plainly that the Ashram was unable to pay their full-timers for the last two months. Hearing this, the gathering exploded on Shyam ji. 'You visit our homes so regularly. You share tales of your work among tribals. You also took our children to tour those areas. They were so jubilant to be among them and sad at their conditions. They narrated us all. We also went there out of curiosity. We had also asked about any financial problem when we had organised a "tour recall" for children and their mothers, but you didn't share anything with us. Why?' they asked almost in unison. Shyam ji had no answer for them. But he knew one thing with utmost surety: He had won the hearts of those families who would now uplift the lives of tribals, their education and the Ekal Mission for the sake of their own children.

□

7
Ekal Brahmastra Se Gram Swaraj

Th lifeline of any movement is its strength of commitment. Swami Vivekananda's eternal words, 'Arise! Awake! And stop not till the goal is achieved' inspired Vishwa Hindu Parishad (VHP) president Late Sri Ashok Singhal ji who called the Ekal a Brahmastra (the ultimate weapon) in 1999. He said, 'Our society has found a Brahmastra and that is the Ekal Vidyalaya. We will be able to solve all the problems of the country through this weapon.' Ashok ji was a diehard devotee of Shree Satya Sai Baba. In 1999, he went to meet Sai Baba. When both of them were conversing, the topic of the Ekal chipped in. Sai Baba asked Ashok ji, 'How vast have you kept the target of these Ekal schools?' Ashok ji said that his organisation wished to open 10,000 Ekal schools. Sai Baba was stunned. He said, 'You are calling it the Brahmastra and your target is merely 10,000. Your target must be one-lakh.' When he heard one-lakh, Ashok ji said, 'Where would we manage to find one-lakh volunteers? Where will the money for such a gigantic project come from?' Baba put his loving hand on his back, 'Ashok, Baba is with you.' When Ashok ji shared this with the Ekal's founding member, Shyam Gupt ji, he couldn't understand the real import of Baba ji's words then. The figure of one-lakh schools was somewhat distant and imaginary for him. However, the spiritual intelligence conveyed it to him that when Baba ji had spoken about 'one-lakh Ekal schools', he must have meant it. So, he also started repeating the same 'one-lakh schools' line.

In 1999, Ashok ji went on a tour to the United States. The people of the Indian diaspora asked him the obvious question: 'What can we do for your mission from here?' To explain his mission, Ashok ji gave a brief presentation about the Ekal mission. When Indian-Americans heard about the Ekal schools and tehir functioning, they grew curious to know more about them. Ashok ji told them that one Shyam Gupt ji was the in-charge of the Ekal School Mission and when he would tour the US, he would explain in detail how the Ekal schools are established and run. When Ashok ji returned to India, he asked Shyam ji, 'You will have to go to America and acquaint the Indian community there with the Ekal Mission.' Later, Shyam ji did tour America in 2001 and gave a detailed presentation about the Ekal schools to Indians living there. He in fact spent three months there, touring various places and explaining how the mission worked. Indians living in America were convinced of what Shyam ji told them, yet they said, 'We will believe you only after we see the Ekal schools functioning with our own eyes.' Thus, a team of Indian-Americans came to India to witness the functioning of the Ekal schools first-hand. They toured several places and closely examined the working of the Ekal schools. After they had finished visiting many Ekal schools, they came to see Shyam ji. Before any conversation could begin, they said, 'Shyam ji, your target is to open one-lakh Ekal schools and we assure that you will never feel paucity of funds. We take an oath here that we will never allow such a situation to arise.'

Then in 2001 itself, Shyam Gupt ji from the Ekal Abhiyaan, Parmarth Niketan's Swami Chidanand Saraswati ji and the president of Vanvandhu Parishad, P.D. Chitlangaya ji, took a pledge of establishing one-lakh Ekal schools while performing the ritual of Ganga Aarti. The witnesses to this historic event were the banks of the Ganga in Rishikesh and a grand statue of Mahadev (Lord Shiva) in front of them. This moment of will and determination to achieve their target was heart wrenching. It obviously was not an easy target to establish one-lakh schools of 'One Teacher, One School' model in rural hinterlands of India. But its dreamer-in-chief, Shyam Gupt ji, was adamant like a rock. With the pledge, the time limit of the target was also finalised. The target was to be achieved by 2011. The date was decided considering the 175th birth anniversary of Ramkrishna Paramhans ji in 2011.

As the pledge and setting of the target were completed and everyone deputed him or herself to complete this task, both the determination and doubt travelled together in this journey. The Ekal schools actually turned into the Ekal Abhiyaan during this period. All the plans conceived by the Ekal team were implemented. They were able to achieve more than desired the results.

In 2005, a Karyakarta Kumbh (festive gathering of Ekal workers) was organised for the first time in Indore, Madhya Pradesh. It turned out to be an unprecedented success and encouraged the Ekal team to organise more such festivals. In 2009, an Ekal Kumbh (Ekal festival) was organised in Delhi and on similar lines, a Sanskaar Kumbh (Festival of Ethics) was organised in Mumbai. Nevertheless, despite all these successes, the year 2011 arrived but the target of 100,000 was still far away. In 2013, India celebrated the 150th birth anniversary of Swami Vivekananda with great enthusiasm. On this occasion, the Ekal team again pledged to achieve their target of one-lakh schools. Meanwhile, many glorious and memorable events were taking place in India, yet the target of one-lakh schools remained elusive. In 2015, the Ekal team reset their target of one-lakh schools. It was also the year when the Ekal was completing 25 years of its inception. To mark this momentous year, the Ekal team decided to organise a Parinaam Kumb (Festival of Results) in Dhanbhad, Jharkhand, where the Ekal was first conceptualised. This event also proved to be very successful and it earned enormous amounts of publicity for the Ekal as well. But still, the target of one-lakh schools was unachieved. Now, a new target, the year 2017, was agreed upon. The Ekal team moved towards this target carefully, ready to face all adverse situations. The target, however, was still not in sight.

The deadline marched past. In the meantime, a session of Bhagwat Katha by Shree Govind Devgiri Maharaj was organised on the banks of Ganga in Rishikesh. It was jointly organised by the Bharat Lok Shiksha Parishad and Ekal Abhiyaan. Shyam ji was also present at this occasion. It was like the repetition of the 2001 pledge for one-lakh Ekal schools in the presence of Swami Chidanand Saraswati ji and P.D. Chitlangaya. However, the memory was saddening for those who wanted to see one-lakh schools established. Shyam ji was both downcast and bewildered. He closed his eyes, folded his hand and began to murmur apologies before Maa Ganga. He was so deeply engrossed in his prayers that it seemed he was talking to Maa Ganga. Maa Ganga perhaps chastised him, 'You have come now. Where have you been all these years? Why didn't you come to me earlier to share your sorrow?' Shyam ji replied with devotion, 'Maa, I didn't come to you, but I have been praying to Mahadev every day.'

Hearing this, Maa Ganga scolded him more, 'My moronic child! Who understands the sufferings of children better, a father or a mother?' Shyam ji was now speechless. He started crying like a child. Maa then comforted him, 'Now, go and move ahead with determination and courage. You will achieve your target.' Shyam ji was now convinced in his heart that the time to achieve the target of one-lakh Ekal schools was near.

On 17-19 November 2019, the Ekal Abhiyaan planned to organise a 'Parivartan Kumbh (Festival for Change)' in Lucknow. As per Maa Ganga's blessing, the target of one-lakh schools was to be achieved by the time this festival was being held. Shyam ji had even told some of the workers: 'If the target of one-lakh schools is not achieved, I will not participate in this kumbh.' Now, the circumstances were getting really complex and difficult for Shyam ji as it was a matter of honour for him. Now, Lord Shree Ram understood the pain of Shyam ji and took the circumstances in His hands. Around the time of the kumbh, the Supreme Court delivered the verdict in favour of the Ram Mandir in Ayodhya and the dates of the festival had to be changed.

Now, the new dates of the Parivartan Kumbh were set as 16-18 February 2020.

On 6 December 2019 the 100,000th Ekal school was founded. On this occasion, a historic gathering was held in Ukai Sugar Maidan, Gursadda, Singpur Road, Songarh, Gujarat. Prime Minister Narendra Modi addressed this gathering via videoconference. Prominent guests on this occasion were Chief Minister Vijaybhai Rupani and Adivasi Welfare Minister Ganpat Bhai Vasava. Shyam ji was the chief speaker and he addressed a huge gathering. The 100,000th school was Kasudi Ekal Vidyalaya (code no HGJ0843310). This school is situated in Panchmahal unit of Pathra zone of North Gujarat. The village head for this school is Gulabhai Dheerbhai Ninma and the teacher is Parul Ben Ninma.

Ultimately, the Ekal reached the target of one-lakh schools. The dream, pledge and blessings of gods came true.

It is evident from the journey of the Ekal that it was riddled with innumerable road blockages and hardships, but it finally helped Hindus to restore their lost self-respect and pushed them towards the path to progress. The Ekal changed both the outlook and conditions of Indian villages. In this chapter, we'll get to know about some of the villages and villagers whose lives changed with the Ekal.

ERADICATION OF MALARIA AND DIARRHOEA

There is a tiny area called 'Taregan Tola' in a hamlet called Paud, Bhandara division, Lohardaga district, which is around 70 kilometre west of Jharkhand's capital, Ranchi. There are around 35 houses in Taregan Tola and around 20 houses sokhta gadhe (soak pits). Every house is connected to a soak pit. In some places, two houses are connected to the same pit. The villagers also managed to build a soak pit near the chaupal (public meeting place) of the village with their own resources and labour. The daily routine activities of these villages—like washing clothes, utensils, bathing, etc.—are conducted in a way that fascinates everyone. The wastewater is neither allowed to go into the street and nor does it gather anywhere. It directly goes into the soak pit. Now, let's try to understand what this soak pit is. To dry up the daily used water, a pit of 4 by 3 is dug up and then it is filled with sand. It is then properly laid out with bricks. Finally, it is covered with a bamboo structure that is further buried with dry sands. Only a hole is opened into this pit from where the water falls into it. This way, the collected wastewater keeps drying itself because of the huge amount of sand in the pit. Such pits help immensely in making the village clean and free of any kind of filth. The wastewater is not thus allowed to gather at any one place, which may lead to germination of harmful insects and mosquitoes. The village remains free from dangerous diseases like diarrhoea and malaria. Besides, the water level also remains balanced. The Ekal school's village head in Taregan Tola, Lakshmi Uraon, informed that when the Ekal was established in 2016, the aarogya yojna was also initiated in the village at the same time. 'Earlier, there was no soak pit in the village and you could see wastewater gathering around every house. There was filth here and there which led to the presence of mosquitoes. Consequently, malaria and diarrhoea were prevalent. However, since 2016 onwards, such cases have plummeted drastically because the villagers built soak pits and didn't let any amount of wastewater to stand still anywhere. Now, the village is completely free from malaria and diarrhoea,' says Ms Uraon.

The total population of Taregan Tola is around 300. But not a single case of malaria and diarrhoea was reported between 2016 to 2019. Though in the same village, two people named Jaggu Uraon and Tunna Uraon died of malaria. One woman named Raimuni Uraon also suffered from a malaria attack. Her case was serious—brain malaria. She was on the verge of death, but she survived due to timely treatment. Now, all the residents of Taregan Tola pledge on every Thursday to keep their village and households clean and free of diseases.

Their pledge includes the following points:

1. Everyone in the family will take a bath daily. He or she will wear clean clothes. They will cut their nails regularly.
2. They will use mosquito nets while sleeping at night. They will use boiled water.
3. If any pit is seen filled with rain or wastewater, it will be covered with dry sands so that it might be soaked up by the sands. Besides, pregnant women will deliver babies in hospitals.
4. Infants will be properly vaccinated. Everyone will wash his or her hands before consuming a meal and after visiting the toilet.
5. There will be a gap of three years between the birth of the first and the next child.
6. Just after the birth of a second child, every parent will go for family planning techniques.

The above pledge has shown results in the villages. Wherever the women of the households wash utensils, they ensure that the wastewater goes into the soak pit. The Ekal's revolution for making villages clean is seen taking proper shape in this village and that's why this village is disease-free. The Ekal's dream of a 'clean village' is seen to have been completely realised here. It was in 2016 that the Ekal school was opened here. Till now, around 60 children have passed out from this school. Presently, there are 30 students enrolled in this school. The village head of the school, Lakshmi Uraon, says that children of the village would waste their time doing nothing before the school was opened. 'But now, they are not only getting education, they are being trained in sanskar and value education,' says Ms Uraon. The villagers are also satisfied that their children are being taught lessons in sanskar. They see that their children have now become disciplined, don't use abusive language, respect elders and regularly go to school for their lessons. For them, it is evident that the Ekal school is different from other schools as value education is compulsory in its curriculum. They have come to know that the Ekal's education is for the whole village, not only for their children. The Ekal has demonstrated its change-worthy values and its contribution will become even clearer in future. The Ekal is empowering villages. A few years ago, women of this village started a campaign against alcoholism. It brought sound results and the malaise of liquor was subdued to a great extent. More importantly, the Ekal has been able to rouse the women. They have bravely put-up fronts in many areas. Men have also become aware of their responsibilities and thus children can focus on their education freely, without any burden on their delicate minds.

WATERSHED CHANGES EFFECTED BY E-SHIKSHA

Today is the age of change and the Ekal Abhiyan has successfully brought about changes in rural education by adopting modern methods. When the Ekal was in its infancy, the tribal children were endowed education through sports, acting and local ways like tilli, goti and kamachi. When the Ekal teachers would teach subjects like Mathematic using techniques of tilli, goti and kamachi, it would be a scene to behold. It was very entertaining for visitors from outside. Now, after the passage of 30 years, the Ekal schools have turned to tablet or e-mode of education. This electronic form of education was introduced in Ekal schools first in Nanakmata block in Uttarakhand state. In the last four years (till 2020), e-education has reached 13 units of 11 zones (states). These states are Uttarakhand, Tamil Nadu, Gujarat, Uttar Pradesh, Jharkhand, West Bengal, Odisha, Assam, Madhya Pradesh, Maharashtra and Rajasthan.

In Karanjo unit, around 30 Ekal schools are using e-education methods. In Namahatu Ekal school, the students were divided into three groups. Group one had students from six to eight years; group two consisted of students from eight to ten years and group three was for students of 10-12 years. All these groups had one group head that was entrusted the job of illustrating the values and interesting aspects of the education for children. When these Ekal students were examined for the quality of the new education method, they proved that the Ekal was successful in imparting e-education in an effective way. As part of the e-education curriculum, Mathematics, Hindi, English, Poetry, Story, Puzzles, General Knowledge, Sports, Prayer and Children's Songs are taught by using tablets for one hour. The students are also shown short videos about e-education and topics of their interest. It begets curiosity in them and they learn with more vigour. E-education has proved to be quite useful for the Ekal schools, as it has increased the presence of students in classes. Their interest in school education has also grown and they feel that the education has become more interesting. Through the use of tablets and listening to the correct pronunciation of words, the diction of students has improved remarkably well. They are showing more interest in learning mathematics. E-education also makes the teachers of the Ekal school more active. Now, they also feel that teaching kids with gadgets is fun. By using tablets, they can easily teach numerical formulas or other calculations by sketching small stories and making colourful drawings. Psychologically, the illustrated explanation is easy to understand and so, the teachers make use of this technique to the hilt. Even the Ekal students say that they like tablet explanations more than the charts shown by the teachers. The tablets also help children memorise lessons more easily. Having learnt how to operate tablets in the classrooms, the children can learn to operate laptops and computers without any trouble. The Ekal school children have even coined a catchphrase for themselves: '*Na Copy Na Kalam, Phir Bhi Hum Ekal Ki Padhai Mein Abbal*' (We neither have copies, nor do we have pen, yet our ranks in the Ekal is lesser to none).

THE ABOLITION OF CHILD MARRIAGE

The unique contribution of the Ekal schools to the villages is that they have changed them for the better by imparting quality education. They have created awareness about every walk of life. Now, the villagers have started realising that they had been following some very abusive malpractices and need to shun them immediately. The Ekal has inculcated its own sanskar (values) in villagers. They have been made to understand what is more important in a person's life, marriage or education? The villagers like those in Donasagar village will now choose education first. Their mantra is first education, marriage later. However, the situation before 2012 was just the opposite. Whenever a boy or girl turned 12-13, he or she would be married. In 2012, the Ekal school was established in the village. From 2014 onwards, child marriages stopped in the village. The village, Donasagar, falls in Kota unit of Bilaspur district in Chhattisgarh. Here, the Ekal schoolteacher is Kumari Krishna Lata Yadav. She informs, 'In Donasagar village, the tradition of child marriage was very old and deeply entrenched in the social mores. As soon as children would turn 12 or 13, parents would find a match for them and get them married. People cared little about educating their kids. They would care that their children must be on their own as soon as possible so that they might become free of the burden. Here, there is one more tradition. To pull the cart of the household, all the family members work in the fields together.' Krishna Lata said that she somehow convinced villagers that marrying children at the tender age of 12 is harmful for them physically. 'They should instead be educated till Class 12 and then be married. I tried to convey this message to them. I also told them that child marriage was not only an immature physical union, but it was illegal in India and might lead to incarceration,' she says. It worked and villagers somehow agreed with Krishna Lata.

Some villagers like Maidi Patel, Vinod Patel, Dilip Yadav, Shreemati Sabhayteen Bai, Vishnu Yadav and Ahil Singh Patel not only supported Krishna Lata, but they also came forward to launch a drive against child marriage in the village. Maidi Patel hasn't allowed his 17-year-old niece to marry yet only because of this. The family is not even discussing her marriage. Rather, they are planning to prepare her for further education. Similarly, the daughter of Sona Bai, Kumari Radhika, who is studying in Class 10, is focussed on her education instead of thinking about marriage. This change of attitude and thoughts took place in the village only after the 2012 opening of the Ekal school there. All those boys and girls, who must have been married at the age of 12, are now passing Class 12 and then are planning further studies.

THE ROAD TO COMPLETE LITERACY WAS PAVED

The Ekal has not made a child literate, but it has also made the entire village literate. It's no less than a miracle! One of such villages is Kutihaiju. This village is in Marampur block in Kalahandi district of Odisha state. This village is 95 kilometres east of Kalahandi district headquarters. The

Ekal team had established a school here in 2006. There are 205 people in this village. Out of them 95 are women, 85 men and 25 children. In 2006, 50% of the people of this village were illiterate. The Ekal school was opened under the shade of a tree and it would run in the evening from 4 to 7 pm. Around 20 children of the village attended this school then. The teacher of the school was a young man (19 years old), Rohit Kushwaha. He had qualified the matric examination to be appointed as the teacher of the Ekal school. Today, he is the in-charge of the Ekal volunteers of Marampur unit. He reminisces about his village: 'Every evening, we would run the school for three hours. On Sunday, the school would organise a special class for the old people of the village for one hour from 6 to 7 pm. In this class, they would get education lessons and as well as advice about different aspects of rural life. Overall, the school ran in this format for about two and half years.'

The special weekly class for oldies and the regular classes for children slowly made the whole village literate. In cities, when a child goes to school, his mother teaches him at home. In villages, when a child returns from school, he teaches his mother and helps her become literate. This is the strength of the Ekal! The Ekal kept its syllabus simple. First, it was the knowledge of letters, numbers and basic general knowledge. Then, they were taught further lessons. The weekly classes for the old villagers made around 200 people literate, able to sign papers and manage their accounts. It meant that the remaining 50% population of the village became completely literate and considerably educated. Among new literates of the village, some names were Gokul Pradhan (60), Devaki Pradhan (65), Shreenath Pradhan (53), Shreemati Saraswati Pradhan (53), Gayatri Pradhan (45), Shreemati Padma Bhui (60) and Shreemati Urmila Pradhan. The weekly class additionally made 20 men, 15 women and 20 children literate. After acquiring literacy, all these villagers conduct their businesses and take care of their accounts on their own. They don't need to give the impression of their thumbs. They now sign proudly.

The Ekal also organises satsang (religious gathering or story-telling class) for the villagers and they are told about Sunderkand (a chapter of epic Ramchritmanas). It helps them understand their religion, Hinduism, and the value of sanskar in life.

Similarly, there is an Ekal school named Maihira Ekal School in

Tarbha unit of Balangir zone in Odisha state. Even in this village, the Ekal school was established in 2012. At that time, only 20 people were literate in the whole village. The Ekal school took it up on its own to make the village 100% literate. It organised classes rigorously, with 100% participation and the Ekal team with the full force of the local unit organised various programmes to motivate villagers for education and ethical values. Today, the whole village is 100% literate. The 80% increase in the literacy in the village has happened solely because of the Ekal. Previously mentioned village Kutihaiju was only 30% literate before the arrival of the Ekal in 2006 and within a few years, the whole village was literate and able to maintain rural life properly.

There is also one more unit, Kuchinda, in Odisha. It is 75 kilometres away from Sambalpur district. Two kilometres away from Kuchinda unit is the village Uluda. In this village, people were unaware of various government schemes run for villages and thus they would always remain deprived of benefits from such schemes. When the Ekal school opened here and the Ekal team launched an awareness drive, around six people of the village benefited by using the Right to Information Act (RTI). They filed an RTI and sought information about benefits of the scheme not reaching them. They were provided both the information and the benefits. Twelve villagers were awarded an old age pension and three villagers were issued ration cards. Thus, the Ekal made the villagers conscious of their rights and the government schemes ran for them. In Odisha, there is also a village that has seen literacy turnaround. Its name is Kuliyari Bahal and it is situated in Senapali block of Navapada district. It is a completely tribal village. Its population of 250 comprises 110 women and 140 men. The Ekal school was established here quite early, in 1998. Until then, not even a government school existed in the village. The first teacher of the Ekal school here was Rikhi Ram Manjhi (Presently, he is a principal in a Saraswati Shishu Mandir). There was a government school around 2-3 kms away from this village. It was not viable for the villagers to cover such a long distance for attending school. The children here first got themselves educated at the Ekal school and then taught their parents at home and were able to make them literate. This village was only 30% literate before the Ekal's advent and later it went on to become fully literate. The key was regular and rigorous regular Ekal classes and the punctual weekly class for elders. A student from this village, Pavitra Mohan Manjhi, was an Ekal student in 1998. After attending Ekal classes for three years, he went to Senpali and did his Intermediate (Class 12) from there. Today, he is a part of Indian Reserve Police and is posted in Nayapara, Odisha. Similarly, another student named Vedang Kumar Manjhi was an Ekal student and went to the city for his Class 12 and later joined the Reserve Police. He is also in Nayapara. One more Ekal student Amar Kumar Manjhi joined as Special Police Officer, Odisha, in 2015. He had joined the service after Class 10.

The Ekal teachers follow a special curriculum routine to make their syllabus effective and result-oriented. Some salient features of this curriculum are as follows:

1. They make students feel comfortable to communicate with their teachers so that the strengths and weaknesses of the students are known to the teachers and students can put forward their views without hesitation. Teachers mostly keep the topics of their conversations with the students around the introduction of the students, details about their families, sports, flora and fauna, festivals, fairs and village markets. It not only helps sharpen the intellect of the children; it enables them to improve their communication skills.
2. The diagrams or pictorial depictions are used to help students improve their optical intelligence. For example, a student is shown a picture of a tree and then asked about its various parts, the fruit that grows on it, the medicinal value of the tree, etc. It is not just a very good exercise to improve linguistic skills, it also inculcates understanding of identifying parts of a living being.
3. Phonetics is the root of understanding any language. Every letter represents a particular voice or sound. In this exercise, the students are taught to recognise various sounds in a word and thus they get acquainted with the origin of the word or etymology.
4. When we Indians learn the English language and its script, we have to comprehend two sounds—one for Indian names and the other for English words. For Indian names, it is comparatively easy to link the sound with the letter. Thus, students quickly learn the names of Indian people, places or things.
5. To make students learn the numbers quickly and effectively, they

are given both oral and written exercises, like they are made to learn numbers orally and count the number of things around. Besides, they are taught to add and subtract from the given number of things before them. They are made to compare things. Finally, they are taught to write numbers in numerical and words.

6. It was realised by the Ekal team that to increase the general knowledge or general awareness of the children, it is paramount that they be aware of the milieu they are living in. They should have a proper understanding of their surroundings. In an interesting exercise, the students go on walks or tour villages or nearby places with their teacher and learn things that are not found in their books. It teaches the difference between the life in books and actual life.
7. The students are taught basic hygienic methods like how to wash their hands, feet and mouths, how to cut the nails and how to take a proper bath, etc.
8. The students are taught to self-recognise their talent and how to express it before their teachers and parents. The teachers, with cooperation from village committee members, also organise programmes to help students demonstrate their special talents without hesitation. One such programmes is called Anand Mela (Festival of Happiness). It is a one-hour programme in which students narrate short stories, act, dance, solve puzzles and perform skits and plays.
9. Then, an evaluation of students is conducted. The teachers try to find out what are the problem areas for students and what ails them and why. Once the weaknesses of the students are discovered, their solution is sought quite easily.
10. Students are encouraged to observe natural and man-made things. They are taught to examine various instruments that people use in their daily lives and also how the society around them functions. When students do so and return with various queries, teachers explain and provide solutions in a way that students can understand well.

MAHARAJPUR VILLAGE: A SYMBOL OF HARMONY

In village Maharajpur, Gwalior district, Madhya Pradesh, the Ekal school has proven to be a Brahmastra (Panacea). Four of its students are now in the government service. The light of Ekal entered this village in 2002.

Since then, the village has seen many constructive changes. Maharajpur village is 25 kilometres away from a place called Dubra. There was a liquor vendor in this area. Besides, some people in the village also used to prepare local liquor. As a result, there were frequent disputes in the village. Men, women and children were deprived of education. When the Ekal arrived in the village, the scene began to change. The Ekal formed a committee of women. This committee held regular meetings. The women would discuss the alcohol addiction of their men. One day, when the meeting took place, it ended with a firm decision that the problem of alcohol would be tackled head-on. First, a police complaint was registered through some former Ekal members (volunteers) against the illegal liquor factories and vendors. Unfortunately, two and three months passed by and no police action was taken. Women then took to the roads, with lathis in hands. Whoever was seen selling or carrying liquor was beaten with lathis. This news spread in the village. The women with lathis began to roam the village, day and night. Now, even the police came to know about them and sensing some order from above, they stood in support of the women. Within one or two months, all liquor vendors went underground. No liquor shop could be seen in the village. Till now, it is so.

Maharajpur village was reeling under another menace—casteism or untouchability. But, the Ekal has broken this barrier also and the village has become free of this malaise. Harmony prevails in the village. There is a temple that is open for all in the village. Though live people with different caste and identities live in this village, the temple is open to all. Earlier, the priests of the temple had forbidden the entry of tribals (low castes) in the temple. But the Ekal launched a drive against this discrimination and called a gathering and persuasively convinced everyone to eradicate this evil discrimination. However, some priests didn't agree even after such persuasive methods. Then, some villagers and members of the Ekal village committee filed a report against this in the local police station. It made this issue a topic of discussion among the villagers and some of them came forward to assist in amelioration of caste discrimination. After the villagers arrived at a consensus, an initiative was taken. As a first step, the tribals were allowed to enter the temple in the presence of the Ekal village committee members. Then, all the villagers started going to one another's house and participated in functions together without any sense of discrimination. This brought about a pivotal change. They started sharing meals with each other. It built an enormous amount of self-confidence in tribal people. The Ekal impressed locals so much that six people joined it as serving members. They remained connected with the Ekal for long and contributed immensely to its cause. More devoted members joined the Ekal Abhiyaan. They rose up to become zonal heads. One of them, Shree Lalita studied for about 5-6 years at the Ekal school. Later, she joined aaganvadi as a government servant. Another girl from this village, her name was spelt as Harita. She was the Adivasi daughter of Jagram and Munni Bai, and she studied up to Class 8 in her village. Then, she studied in a government school in Dubra to qualify her 10th standard exam. She stayed in the village and became the Ekal school teacher. She taught the students with full enthusiasm and devotion for two years. Impressed with her work with the Ekal, the local village panchayat recommended her name for a job in aaganvadi and she ultimately joined there. One more Ekal student, Kalicharan son of Raghuvar, studied at the Ekal school for three years (2003-06). Ekal whetted his interest in education. At that time, the Ekal school teacher was Gopal ji. He got Kalicharan admitted in the Seva Bharti Hostel in Dubra, where he studied very hard. He then appeared for Class 10 exam from his village government school. Ten years later, he applied for a post at the Post Office and was selected. He shared his views about the Ekal: 'Had I not studied at the Ekal school, I would not have reached here. I will always be indebted to Ekal.'

The Ekal miraculously turned around Maharajpur. The success of the Ekal-educated villagers raised the ranks of the Ekal in the nearby areas. Now, people became supportive and take keen interest in joining the Ekal Abhiyaan. They think that the Ekal was their own movement. The Ekal keeps organising various programmes in collaboration with the villagers so that the harmony and aspirations of the villagers remain alive. Before the entry of Ekal, there was about 30-35% literacy in the village. Now, it is 100%, suggesting that the Ekal brought about 70% literacy in just a few years. The villagers of Maharajpur say, 'We wish that the Ekal will always remain among us.'

ALIGANJ: ON THE ROAD TO SWARAJ

The soul of India resides in its villages. If every villager takes part in its development, the village will be prosperous and march ahead on the path of progress. And how much a person can be responsible, it depends on the ability of their decision-making. For an ideal democracy to flourish, it is imperative that the public takes part in every aspect of the ruling system. The participation of the society in administrative works is a constructive initiative for the masses. The Ekal Abhiyaan is very aware of it and has been making constant efforts to achieve this goal. Aliganj is a village in the Ayodhya district in Uttar Pradesh. This village is being made completely self-dependent through various initiatives. One such initiatives has been to plant around 350 saplings on both sides of the road to the village. Hundreds of these newly sown plants are flowering plants. All these plants have now grown up and if you visit the village, you will find that it looks beautiful and filled with scents of various flowers. It looks green and clean. In addition, the informal education of the Ekal school has made education popular in the village and now more children and elders take interest in being taught. Today, all the children of the village in the age group of 6-14 are literate.

Earlier, the rainwater could be seen gathering in several places. There was no proper drainage system. A serving member of the Ekal village committee, Ramchandra Verma, took it upon himself to engage other villagers to build drainage routes. It helped take rainy water out of the village. The village thus became free of malaria. Not only this, the villagers also built a garbage house outside the village. There was no temple for the villagers to worship in the entire village. Now, a temple is being constructed in the middle of the village on the same spot where villagers once collected their garbage. This place was actually a pit of around 20 feet. The villagers filled that with dry sands and now they are themselves trying to construct the temple. Some steps have also been taken to produce permanent employment in the villages. The villagers have boycotted Chinese products and are making fairy lights. It's a positive initiative for the development of the villages. The villagers have also started producing mustard oil in the village. These two steps have led to monthly savings of around Rs 12,000-15,000. Besides, the Bharat Lok Shiksha Parishad has taught the village children how to make various items from scrap paper. All these items are sold at the Ekal Carnival and children earn some amount for themselves. It is helping their family economically. Thus, making the villages self-dependent was only a dream some years back, but the Ekal has made that possible today. The Ekal has stirred the self-respect of the villagers and they have taken their fate in their own hands. This is true self-dependence.

GULABI GAON OF MAHARASHTRA

The Ekal has developed a village called Bhintghar as a gulabi gaon (pink village) in the Pratapgarh unit of Nashik district. The name denotes that multi-dimensional development is taking place in the village. Around 15 years ago, the Ekal schools were established in almost all the Scheduled Tribe and Scheduled Caste villages of the forest area. At that time, most of these villages were in pathetic conditions. The road links to the villages, transportation, sources of employment and agriculture were all in doldrums, and improper arrangement of education and frequent famine were lingering problems. In addition, poverty, superstition and paucity of awareness about health issues were prevalent in the villages. The villagers had to migrate to other areas for better living.

It was under such circumstances that the Ekal opened its school here. The Ekal's five-dimensional education left an impression within five years. The villagers became aware with the arrival of education. The elders began to attend weekly classes and learnt various things to develop their village. They not only got to know what they had to do for their village, they were also informed of their fundamental rights enshrined in the Constitution of the country. The villagers were inspired to take concrete initiative to make their village green, healthy, clean, developed and self-dependent in the modern sense. Slowly as the villagers invested themselves in such tasks, the results became visible. Not only did the village look better, the children showed extra interest in being taught at the Ekal school. The students now attend the Ekal school with religious devotion and they not only learn the basic lessons in maths and language, they are also imparted education of values. As a part of the village education, the villagers have learnt new techniques of organic farming, village development, health, hygiene and awareness about the environment. The villagers also gather in the evening for satsang. Once, all the villagers decided that there must be equality in the village. What should be done for its sake? Then, someone suggested that all the houses, school and other construction sites in the village should be painted pink. That way, they all would look alike and share the message of equality.

Since then, the whole village has been painted in the pink colour and the villagers have ensured that the village remains completely clean. Villagers themselves clean every street. They have also kept separate buckets for toilets, nutrition nurseries and bio-pits.

TEMPLE CONSTRUCTION BY THE EKAL

There was a man called Dharam Singh in Doli village of Rajouri district in Jammu. He had constructed a temple in the village with the help of villagers. He died 10 years after construction of this temple. Later, the temple was closed. In 2008, the Ekal team opened four schools in the entire unit of the area. This unit was named Akhnoor unit. An Ekal worker named Tarun Singh was appointed the unit in-charge. When he visited the Doli village, he saw that the temple was closed. He discussed it with the villagers and with their consultation, he decided that the temple would be reopened. The villagers told him that he would have to first take permission of the family of Dharam Singh who had built the temple. The villagers also opined that the temple would be opened only if it would benefit of the villagers. This temple was in fact a Kali Mata mandir (temple of goddess Kali). The temple had been closed for about 20 years. The Ekal team got it renovated and opened it to the public. The usual worship started in the temple. Today, various kinds of religious festivals are organised here. Every year on the occasions of Krishna Janmashtami and Ram Navami, the enthusiasts lead processions with a tableaux. On 31 December a jagaran (whole night festival) is organised here. On 1 January a free bhandara (food distribution) is organised. The Ekal team, with the assistance of students and villagers, had also built a fence around the temple and made a proper space for people to sit within the premises. Besides, the Ekal team is also planning to build a Durga temple in the village.

THE EKAL NETWORK REACHES PAKISTAN BORDER

In Panchayat Valdo of Tehil Kod in Jammu district, there were six villages where there had been no communication medium since Independence till 2018. An Ekal worker named Suresh Sharma of village Kala also complained to the authorities about it, but no one paid any attention. The absence of communication meant utter inconvenience to the people living in these six villages. Villagers could send no messages to anyone outside the village. If a student had to apply online for some course, they had to go to the tehsil. In a way, these six villages were cut off from the real world. For any digital work, they had to cover the distance of 50 kilometres. The Ekal team assembled the villagers and launched an agitation against the apathy of the administration. They handed a memorandum of demands to the concerned authorities. As a result of this Ekal protest, Airtel sent their team with instruments to the Valdo panchayat area. Thus, all the six villages of Valdo panchayat were connected through the Airtel mobile network. All these six villages—Vadaun, Batal, Kala, Dakhal, Makheriand and Jogwa—are on the India-Pakistan border.

GRAM SWARAJ MANCH: ONE POSITIVE ASPECT

The Gram Swaraj Manch (Organisation for Village Self-rule) is a part of the Ekal Abhiyaan. It is a known fact that the Ekal schools are doing wonderful work for education. Every Ekal teacher lives in the village with his or her family. So, it is easy to spread the wings of the Gram Swaraj Manch with these teachers' help. In this way, the problems and requirements of the villagers are looked after in an organised way. The villagers are instigated to find out their problems and ways to solve them on their own so that the road to the self-reliance of the village may be paved. This will also help generate within them a sense of belonging to the village and make them consider the problems of the village as their own.

In 2015 or 2016, a seminar was organised in Lucknow. Its subject was 'How can the farmers get the due value of their crop?' It was advertised widely so that a large number of people might attend the seminar. Satish Sachan ji of Kanpur also got to know about this seminar. He had resigned from his government post after getting frustrated by the corruption. His story was: 'I had resigned from my post after being unable to see rampant corruption in the government system. I wanted to do something for the village. And for this, I had to do some rural work. So, I started farming. I wanted to find out why our village was lagging behind in development? I was wrestling with all these thoughts, and one day, I got an invitation to a seminar about farmers in Lucknow. Shree Madhvendra ji was supposed to be the chief guest of this programme. He was the general secretary of the Ekal Abhiyaan. I was introduced to him after the seminar. After listening to his thoughts, I was assured that what I was planning could in fact be possible. This was my first introduction with the Ekal.'

The seminar cast a magic spell on Sacha ji and he began to take part in activities of the Gram Swaraj Manch. Gradually, the working area of the Manch expanded. When the Manch volunteers became active in a vast area, they realised that however hard they might work among the villagers, the desired results would be achieved only after the villagers were made socially, economically and politically conscious and empowered. The villagers in fact looked broken and hopeless before the Manch began to invigorate them. First and foremost, these villagers had to be told that they could do something for their village or the country. The apathy of the government had filled them with despair. Thus, they had to first shun this negative sense of despair and a new stream of enthusiasm had to be inserted into their veins. They had also to be told that the entire government system was not corrupt and inept. This also gave the Manch an idea of what exactly they had to do in villages. They had to bring awareness to the villages. They had to teach villagers ways to make their villages empowered.

To provide leadership to the Gram Swaraj Manch at the central level, the name of Satish Sachan ji was proposed. Observing his effective way of communicating with farmers, his dedication and labour, he was appointed the central in-charge of the Manch in 2018. Hence, Sachan ji became part of the Manch forever. Now, the Manch prioritised and divided its work in an organised way. The targets of the Manch were as following:

1. To make the village committees and villagers empowered.
2. To understand the sufferings of villagers and make them heard at the official level.
3. Chemical-free agricultural fields and liquor-free villages.
4. Conservation of Indian culture
5. Equal opportunities for all

To achieve above targets, following programmes were planned:

1. To prepare the village to become economically empowered and ideal. To get proper value for their crops, the villagers must be encouraged to adopt innovative ways of farming and master communication skills to convey their demands before the authorities. To teach villagers

skills other than agriculture so that their labour might be utilised elsewhere too. Among these works were domestic industrial work, agriculture-based work, carpentry, embroidery, sewing, art works, etc.

2. The Gramothan Yojna is also doing the above-mentioned works, but the Manch is trying to do it as an awareness drive so that the villagers can understand the real value of them.
3. To inform the villagers about various programmes launched by the government for their development. To organise small workshops or jan panchayats so that the villagers are able to take benefits of such government schemes.
4. To inculcate self-respect in the villagers, they are informed about the panchayati raj system that empowers them through self-rule at the rural level. To constantly instigate them to search for solutions to their problems on their own so that they can generate leadership capabilities. To achieve these purposes, a series of events like jan panchayat, unit sammelan, sankalp divas, yuva divas and voter awareness programme are held.
5. To organise villagers so that they can protest if they are denied the proper price for their crops and labour. They are also trained to use the RTI, communication through newspapers, magazines and TV channels.
6. To make the Manch more powerful, villagers are encouraged to make a district committee, block committee and village committee.
7. To organise sammelans (seminars, workshops and other gatherings) for villagers like elected panchayat representatives so that they may learn the value of organised activities and channelise their energies properly.
8. To make the panchayati raj system more powerful. The Indian Constitution has made up a three-dimensional ruling system for Indians. First is the Parliament of India. In the middle are the state assemblies. Then come the gram sabhas (panchayats). Today, the Parliament and state assemblies are very powerful but gram sabhas are still crying to get their dues. They are in fact oblivious of their own strengths. The Manch is devoted to guiding gram sabhas and its members about their rights and how to exercise them.

9. The Gram Swaraj Manch aims to conserve all aspects of the rural milieu like water, jungle, fields and animals. It in association with gram sabhas is running various programmes for the guidance of the villagers and to make the rural panchayat system transparent and more powerful.

Today, when urban life is dominant, the Gram Swaraj Manch is trying to make rural lives equally attractive and lucrative. For this purpose, it is running some key programmes such as:

1. **Nadi Bachao Abhiyaan (Save the River Campaign)**: It is a programme to worship rivers and find ways to conserve their purity.
2. **Paryavaran Jagran Abhiyaan (Environment Awareness Movement)**: As part of this programme, every Ekal student has to plant a tree.
3. **Dharti Bachao Abhiyaan (Save Earth Campaign)**: This programme aims at encouraging farmers to pick organic farming and preparing a nutrition nursery.
4. **Pashu Suraksha Abhiyaan (Animal Safety Campaign)**: This programme is primarily aimed at protecting cows, promoting agriculture based on cows and establishing local industry based on agricultural products.
5. **Mahila Sashatikaran Abhiyaan (Women Empowerment Campaign)**: As part of this programme, women are encouraged to create employment for themselves and self-help groups.

The Gram Swaraj Manch is religiously organising the above campaigns. It not only organises these campaigns only on village level, rather they are regularly held at block, district and state levels. For this purpose, the Manch has constituted committees of devoted villagers, farmers, women and youths. Overall, the Manch is giving voice to the pain of tribals and empowering them to overcome this.

□

8

Encouragement and Enlargement Through Social Connect

There is one secret for achieving a target—never let it disappear from your thoughts and actions. The means to arrive at your target are planning, organisation, training, labour, sacrifice and devotion. The target of the Ekal Abhiyaan is clear—it is to empower tribals living in distant hinterlands of India and ensure multi-dimensional progress of India by generating self-respect in its tribal population. For this purpose, the Ekal envisaged a five-dimensional educational model and many other programmes. To make them functional, a devoted organisation and its working methodology was established. It worked so well that the Ekal has been able to steer the society on the path of self-ascent.

It was 1987 when the Vanvasi Kalyan Ashram was celebrating its anniversary. In an event in Kolkata, Prema ji wished to tour tribal areas. Thus, a programme was prepared for this tour that would also include some influential and affluent families of Kolkata as well. A young girl of such a family was also part of this touring group. The first halt of this tribal tour was in a village of Phulwani district. Prema ji was the attraction of the touring group and her arrival in Odisha was already communicated in various parts of the state. She was renowned for her story telling of Ram Katha and Bhagwat Katha. Tribals from far and wide assembled to see her and listen to her stories. They all also wished to be blessed by her hands. It became so crowded that it began to seem like a fair. They all wanted to touch Prema ji. Among the crowd was an old woman who was trying hard to reach Prema ji but she was unable to do so. Then, some women came to help and pushed her towards Prema ji. Suddenly, everyone realised that this old woman was blind. It became a very emotional scene. The blind woman was so overwhelmed with emotions that she was in a totally dishevelled condition when she touched Prema ji with her hands. She broke down as she touched Prema ji. Even Prema ji was struck with her touch. Both of them didn't utter a word, yet communicated through their eyes and hearts. This scene brought tears to every eye. Even the young girl who was accompanying the touring team started crying. Her mother tried to calm her. She thought that some insect had bitten her daughter. But, when she checked, everything was fine. She was asked why she was crying? She replied that her mother's almirah was full sarees and that old grandmother didn't even have one. True to these little kids' words, almost all ladies of the village didn't have one full saree. 'How could it happen? All this is making me cry,' she said. Her response melted every heart and made them question themselves.

This tribal tour touched the heartstrings of all the women in the touring team. Prema ji announced that until she would arrange for a saree for every woman of the village, she would not buy any for herself. This tour and its experience moved her so much that she started mentioning this in every katha she attended and even made appeals for saree donation. It worked miraculously. Bundle after bundle of sarees were donated for those deprived Odisha women. When these sarees were sent to that village and those women were told that Prema ji had sent them as a gift to them, they wept in gratitude.

After taking a tour of the tribal areas, the city women and their associates started working with devotion to uplift the lives of the tribal people in any way they could manage. When the Ekal ushered in its mission in the tribal areas, their self-improvement was its foremost goal.

Once Chitlangaya ji, who carried a deep impression of tribal life on his heart, met Shyam ji. He was eager to know more about the tribal affairs. After hours of discussion, he asked, 'What is the worst suffering of the tribal people?' Shyam ji replied plainly, 'The absence of health facilities.' Then, Chitlangaya ji enquired about the health centres run by the Vanvasi Kalyan Ashram and whether they were facing some difficulties? Shyam ji told him that there were limited manpower and financial resources and the road connectivity to far off tribal areas was non-existent and thus the ailing tribals weren't able to come to the Ashram-run clinics themselves. 'Besides, religious conversion is rampant in Odisha's tribal areas. The tribals are being forced to become Christians in exchange for health facilities. To make the matters worse, there is acute apathy on the part of the government machinery that is tasked to work for the tribal welfare and thus they are easy prey to Christian missionaries. We, however, have been able to rescue many of them and brought them back to Hinduism by organising various activities among them to win their confidence. Now, they are determined that they will not turn towards the Christianity and will defy inducement of health clinics. They are ready to face health hazards for the sake of Hinduism. Hence, the onus of taking care of tribals' health is now on us. They have trusted us. We have to procure medicine and supply them to the tribals. For this purpose, we need a medical van or ambulance. At the moment, we need four such vans,' Shyam ji explained the whole situation to Chitlangaya ji.

Chitlangaya ji didn't even blink for a second and wrote a proposal for four medical vans.

Four medical vans for the tribals! This was a big news in the rural areas of Odisha. It spread like wildfire. Everyone was upbeat. The Ashram thought of a plan to inaugurate the occasion of starting medical vans from tribals in the presence of Swami Lakshamanand ji Maharaj. It was a big achievement for Shyam ji and his colleagues who were just beginning to register their foothold in the tribal areas. A tea session was hosted at Chitlangaya ji's residence after the inauguration. Some dignitaries of the city were introduced to Chitlangaya ji there. Then, Chitlangaya ji asked Swami ji what would he do with those four medical vans? Swami ji went into a trance and hit his stick on the ground in anger. He then said in a rage, 'I would free Phulwani district from the Christianity and will bring back all converts back to the fold of Hinduism.' A Communism-inclined industrialist like Chitlangaya ji didn't expect such an answer. He looked at Shyam ji and said, 'Why did not you tell me this earlier? You were talking about the welfare of the tribals. Had I known that it would be for a religious purpose, I would never have agreed to provide you even a single van.' As Chitlangaya ji said this, Swami ji handed him keys of two vans that were given to him for inauguration and said, 'Keep them. They are right here. I will go now.' Everyone stood up from their chairs. The atmosphere had become very grim. By now, Chitlangaya ji also came to know that he was not any ordinary swami. So, he somehow assuaged Swami ji and handed him back the keys of vans. This event hardened the resolve of Chitlangaya ji for the welfare of the tribals. He then backed Shyam ji with all his resources.

TOUR TO AMERICA SHOWED A NEW INDIA

In the 2001 American tour of Shyam ji, Shree Ramesh Bhai Shah became his guide and his two daughters and son were his colleagues. Rameshbhai's wife Kokila Ben also contributed to make this tour a success. Rameshbhai's house was the Ekal office in America at the time. He would work the whole day for his business and take care of the functioning of the Ekal at night. His dedication and unstoppable labour for the Ekal won Shyam ji's heart. Rameshbhai later became the front man of the Ekal Abhiyaan in America and all his family members assisted him in this mission. From 2001 to 2014, Shyam ji went to America for the sake of Ekal several times. If we sit to write down his American experiences, it will turn out to be a separate book. So, let's discuss here his activities related to the Ekal. First, Indian-Americans did not believe that a school could be run with such meagre resources. They had never heard of people working without any remuneration as Ekal's volunteers did. They thought a person would work only when they were promised suitable monetary return for the work. Their second wonderment or objection was that how could 90% of a budget be allocated for a school because they had seen NGOs in the US working on an entirely different model. In budgets of almost every NGO, almost 50% would be overheads, meaning that the workforce attached with the NGO would take 50% of the amount they would collect for the NGO's work. How could this amount be merely 10% in the case of Ekal?

One meeting of the Ekal was organised at the residence of a neurosurgeon, Dr Veena Gandhi, in New Jersey. Dr Gandhi was related to Mahatama Gandhi's family. In this meeting, many people who were running international level NGOs also took part. They got so angry at Shyam ji's description of the Ekal that the meeting was on the verge of breaking out into a scuffle. They accused Shyam ji of misguiding them about the Ekal's functioning. They asked Shyam ji how much was his salary? Shyam ji didn't know how to respond to them. Then, an RSS pracharak, who was present there, explained to those gentlemen how the system of volunteering at the Sangh worked. They felt somewhat satisfied, yet their curiosity still lingered. When Shyam ji was being introduced as the Sangh pracharak, the NGO fellows were not unable to fathom what Shyam ji actually did at the Sangh and with the Ekal. The RSS was little known overseas at that time. Whatever reputation it had was for all the negative reasons. Then, the fact like a man wears clothes given by someone else and works without any salary and that a man can be a volunteer for lifetime was completely unbelievable for them. When that RSS pracharak explained to them that thousands of people work as volunteers, they came to know that such a big group could be organised for a purpose. And when the pracharak said that a senior person like Shyam ji was merely a pracharak of the Sangh, they understood that youths would also be ready to dedicate their lives for the Sangh.

Shyam ji tried to explain all these things in a different way, 'All the good manners or discipline that we have in our lives have originated from nature. Mother Nature gives birth to the culture. All these natural things like mountains, seas, trees, earth, rivers, etc., endow us with the ethical values. It is the reason that our ancestors invented pilgrimage tours to places right in the lap of nature so that we can connect to our Mother Nature. The society that is still living as an offspring of Mother Nature in its lap is the tribal society. These tribals are thus naturally patriotic. Patriotism is like a value that is practiced daily. We have only taught the tribal youths that the Ekal is a mission for Lord Ram. The purpose for which Lord Ram had appeared as an avatar, the Ekal is devoted to the same purpose. Hearing this, they readily agree to join the Ekal mission. How much salary was Ram ji's army given? Why are we expecting the salary for Ram ji's troopers now? The tribal families think that "Ram ji's work" means building the Ram Mandir in Ayodhya and thus they happily hand over their young sons to the Ekal? This is our strength.'

There was one more objection to the budget of the Ekal. People asked why was only 60% of the budget kept as an overhead for the salary of the Ekal teacher? Then, what happened to the other 30%? Shyam ji delineated that the 30% was spent on various layers of the training for the teacher. But, the gentleman who had raised this question was not ready to accept this. He had this impression that the government trains the teachers and that is why they are appointed in schools as teachers. He doubted that the 30% of the budget was being leaked out to some other sources. He had reached such a conclusion because he had seen such a system in America. Since he had been away from India for a very long time, he had no idea how the government functions in Indian villages. It proved to be quite arduous to make Indian-Americans understand why the Ekal teachers needed to be from the village itself. They were also very doubtful about the syllabus of the Ekal school. And when Shyam ji told them that there was no fixed place or building to run the school, they thought that Shyam ji was hoodwinking them into donating money and that he would run his own business with that. They were also not able to digest the remuneration paid to Ekal teachers and volunteers. They firmly believed that the Ekal was merely a tool to collect money, as it was impossible to run a primary school with such a small amount in the budget. At last Shyam ji had to say that they might send some relatives or a delegation of people to India so that they might be informed credibly about the Ekal project. This, to some extent, sounded trustworthy to them. Hence, Shyam ji's first tour to America was more about convincing Indian-Americans about the credibility of the Ekal than collecting money.

In one more meeting, a very awkward question was posed to Shyam ji. One gentleman asked, 'You are not cheating us? Could you provide any evidence to prove this?' He added that he had seen many people coming from India to collect money in the name of some social service and they finally spent it for their personal use back in India. 'And you are not one such person, how should we believe that?' he asked. One gentleman from the crowd tried to assuage him saying that Shyam ji was a Sangh pracharak and hence he would never lie. Hearing this, that questioning gentleman lost his cool. 'People who call themselves truthful and saintly prove to be real frauds. They have brought bad names for India all over the world. Why should I accept that Shyam ji is not one of them?' he said in a fit of rage. Shyam ji asked him very humbly how he came to such an understanding? In his reply, he first appreciated Shyam ji that he didn't mind his straight allegation and rough language; he then shared his life experience. 'One incident has hurt me so much that I often lose control of my language,' he said and everyone in the gathering heaved a sigh of relief that now his anger was subdued. Then, he continued his story: 'There is a temple in our colony. We all assemble there on Saturday and Sunday for various functions. Once, a saintly person named Narayan Swami came from India. He stayed in the temple and proposed to narrate the Bhagwat Katha. Everyone agreed. So, he would narrate the Bhagwat Katha on Saturday and Sunday and meet Indian families on the rest of weekdays. Once during the Katha, he proposed to build a Narayan Mandir in India. Naturally, nobody would object to such a noble suggestion. For the construction of the proposed temple, it was imperative to collect money. I was overzealous and announced to donate a big amount. All became impressed with my zeal and they appointed me the head of the money collection committee. With proper consultation with Swami ji, we prepared a budget for the proposed temple. Fortunately, the collections went beyond the expectations and it was much more than the budget. Swami ji was very satisfied and he left for India in a jolly mood. A year after Swami ji's departure, I got an opportunity to tour India regarding some business-related affair. I thought it was a good opportunity to meet Swami ji and pray in the newly constructed Narayan Mandir.

'I took some of my friends with me and left for a tour of the mandir. We reached the address, but there was no trace of the mandir there. When we inquired the locals there about the temple, they said they had never heard of any temple construction in the area. We then somehow got the address of Swami ji and reached there. Fortunately, he was there. After exchanging formalities, I requested Swami ji that he must take us to the temple so that we could pray there. We hoped that the temple would have been built by now. Swami ji nodded, "Yes, the temple is ready." Then, he went inside and brought his wife with him. He said, "This is my wife Laxmi and I am Narayan. And this house where you are sitting is the temple of Laxmi-Narayan." We all were stunned. I was dumbfounded and unable to utter a single word. I just put my hand on my forehead. Since we could not do anything, we thought it best to take leave of Laxmi-Narayan. On my way back, one of my friends asked me why I was there. One of my friends who was with me told him the whole story of the Laxmi-Narayan temple. He didn't feel surprised and said that we were befooled by a crook. "This crook Narayan has fooled hundreds of people here and now he even went to America to cheat people," that friend murmured in anger.'

Hearing this story, every head in the gathering turned down with shame. That gentleman was also unable to control his emotions while narrating this tale of deceit in the name of Laxmi-Narayan. He and Shyam ji were unable to look at each other. After a pause of a few seconds, Shyam ji said, 'I can understand your feelings, my friend. I also respect your emotions. You have opened my eyes. I could not even imagine such deceitful conduct on the part of a religious person. Now, I have to only say this much to you that I will first build the temple and then will come to you.' The story of Laxmi-Narayan cheat taught Shyam ji a very important lesson that he would have to win the hearts of people first before connecting them with the Ekal Abhiyaan. He asked the whole gathering that they all must browse the website of the Ekal and zero in on any mentioned school in any district of any state of India and should ask their friends or relatives to visit that school. 'When you are fully convinced, only then you must trust me,' he said. The gathering dispersed with this announcement. However, Shyam ji felt a huge burden on his heart. That story-telling gentleman came to Shyam ji and showed great affection. He insisted that Shyam ji must visit his home. Shyam ji also felt that he must go with him and meet his family. After meeting his family, Shyam ji felt very relieved.

This same gentleman later became the head of the Ekal Chapter in his area. Such has been the miraculous functioning of the Ekal!

Time never stays the same. It tests all its travellers. The Ekal also faced testing times. Some occasions came when serious doubts developed in the minds of its overseas donors. In fact, it happened because of some events. One of such events took place in Gorakhpur of Uttar Pradesh. It was 2002. Shyam ji was on an American tour at the time. One Ekal School in Gorakhpur district was under the patronage of a donor based in America. He was a big shot in America and owned a high-profile company. The branches of this company were also present in India. He once asked his employees in India to pay a visit to an Ekal school. He had browsed all the information about the school from the Ekal website. His employees went to visit the school without any prior notice to the Ekal team. When they reached the address, there was no school there. They enquired the local villagers whether they knew about the school, they refused. The employees went back and prepared a report based on their tour and despatched it to their employer in America. Shyam ji, who was in America, was informed of this. He called the Ekal team in India and enquired about everything. It came true. Shyam ji was told that the local village committee head had betrayed the Ekal team. Shyam ji was numbed because of shock and embarrassment. American donors called a meeting after this episode. Some unsuitable words were used for Shyam ji in anger. A rock-solid man like Shyam ji came to tears after hearing upsetting and insulting words. Comments were being passed on him in the meeting and he was seething with anger within. He was making up his mind that he would not accept a single penny from American donors in the future. 'A mistake has been committed and accepted. You will use abusive words for this? This is enough!' Shyam ji was going to say these words, but a friend grabbed his hand and asked him to stay calm. That friend explained the whole episode to American donors in his way. This episode hurt Shyam ji a lot. He also wept a lot. But he learnt a lesson. From then onwards, he began to say in every meeting, 'We do not claim perfection. But our commitment to perfection is perfect.' He meant to clarify that the Ekal was susceptible to making mistakes, however, it would always be ready to rectify the mistake. American folks also realised that there are all types of people working for such a big organisation and hence, there was always the possibility of mistakes and even mischiefs. Thus, honesty and full devotion to duty became the identity of the Ekal.

USP OF EKAL: DEVELOPMENT OF VILLAGES

A new question came before the Ekal in America itself. In one meeting, Shyam ji was asked why his endeavour should be supported by Indian-Americans as hundreds of people, both saintly and social, come from India to collect money for ventures back in India? They said that they all were connected to some social cause in India, what was unique in his cause? 'This is called in business terms—the unique selling point (USP)? What is your USP?' they asked Shyam ji. Shyam ji had heard the word USP for the first time. He was at sea. He was unable to muster any answer. One of the Sangh workers was luckily with Shyam ji. He answered on his behalf. 'You were listening to Shyam ji for such a long time. You must have noticed the difference. Other people who come to collect money say that we will run such a venture in India and so support us. Shyam ji has been saying that please support us so that we can make villagers self-reliant. It means that his Ekal schools will educate villagers or tribals and make them stand on their own feet. This is his USP,' he said. There was a round of applause on this answer. Yet, the questions continued. The same gentleman who had asked Shyam ji the previous question asked him again, 'Do you agree with this USP?' Shyam ji said readily, 'Yes, 100%.' Another question came, 'Then, what is your strategy according to this USP?' Shyam ji explained to him the five-dimensional education pattern of the Ekal and told them the importance of the 'service to organisation' route. He explained to them how the organisation leads to self-reliance and self-reliance to self-respect. The questioner was satisfied. Then, another gentleman raised his hand and asked, 'How much time does this whole process take?' Shyam ji answered, 'It takes about five to seven years.' Then, he asked why it takes so much time? Shyam ji explained that it was because the local churches and the government provided villagers enough freebies and now, they were used to them and hence, it took time to make them understand the value of labour and self-reliance. 'We first have to make them shun their habits of getting things for free and then will have to turn their habits into self-reliant ones. It will take time,' said Shyam ji and everyone felt satisfied. This meeting ended on such a satisfying note that the gathering decided to open an Ekal Chapter there.

The Ekal was making fast strides into getting new techniques for pedagogy and other functions. The Ekal learnt to make use of reporting, filmmaking, email and websites in America. In India, people don't ask many questions when they donate money, but people in America are different. Here, the more the money, the more the questions. They will ask 10 questions before giving you one rupee. Even today, if someone comes from America with a purpose to do something for the Ekal, he comes with questions prepared based on information given on Ekal's website. The first concern in the mind of the donor remains the transparency about the functioning and review of the whole Ekal organisation. On transparency, the Ekal has always maintained that instead of 100%, it would provide 125% transparency to the inquirer. Once Shyam ji was flummoxed, how could Ekal provide 125% transparency? He was told that to answer satisfactory answers to all the questions of the inquirer is

100% and then tell him even those things that he did not ask or did not know is 125%. In this way, the Ekal passed its tests of transparency with 125 marks out of 100!

PROTEST AGAINST ASHOK JI IN BOSTON

This incident belongs to the days when Shyam ji was on an American tour. It was winter. Shyam ji was staying with a family. He was having a discussion with the family and others in a meeting and the Ekal was an obvious topic. Someone asked Shyam ji why he opened Ekal schools only in rural areas, while there was a requirement for such schools in cities as well. Shyam ji answered this question by giving an example. He asked everyone to look outside the window and showed them that most of the trees have shed their leaves in the season of winter and they all looked like naked skeletons. 'Now, if owners of trees wished for new leaves to grow on their trees after the end of winter, which parts of the trees they would nourish?' he asked the gathering. All of them said that it would obviously be the roots. Shyam ji was very happy with this answer and tried to prove his point. He said, 'Indian society has three parts—first is visible, second is semi-visible and the third is invisible. The first visible part is urban areas or cities. You can see it everywhere, on TV, in newspapers, even in government bodies and administration. The second are villagers who are in the vicinity of cities and they remain semi-visible. However, they are fast catching up with the culture of cities and nearing them as far as standard of life is concerned. All types of modern facilities are reaching these villages (or qasbahs). The third part of the society that remains invisible is the tribal society or extreme rural areas. In short, we can say that Indian society is divided into three parts:

1) Urban India
2) Rural India
3) Remote India

Our aim is to empower the tribal society through the efforts of Ekal. This is the society, which is the bedrock of Indian culture, religion, values, democracy and even its security. Once this society that has been deprived of mainstream attention for ages will become empowered, it will automatically make India stronger.' This long harangue satisfied everyone in the gathering, yet a member of the family asked Shyam ji that if the tribal society was so pivotal, why had it been ignored for so long and who kept exploiting them? Shyam ji replied that the people responsible for the plight of tribals were the urban-dwellers. 'We have ignored the development of the tribals and have also been exploiting them for our own interests. The Ekal Abhiyaan is actually a tool of repentance for our past misdeeds,' he said. That young man was convinced with this answer. However, he shot another question: 'We live in America. We were in fact born here. Why should we be sensitive about problems prevalent in India and care for them?' This question perhaps dwells in every young man who was and is born in America and sometimes in his life, this must have stirred his conscience. So, such youths are told that since they were born in America, they must be completely devoted and sincere in their duties towards America, however they also have responsibility towards the country of their parents' origin. It is the land of their ancestors and thus warrants as much of their attention as America.

Here, it also becomes evident that those youths whose parents keep taking them on an Indian tour understand the fact that India is the land of their ancestors, but those youths who have never visited India, they are hard to be convinced of this fact and neither they themselves feel any emotion for India. There is a graver problem and that is the media-created image of India. It is a maligned image and has been created after reporting only negative things about India. It has repulsed youths of Indian origin more than anything else. Actually, anti-India forces dominate the media discourse and it is a very serious issue for those who want to clean India's image before the world. This became crystal clear when Ashok Singhal ji toured America. Ashok ji stayed with a family in Boston. Shyam ji also got a chance to be part of one of his planned programmes in Boston. As per this programme, Ashok ji had to address a gathering of students in a reputed university in Boston. Some volunteers and colleagues accompanied him. As soon as they arrived at the gate of the university, they were shockingly greeted with 'Ashok Singhal Go Back' slogans. All of Ashok ji's colleagues encircled him anticipating some trouble. The administration also became alert. So, Ashok ji, though opposed by slogans, entered the university without any problem. As he treaded inside the campus, he saw the walls were festooned with posters and slogans against his arrival. It didn't even call for calling off his interaction; there were remarks against Rashtriya Swayamsevak Sangh (RSS) and Vishwa Hindu Parishad. Anyway, Ashok ji and his colleagues marched past these slogans to reach the auditorium where a large number of students had gathered to listen to him. His colleagues also remained alert that any untoward incident might happen. However, Ashok ji delivered such an impressive lecture that it was listened with rapt attention and nothing unpleasant happened. Even the question-and-answer session went well. Students asked relevant questions and Ashok ji replied quite satisfactorily. After the event was over, Ashok ji's colleagues tried to find out who was the protesting party? Shyam ji told them there was an independent organisation called ASHA that claimed to do social work in India and was active in almost all the universities of America. In America, this organisation was known to be a supporter of Communist thoughts. The newspapers of America had considerable influence of Communists and Muslims and thus they kept publishing articles against RSS, VHP and similar Hindu groups.

The revelation about ASHA was both shocking and disheartening, as everyone had heard about it in India but nobody cared to peel layers of its real ideology. Till now, people had a positive view of ASHA, but now it had exposed itself. However, more than scorn, the people felt the need to help change the ideology of the organisation. Since Shyam ji had just landed in America, nobody tried to disturb him with such an idea.

When Shyam ji had started touring the US, most of the people who would descend to meet and listen to him were above sixty people. Shyam ji and others also felt curious to know about people who opposed Hindu organisations, but he was making a start in America, so he thought it was wise to limit his activities to listen to people and the American scene in a better way. After some time, he asked colleagues based in America why it was so that only sixty plus people attended his gatherings? He was told that there was an IT sector boom in India in 1970's. At that time, hordes of talented people migrated to America and later were granted citizenships here. Since most of them retired at the age of sixty and had settled their children, they had time for reminiscing about their birthplace India and taking part in activities like Shyam ji's gatherings. There was one more valuable piece of information that this age group had a lot of savings and if it remained unutilised in their lives, the government would take that over after their deaths. There was one more thing: children in America considered it below their dignity to accept property or money from their old parents as they themselves have enough. In such a scenario, these sixty plus people remained anxious about how to spend their saved money. In America, there is a 'Health Guarantee Scheme' and thus all health-related problems of people are the responsibility of the government. Hence, the people of this age group seek some 'meaningful and constructive work' to spend their savings on. In Shyam ji's Ekal meetings, one important thing discussed by this age group of people was: 'You care for the children of India. We care for our children here. Your children need education, our children need to learn Indian values. What solution do you have for this?' Shyam ji would hear these questions, note them in his mind, but he did not have courage or a solid plan to come up with any solution. He would keep his head down in contemplating posture and say nothing. But in his heart, he had one conviction that Ram ji would definitely suggest a way out.

A YOUNG GIRL TAUGHT HOW TO WIN HEARTS

Once Shyam ji was staying with a family in America. All the members of the family urged him to explain how the Ekal worked to them. They gathered around him. Shyam ji told them basic things about the Ekal and then showed them a film. Then the family started questioning him. The youngest member of the family, a 10-year-old girl, was the first to ask the question. Everyone was puzzled about what she could ask? She said, 'What can I do for the tribal children? I cannot donate money. I cannot go to India either to help them. So, please tell me what I can do for them from here?' Shyam ji was baffled. He never expected such a question could also be posed before him. He posed a counter-question, 'Daughter, why do you want to do anything for them?' She replied, 'When I was watching the movie, I carefully observed that there was a spark in their eyes that said that their lives had changed after they became part of the Ekal. The Ekal is thus changing the lives of the tribals for better. I want to be part of this abhiyaan.' As she finished her answer, the elders of the family felt ashamed of themselves, as a kid was able to observe the change being brought by the Ekal by observing the spark in the eyes of the tribal children on screen, but they failed to notice this important detail. Shyam ji asked that little girl whether she would like to become friends with tribal children? She was elated and readily agreed. She asked Shyam ji what she would have to do for this? Shyam ji suggested to her to write a letter to the tribal children. 'I would translate that letter into the local language for those children and I would get their reply and would send that to you translated into English,' he said. That girl was extremely delighted with this idea. All other members were also very impressed with this girl's conversation with Shyam ji. Shyam ji then realised that the Ekal communicated in the language of love and it works miraculously. This is the strength of the Ekal, he said in his heart. That girl quickly wrote a letter and handed it to Shyam ji. The first line of the letter impressed everyone so much that they found it difficult to believe that that little girl wrote it. Since it was obvious no one wrote it on her behalf, they had to believe it. The letter was purely her emotions and it read, 'My brothers and sisters of the Ekal, salaam to all of you. Both you and I go to school. However, there is a difference. When we go to school, we make our lives better. When you go to school, you make India better. Thus, you people are really lucky that you have become part of the enterprise to make your country greater. That is why I salute you.' Reading this letter, Shyam ji closed his eyes and sat on the chair in that posture for a while. The atmosphere in the house had become almost divine. It seemed as if the sun was rising in the house and the whole house was filled with its light. They thought it was all because of the blessing of Lord Ram and they paid obeisance to Him in their hearts. After a while, the atmosphere became normal. They asked Shyam ji why he was sitting silent with his eyes closed. He said that the episode was like a life lesson for him. I tour places after places explaining the Ekal to people. 'Even in India, I have to make so many efforts to convince people of the importance of the Ekal, but the way this little girl has explained the Ekal, it never occurred to me as well. It was mesmerising. I wondered how such a precise and noble idea came into her delicate mind. I was just lost in these thoughts,' he said.

The family members realised the curiosity of Shyam ji and told him that the family went to India during holidays every year. 'Though our residence now is in a big city, we are originally from a village. We husband and wife make sure that we will spend at least a day in our village. When we meet our family members there, I can't express what feelings overcome us. This little girl also accompanies us to the village. She becomes a bemusing doll for the village kids. They don't know English and this girl does not understand their language. She becomes the centre of everyone's attention. When people in the nearby villages hear about a family from America, they also come to see us. They bring their children to show her to them. She also likes to play with them. Once we did not have much time to visit the village, but she insisted and we had to surrender before her wish,' the patriarch of the family said. As he stopped, Shyam ji discerned a new message in his description. He knew that all the urban members of the Ekal felt impressed with the mission of Ekal when they themselves visited villages and tribal areas. But he was not aware that Ekal's work could impress such a young mind as that of that little girl. This gave him an idea that the young generation of Indian-Americans would not have any trouble connecting with the Ekal provided they had first-hand village experience. A little girl had shown Shyam ji the route to the hearts of young Americans.

A DEEP IMPACT ON THE WORKING MECHANISM OF THE EKAL

One event during Shyam ji's America tour was so deep that it impacted the whole strategy or working mechanism of the Ekal. The story goes like this. One youth from Chicago cleared the medical entrance test but he fell one year short in the age criterion. So, he had to wait for one year. In order to utilise his one year, he planned to tour some interesting places on the earth and to do something extraordinary. He searched many websites and brochures of many institutions. Normally, American youth think that only Africa is a place on the earth where they would find challenging situations. The Church has even built some attractive destinations for them there. Suddenly, he came across the website of the Ekal. He became curious to know more about the organisation. By coincidence, Shyam ji had to tour Chicago after a few days. That young man read the introduction of Shyam ji and got complete information about his Chicago tour. So, that young man arrived to attend one of Shyam ji's programmes in a Chicago auditorium with his mother and niece. Shyam ji was also informed that a curious young man would attend his programme. Shyam ji showed the audience a film about the Ekal. It was a part of his presentation. Then he spoke about the Ekal for some time and asked questions from the audience. Since he was brimming with curiosity, that young man raised his hand first to ask a question. Shyam ji asked him to introduce himself first. He said that his name was Sanjay. When all the questions had finished and Shyam ji had free time, he asked Sanjay's niece, 'How was the film?' Like all enthusiastic children, she was very excited to know about the tribal people and their children. Then, Shyam ji asked her that as his uncle Sanjay wished to go to those tribal villages, would she permit him? Hearing this, the girl became sad and her eyes filled with tears. Shyam ji then asked his mother whether she would permit Sanjay to visit tribal lands in India? She said, 'When he was born, we named him Sanjay. When he grew up, we thought that he had become SonJoy. Now, when he has decided to tour those tribal villages, we think he has become SunJoy in a real sense, illuminating those around him.' Everyone that was around there became emotional on this and applauded for Sanjay's mother. Sanjay's mother was Darshana ji. She urged Shyam ji to visit her home. Shyam ji agreed. When Shyam ji was at their home, Darshana ji asked him, 'We know that Sanjay has decided to go to India and will live in villages. We don't have any objection to that as we old generation Indians were ourselves born in some village of India. We have always felt ashamed that we could not do anything for our mathrubhumi. Now, when our son has thought so, we think it's our good fortune. However, one thing is worrying me: who will take care of him when he will be in villages?'

Shyam ji comforted her, 'I am there for him.' At this, Darshana ji said, 'Should I think that Sanjay is visiting his mama ji's place?' Shyam ji was pleasantly shocked. He said, 'It would be my pleasure.'

Now, Sanjay was Shyam ji's responsibility. Darshana ji put vermilion on Shyam ji's forehead and tied a rakhi on his wrist. Thus, Shyam ji became her brother. Now, her second wish was that whenever Shyam ji would come to Chicago, he would stay with Darshana ji's family. This was a kind of proposal that would require permission of local Ekal team members. Coincidentally, they were there on the spot. So, Shyam ji looked at them and they nodded in agreement. Thus, it became final that Shyam ji would stay at Darshana ji's place whenever he would be in Chicago.

Darshana ji even finalised his room. Sanjay also spelt out his programme to visit India. But, now the question was how he would tackle the problem of language while living in Indian villages. Sanjay did not know even a single letter of Hindi. As a solution to this problem, it was decided that Sanjay would spend some time with Shyam ji during the latter's tour to America. Shyam ji was entrusted with the job of teaching working knowledge of Hindi to Sanjay. Ultimately, a plan was charted out how Sanjay would visit India. He was supposed to land in Delhi and then straight away meet Shyam ji. He would then follow Shyam ji's plan of living in villages. Initially, it was planned that Sanjay should visit an Ekal school near Delhi and spend a week there. Then onwards, he must be sent to villages. After his arrival in Delhi, he was sent on a motorbike to Ekal schools in villages around Delhi. He was asked to spend a day in a village. After a week, he returned. Shyam ji sounded him out and was satisfied that he did not have much trouble spending nights in villages.

The second experience for Sanjay was that no other vehicle than motorbike could traverse through villages. Now, Sanjay was ready for a yearlong stay in the villages. A plan was prepared for that. It was kept in mind that he must stay in almost all provinces of India. Some workers who had some knowledge of English were made his colleagues. Besides, Sanjay himself learnt working-level Hindi. It was also decided that once in a month he must meet Shyam ji somewhere and he should spend two to three days with him. Whatever Shyam ji conversed with the Ekal workers, Sanjay would analyse it. The Ekal team also ensured that while Sanjay was living in villages, some member of the Ekal's urban organisation should be in contact with him so that he must have diverse experience of the Ekal's working. Sanjay had carried a video camera with him and he shot videos of every important thing happening during his stay. He spoke to villagers of all kinds and deeply enquired about the impact of the Ekal schools on rural life. He would shoot videos whenever he felt something important was being discussed or done. He minutely observed every little happening of the Ekal and shot videos accordingly. He interviewed the Ekal teachers and recorded them.

In the name of the urban organisation of the Ekal was only the Vanvasi Kalyan Ashram then. So, Sanjay spoke to the members of the Ashram as well and shot their videos.

Amid such experiences, his one-year among tribals and Ekal schools was over. To learn about his experiences, a meeting of senior Ekal members was organised. He first showed some of his videos to the Ekal team. The Ekal members then asked him questions about the three-hour syllabus of the Ekal schools. He answered all these questions by showing videos. The Ekal team was stunned to note Sanjay's sharpness in catching such minute details on his camera. Similarly, the Ekal team knew how the Ekal had impacted the lives of villagers, but when they saw the videos shot by Sanjay, they felt anew and satisfied that now there was video evidence of that. The most important was that Sanjay had shot special videos to demonstrate the functioning of the Ekal to people living in America. Everyone in the Ekal team was proud of such work. When he was asked to summarise his conclusions in three sentences, he said:

1) The views of the central Ekal team about its mission have not percolated down to the villages.
2) The rural or tribal people think that the Ekal is either a government scheme or a charity organisation of wealthy urban people.
3) There should be more focus on the utilisation of voluntary members of the Ekal.

In the question-answer session, he was asked how many of the thoughts of the centre were trickling down to the villages? He said it was merely 40%.

With this, Sanjay's India tour came to an end.

Shyam ji was of the view that Sanjay could not express certain things before the Ekal workers. So, he decided to have a one-on-one session with him before his departure to America. Shyam ji told him that he was the first overseas person who had come to tour and study the functioning of the Ekal and thus people in America would ask him about the Ekal. What would he answer if he came across such questions? 'I will tell them that none but the Ekal has cared for tribal people living in distant forested villages of India. Yes, the Church is also active on this front, but it can't match the devotion of the Ekal,' he said. He promised Shyam ji that he would connect youths living in the areas around every Chapter of Ekal in America. Meanwhile, Sanjay also asked Shyam ji, 'What is the purpose of your visit to America?' Shyam ji explained, 'To introduce the Ekal to people there and also keep them informed of its progress. If people have any doubt about the Ekal, I try to remove them and convince people.' Sanjay then asked him that if any alternative could emerge, how would he react? Shyam ji said, 'I would be happy. What could be better than that?' Then, Sanjay suggested, 'These days, all such types of orientation works are done through websites. I will prepare such an audio-visual website that it will serve all the purposes for which you tour America.' Shyam ji was surprised and a little iffy, but ultimately, he gave his go-ahead to Sanjay for this task. Shyam ji connected the web designing team of the Ekal to Sanjay and he updated the Ekal website within six months. The new website appealed to everyone and it was ushered in with a warm welcome.

Those days, websites were not known at a large scale in India, but in America, life could not be imagined without web portals. It still is the same in America. The Ekal website was checked by those associated with the Ekal in America. They shot different kinds of queries and found their answers on the website. Hence, the Ekal passed the portal pareeksha (exam) successfully. Even the small queries about the three-hour syllabus of the Ekal had video answers prepared by Sanjay. Every donor could search for the Ekal school he was donating to with every possible detail like the name of the school, its village, its rural organisation, the number of students, their names, teacher's name, the daily functioning of the school, examination details, results of the exam and the impact of the Ekal school on the village where it was situated. There were also videos with such details. As Sanjay had promised in India, he devoted himself to work for the Ekal in America. He widened the Ekal network among the youths. Today, if you browse the Ekal website and see a number of stories about the youth connected to the Ekal in America, the maximum number of them have joined the Ekal because of Sanjay's efforts.

When he returned to America, his family thought that they must mark the occasion with a celebration. Shyam ji was invited as a special guest on this occasion. In the beginning of the programme, Shyam ji shared the conclusions of Sanjay's India tour to tribal areas. Then, Sanjay shared his experiences. Then, it was the occasion of the question-answer. Someone asked, 'When did you miss your mother the most?' Another question was, 'When did you feel the most uncomfortable in the villages while living there?' The third prominent question was: 'After spending one year in rural India, what did you feel was the most enjoyable?'

Sanjay answers all the questions one by one. He said, 'I remembered my mother most when I fell sick. It was a fever. One of the ladies among the villagers nursed me. She put my head into her lap and lulled me to sleep. Then I definitely remembered my mother because I knew that my own mother would not care for me that way in America.' About the second question, he said, 'I felt most uncomfortable when I had to wash my clothes, as there are washing machines in America. I had never washed my clothes here. So, when I tried that in the village, I would sometimes slip the soap and sometimes, my clothes would not dry up easily. The village kids would look at me and chuckle. Then, I used to feel embarrassed that I could not manage even such an easy task.' Now, he came to the third question. He said, 'Before deciding to go to India, I was planning to go to some African country as most of my friends did. We youths had this belief that perhaps only the Church takes care of the underprivileged and the poor in the world. But after travelling to India, I can say this with full confidence that in my ancestors' land, I have been witness to the finest kind of human service in the very difficult rural locations. I am proud to be among those people. I am proud of being part of the Ekal.'

The whole room reverberated with applause when he stopped talking. Now came the turn of Sanjay's parents to say thanks to everyone. His mother, Darshana ji said, 'When he was born, we named him Sanjay. As he grew up, he began to be known as SonJoy. Now, we feel that he has become SunJoy. There is a reason for this nomenclature. A year in rural India has changed him so much that now he will illuminate our lives like the son of sun. I am his mother. I feel that I should quit my job and devote my life in the service of Bharatmata. I did not know anything about the Ekal, but Sanjay's experiences have shown me an entirely new life. He has opened my eyes.' She then addressed Shyam ji, 'Shyam ji, you have become an elder brother. Now, the life of your younger sister is devoted to your mission.' Sanjay's father Anil ji was equally emotional. He said, 'When Sanjay decided to go to India first, I took it very lightly. Now, I deeply regret why I weighed the Ekal so lightly. Shyam ji, I can't think of a better gift on our marriage anniversary that I have found the mission of my life.' Like everyone, Shyam ji was also full of joy, but he controlled his emotions and addressed the gathering, saying, 'Whatever you are seeing in this family is the result of the scent of our soil, the soil of our villages. This is where our culture takes birth. This experience has the power not to change youth like Sanjay, but it can change the youths of the whole world. Today, I am happy that I can see the rise of a "new India" in this foreign land as well.'

A YOUNG COLLEGE GIRL COLLECTS MONEY FOR EKAL BY POLISHING SHOES

One more incident in the journey of the Ekal left an indelible impression. The Ekal's founder Madan Babu's eldest son, Shree Anand Agrawal (now he is no more) lived in America for a very long time. Before Shyam ji started touring America, he had held the front of the Ekal there. Thus, whenever Shyam ji visited America, the visit to Anand ji's family would be like a pilgrimage for him. Once, Shyam ji was watching the latest film on Ekal with the children of the family. The children were very curious and excited to know about the tribals. They would call Shyam ji dada ji. The youngest of the children, Shruti, was the naughtiest. She would always sit beside Shyam ji and ask many questions. Even Shyam ji was fond of her and would feel a divine happiness by talking to her. Once she asked, 'Dada ji, you people have built such a big enterprise, but should it not have a role for children?'

For Shyam ji, this question was nothing less than a divine wisdom. He became very emotional. Little Shruti said whatever her heart suggested. But, it was like a challenge for Shyam ji. He had never bothered to think about it. Shyam ji said that he couldn't think of any answer and that Shruti should herself suggest something on the subject. How could she help in this regard? She said that she would also adopt an Ekal school. Shyam ji said, 'Okay, whatever your father donates for the schools, he would put that under your name.' But Shruti said, 'No, no. I will collect my own money.' Her father, mother and Shyam ji together said, 'How would you collect money?' She said she would collect that in her own way. She then put a condition before Shyam ji. 'The condition is that you will have to come to my college to collect this money,' she said.

Shyam ji promised her that he would come to her college. Her determination surprised everyone, but no one had the courage and any reason to say 'no' to this gutsy girl. The next year, when Shyam ji went on an America tour, his itinerary also had a programme in some university. Shyam ji had forgotten last year's promise to Shruti for collecting money. When he was told that the university where his programme was scheduled was the one where Shruti studied, he was reminded of the pledge of a little girl. He was also reminded of his promise and so he agreed. Shyam ji reached that university and came to a room adjacent to Shruti's classroom. Shruti's classmates were present there. In the beginning, Shyam ji showed them a short film. Then, he gave a presentation about the Ekal. Later, the question-answer session took place. One American girl raised her hand. Shyam ji was fear-struck that he might have hurt her feelings inadvertently. She said, 'Sir, you have said in your presentation that you provide value-based education to the tribal or village children in India. I have a question for you. What ethical values can you teach to those people? I feel that you must learn ethical values from them.' Shyam ji felt as if he fell from the sky flat on the earth. That American girl had challenged him and she was also speaking the absolute truth.

Shyam ji humbly asked that girl how did she know that he and his colleagues needed lessons in ethics from the rural people? She explained, 'I had gone to India to work on some rural project on behalf of the college. I stayed in many villages. I also spent nights in villages. I really felt that not only India, but also the entire world could learn a lot from the Indian village life and rural culture. We urban-dwellers cannot teach a single thing to them. Instead, we must learn from them.' Shyam ji patted this girl's back with affection and encouragement. She shared such a wonderful experience that was hitherto unfelt by Shyam ji and the Ekal team. He also thanked and patted Shruti for making him and the team experience such an important learning. Now, the time came to hand him over the cheque. Shruti handed that cheque to Shyam ji. When he checked the amount of the cheque, he was surprised that it was for $500, while the total budget for an Ekal school was fixed at $350. He looked at Shruti with dismay. He asked her how she collected this much money? She said jokingly that she would not share that with Shyam ji. Suddenly, one of her friends raised his hand and said that he could share the secret. Shyam ji thought for a moment what was so secret about this that Shruti was coy to share that the information. He thought all of her classmates and friends must have collected that money together and that is why she was not willing to share that. But when his friend shared the secret, Shyam ji felt that he must hold Shruti in his arms or touch her feet in respect.

Her friend told Shyam ji that Shruti prepared a banner with something scribbled about the Ekal and hung it on the gate of the college. She then sat under it to offer boot-polishing services. There was also a short introduction of Shruti written on the banner. As people would pass her by, they would read the message on the banner and also contribute even without getting their shoes polished. She quickly collected $500 by donation and by polishing shoes. She wanted to conceal this from her family and that is why she called Shyam ji to college.

What an experience it was for Shyam ji and the Ekal! A girl polished shoes to fund a school. Could anyone imagine greater devotion than this? It also proved one thing that the hearts of children are always clean, whether they are in India or America.

A TEENAGE BOY VISITS AN EKAL SCHOOL ALONE AND BRINGS THE MESSAGE OF EKAL TO AMERICA

One more incident left a deep impression on Shyam ji. It forced Shyam ji to contemplate a lot. He was staying with a family in America. Both the husband and wife would go to work. The children would stay alone for some time and thus Shyam ji developed a friendship with them. The elder son was 13-14 years old. He was of a very curious nature and would ask a lot of questions. When he got to know that the Ekal taught children of his age who could not afford their school fees, he became extra curious to know about them. However, he was unable to fathom poverty properly. After watching the film, he became emotional as he saw penury-driven children. He asked his parents to take him to those places where those children lived. In order to get him first-hand tribal experience, his parents would have to bring him to India and they were not in a position to do so because of their professional commitments. Since his parents were not in a position to travel, he said that he would travel alone to India. He was adamant. It became very strange for his parents to say 'no' to their beloved son. They finally dropped their objection to their son going to India alone, but his tender age was a worry for them. The parents contacted the Ekal volunteers and shared their predicament with them. They advised them that the boy could be boarded on the flight from America to Chennai and at Chennai Airport, someone from the Ekal team would receive him. 'There would be no problem for him, please be sure,' they assured the parents. The parents were Tamil and they agreed on sending their child to Chennai.

At last, that boy landed at the Chennai Airport. A number of Ekal volunteers, including some mothers, were at the airport to receive that boy. As he came out of the airport, a group of people welcomed him. He was so perturbed that so many people came to receive him. But, it was a new experience for him. Everyone lovingly took him to the car. As soon as he got into the car, he asked, 'Where is the Ekal school?' He was told that since he had come from such a long journey, he must freshen up first. 'Then, we will take you to the Ekal school,' the Ekal team assured him. But that boy was adamant that he would directly go to the Ekal school. His innocence and love for the Ekal won everyone's heart and the volunteer who was supposed to take him to the Ekal school was finally called. He had come on a motorbike and he was asked to come before the arrival of the American boy. When the boy came to know that the man on the motorbike would take him to the Ekal school, he insisted on going with him to the Ekal school at once. He had never ridden on a motorbike in America and so he was also childishly thrilled to ride one in India. Ultimately, the Ekal team had to give into his demand and had to send him on the motorbike to the Ekal school. The boy's enthusiasm impressed everyone. That boy toured the village on the motorbike. When he saw the tribal children washing their own clothes in an impoverished condition, he started crying. He had never seen such poverty in his life, but he was surprised to see children smiling everywhere. He was unable to understand how those children were so deprived yet so happy. When the village mothers cuddled him and treated him like their own son, he was overjoyed but he was unable to understand what his relation was with them. He did not feel that warmth of motherhood even when he was with his own mother.

When he returned to America, he prepared a presentation. He had also clicked photographs in the villages he had visited. Coincidentally,

Shyam ji happened to go to the annual Ekal meeting in America. When that boy saw Shyam ji, he came running towards him and embraced him. Shyam ji was unable to understand why he was so happy and so emotional. His presentation was given 10 minutes in the programme. In his presentation, he showed and spoke about the Ekal school, but he described the poverty and resourcelessness of the tribal children in such an emotional way that every eye in the auditorium was moist. When this boy was mentioning the love and affection he got from the villagers, especially from the mothers, he broke down. When he finished his presentation, the people who were also crying with him gave him a standing ovation. Some mothers in fact rushed towards him and put their hands on his head. This boy won every heart gathered there and changed the atmosphere of the whole programme.

Shyam ji was standing in a corner. He thanked Ram ji that He had bestowed so much emotion even to the young generation who had taken birth in America. Really, young examples like that of young boy are still to be found in India.

□

9
From Sanskar to Expansion of Service

It is known universally that mothers have a higher degree of affection for their children than fathers. The Ekal team also realised the fact that if mothers could be made part of the Ekal programmes, the guarantee of their success would be multiplied, as mothers are the first nurseries of value education for the children. Keeping this in mind, Shyam ji thought out a plan. As part of his plan, he would take some students of Chakapad Hostel in Odisha to Kolkata. These children were supposed to live with Kolkata families in groups of twos for two days. The host families were selected after meeting two conditions—first, there should be children of the age of hostel children; second, the mother of the family must be so sensitive that she could take care of the hostel children as her own. Thus, 20 families were listed and Shyam ji took responsibility for taking 40 children to live with these families. Ultimately, the day arrived when Shyam ji reached Howrah Station with 40 hostel children. Children of 20 families were already waiting to welcome these children at the railway station. For the vanvasi (or tribal) children, it was the first train journey of their lives. They were awed by seeing such a huge railway station. Shyam ji made them feel at ease and told them that the children from the city had come to welcome and take them with them. As the urban children caught their hands to take them out of the station, they were shocked to see their bare feet. They did not even have chappals. They did not have any baggage except a satchel hanging on their shoulders. The urban children thought the tribal children had forgotten their luggage in the train bogies. Since there was a linguistic barrier to communicate with the tribal children, they asked Shyam ji to ask the tribal children to bring their chappals and luggage from the train compartment.

Shyam ji explained to the urban children that the tribals do not possess chappals and neither do they have any additional belongings other than a small satchel. The urban children were shocked with disbelief. Anyway, both the groups of children proceeded to board the van that was to carry them to the city. Suddenly, something happened. There was some commotion and the urban children came running towards Shyam ji. They told Shyam ji that the tribal children were not boarding the van. Shyam ji understood the matter and said to the urban children, 'They have never seen a van in their life. They are feeling awkward and afraid. You must hold their hands and help them board the van with assurance.' Somehow, this problem was solved exactly as Shyam ji had suggested. Now, the children reached the houses where they had to stay. It was an apartment building with a lift to go up. As the tribal children entered the lift and it began to move up, they started crying. They had heard from their elders that everybody will go up one day after death, and thus they thought it was their moment to go up. And, they thought, they were so unlucky that they were going up without their parents by their side. They kept crying so much that even after coming out of the lift, they were not calming down. Finally, mothers of the adopting families comforted them as their own children and in the warmth of maternal affection, they felt they were 'safe and alive'. Meanwhile, Shyam ji was very nervous. 'Had any untoward accident or bad experience taken place within any family, I would not be able to enter villages after that,' he kept thinking, with constant fear-struck reminders. Therefore, he decided that he would keep enquiring about all those tribal kids by visiting each family with whom they were staying. He knocked at the door of one family. The patriarch of the family warmly welcomed him. When Shyam ji got seated comfortably and had water, etc., the man himself brought refreshments for him. Shyam ji asked, 'Where is behen ji?' He said, 'She is in the washroom.' Then, Shyam ji asked, 'Where are the tribal children?' He answered, 'They are also in the washroom.' Shyam ji thought he must wait for a while. Anyway, an hour passed but neither the mother nor the tribal children were seen. Shyam ji became anxious and he asked the man why it was taking so long. He said in a relaxed manner, 'Shyam ji, if you remember, when you came with the proposal to our house, you had asked my Mrs to treat the tribal children as her own. She actually heard that she had to make those children just like her children. So, she is rubbing soap after soap to turn the blackish skin colour of these children into whitish complexion like that of her own children.' It was somewhat hilarious and highly surprising for Shyam ji. However, he was extremely joyous that ultimately the tribal children had won the heart of this mother and vice-versa. He was reminded of this universal and proven wisdom 'a mother of this country is always a mother, whether she is in a tribal village or in an advanced metro city. You can replace a child with any other, but the heart of the mother will remain unchanged.'

In order to herald the arrival and stay of the tribal children to the whole Kolkata, the Ekal planned a big group yagya (oblation ritual).

The programme was organised in the evening and 20 yagya vedis (sacred fires) were prepared at 20 different places in a big hall. The tribal children and their 'adopting families' sat around these vedis. Since all these tribal children knew the ritual of hawan (chanting mantras around sacred fire), a tribal child was asked to chant mantras on loudspeaker and all the children and family members sitting around would repeat the mantras recited by him. All the tribal children were dressed in similar looking clothes and they looked smart and attractive. They actually looked like a kid battalion of patriotic soldiers. Their diction of chanting mantras was so perfect that the urban people present there gushed over them. After the yagya was over, Shyam ji introduced these children to the guests. The mothers of the families and others from the gathering hugged and cuddled all these children so much that they got overwhelmed and tears rolled down their eyes. The mothers were also crying with affection for them. This gathering became memorable for the tribal children. All the guests admired the families who so affectionately and successfully cared for these children and made this experiment a glorious success.

In this experiment, Shyam ji discovered a new route to enter into the hearts of the urban people (women or mothers) and the tribal people (especially children). From this route, he had to build a bridge between the tribal society and the urban society.

At the time of the departure of these tribal children, a parting ceremony was organised. All the connected urban families assembled at a designated place. This programme was designed to listen to the experiences of the tribal children and the families with whom they stayed. All the families participated in it with full enthusiasm. From the families, only mothers were asked to speak, even though some kids chipped in to share some interesting tales. In short, everyone was elated and thrilled to share his or her experiences with this home-stay experiment. From their experiences, it was known that every morning after taking bath, the tribal children would conduct the hawan and puja on their own in a very attention-seeking manner. It was as if they were following the routine of their hostel. But, one of the most attractive aspects of the training of tribal children was how one can communicate through the language of the heart even without knowing the real language of people. Even the mentality of these tribal children became evident to the urban families. Whenever they were offered any gift, they became hesitant to accept it. It meant they were full of self-respect and did not allow their dignity to plummet on any occasion.

In the end, the tribal children were asked to share their experiences. Since they had difficulty understanding Hindi or Bangla, Shyam ji became their moderator. He asked those kids in Odia how would they respond if their parents and others back in their village would ask, 'What did you bring back from Kolkata?' Shyam ji was expecting that since these kids had come with mere satchels from their villages and now, they were showered with so many gifts, so naturally they would say that they had returned with a sack full of gifts. But to his dismay and chagrin, they said, 'We have brought a new mother from Kolkata.' The answer numbed everyone. Emotions pervaded every soul in the hall. The mothers were in tears. They were moved by the fact that those kids did not forget the affection they had received from their mothers for two days in a city. They forgot their gifts but not their mothers.

The tribal children returned to their villages as scheduled. The villagers welcomed them as if they had returned after a journey to the moon. It was full of thrill and elation for tribal villagers that their children had returned from a big city like Kolkata after staying with urban families there. In fact, the whole village gathered at one place to listen to the experiences of the just-returned children. They told them about their first experience in a lift and how they went up and thought they had died and were rocketing up as souls. They told them a car picked them up from the railway station and they toured various places in Kolkata in the car. They turned emotional while reminiscing how city mothers cared for them while they were staying with them. They recalled the affection they showered on them. They also narrated how they intermingled with urban children and had fun with them. They went shopping in the bazaar of Kolkata. They mentioned that the city mothers had made them sit in their laps while performing a group hawan. They told everyone that when they were saying goodbye to their 'adopting families', they all came to see them off. The children also showed the villagers the gifts they had brought with them. The villagers were seeing some of the toys for the first time in their lives.

After hearing the experiences of their children, the first reaction of the villagers was that they invited the Christian priest appointed for their village by the Church. The Church had appointed Popka, or priest, for every village. In the village language, he was or is still called Popka. When the Popka was informed about the invitation from the village. He was upbeat as he expected that it would be for some feast. When he arrived in the village, he saw that the whole village had assembled at one place. An elder of the village addressed him, 'You used to brainwash us into believing that the city-dwellers exploit us and look down upon us. And that is why you would convince us to convert to Christianity. But, one child in our village has just returned from Kolkata. He has shared his experience with us. His experience is just the opposite. According to him, the city-dwellers love us. Besides, the way people in Kolkata treated him, we could not even imagine that we are loved so much by our city brethren. Why did you keep us in the dark for so many years?' Then every villager asked the same question in a chorus. Popka had never prepared himself for such a reaction in the village. He had never imagined that he would face a volley of such piercing questions. He neither had any answer to these queries. The villagers were waiting for such a moment to vent their long held-up anger. They all started beating Popka and beat him so much that he never mustered the courage to return to that village again. The news of Popka being thrashed by the villagers spread like wildfire in the neighbouring villages. The villagers were so influenced by this news that people who had turned Christians because of the Church's chicanery returned to their original Hindu faith. It instilled a faith in Shyam ji that Kolkata-like experience could actually make the whole tribal belt free of conversion. Now, every village was ready to beat the Popka or Christian priest and they feared to tread into the villages. However, villagers were still seething with anger and nobody knew the exact reason for that.

Then one day, it was announced that the then Prime Minister Rajiv Gandhi would tour Odisha. He would come to Odisha's capital Bhubaneswar. As soon as the tribals heard the name of Rajiv Gandhi, their anger mounted several notches up because the Christian priests would use the recorded tapes of Sonia Gandhi, Rajiv's Christian wife, to entice innocent villagers towards Christianity. The villagers held a meeting and decided to teach Rajiv a lesson. The state Congress has organised a big event in Bhubaneswar to welcome Rajiv. At that time, Odisha was divided in two parts—one was East and it included Bhubaneshwar; the other was West and it connected to the East only via one pucca road. The tribal villages would fall on both the sides of the road that connected the East and West. The villagers cut big logs of trees and threw them in the middle of the road. It was completely blocked. Now, no bus could pass from the West to the East. Since Rajiv Gandhi was not only the Prime Minister of the country, he was also the president of All India Congress Committee, the local Congress workers, a large number of them from the West, were supposed to go to the Bhubaneshwar function. However, the road was blocked and they could not go to attend the function. The road blockage was planned so discreetly that no one got a wind of it. The next morning when Rajiv Gandhi arrived for the function, he saw that half the pandal (tent) was empty. He was flabbergasted and became angry with the state Congress leadership. When he enquired about the absence of workers in the party event, some of them dared to tell him that there was anger against his wife, Sonia Gandhi, whose name was used to convert people to Christianity.

It was a new dawn. Now, you imagine that only because a loving mother of Kolkata showered her affection on tribal children and it rattled the Sultanat (government) of the Congress in Delhi. This is the power of values and love!

It was an insult to Prime Minister Rajiv Gandhi and so the state Congress government and the Central government took it personally.

They found out that the Hindu resurrection in Phulbani district was happening because of Swami Lakshmanand ji Maharaj. The Church had already opened a front against Swami ji. When two governments backed it, the Church became aggressive. There was one more reason for the Church's aggressiveness. As per the Reservation Act, if any person belonging to the Scheduled Caste (SC) converts to Christianity, he or she loses the right to get reservation due for SCs. However, despite the clear stipulation of the law, many SCs, even after conversion, were taking reservation benefits and had occupied high positions in government jobs. They had fudged the SC/ST certificates. Swami ji had launched an agitation against this fraud. As a result of Swami ji's indefatigable efforts, many Christian SCs/STs lost their jobs. Cases were filed even against senior government officials who had embraced Christianity and availed of SC/ST quota. Several of them also lost their jobs. One of those gentlemen, who was from Phulbani district itself, had even become the chief secretary in the Odisha government. He had also used a fake SC certificate to get a government job and was the key figure in hatching the conspiracy for the Church to start a conversion campaign in the tribal belt. He also had to lose his job. This infuriated the Church a lot and it planned to take revenge against Swami ji. It already had the support from the government system and thus a number of assassination attempts were conducted to kill Swami ji. But, he was saved because of the local tribal support. This support was the result of Swami ji's careful building of the organisation of dedicated tribals through his regular satsang and meeting with children's parents who would attend the night classes of the Ekal for the elders. Meanwhile, one more aspect of tribal enthusiasm became obvious. Not only tribal youth but also the tribal women took part in the activities with great enthusiasm. They were also more aggressive than their men folk. Therefore, the teacher was not paid for his night classes. The villagers themselves arranged everything, even the stationery. Similarly, the satsang was organised in the similar spirit and it filled the tribals with an aggressive sense of defence of their religion. It later became the guiding light of the Ekal.

CHAKABAD BUILT A BRIDGE OF TRUST

To build a bridge between the tribal society and the city folks, the Ekal conducted another experiment. It was 1986. The Ekal planned a three-day long programme on the occasion of Shivratri in Chakapad, Phulbani. In tribal culture, the Ashta Prahar (108 Melodies) has great importance. It means that eight groups of devotees sing devotional songs in a single mandap (porch) for three long hours. It is so endearing to the tribals that if you give them Rs 10 for dinner and at the same time invite them to the Ashta Prahar, they would sacrifice their dinner for the Ashta Prahar. In the planned Ekal programme on Shivratri, around 108 mandaps were erected. One singing group gets only one chance. Around 150,000 tribals assembled for this programme. At the invitation of Swami ji, almost every village sent a group of people to take part in the programme. The Ekal arranged for their lodging and food. This Chakapad programme was aimed at connecting tribal and urban societies. So, a number of families from Kolkata were invited. The rich families of Kolkata also contributed handsomely for the success of this programme. The secretary of the Vishwa Hindu Parishad was from Agra. He also came to attend the programme at the invitation of Shyam ji. The governor of Odisha also graced the programme for one day. Similarly, Shankracharya of Puri also registered his presence for one day. The participants also came from all prominent towns of Odisha. Madan Babu's son and daughter also came with the group from Kolkata to attend the programme. The head of this group was an elderly man. Everyone was surprised to see this old man leading the group of elites from Kolkata.

The city-dwellers were seeing the tribals in such a large number for the first time. Their cultured and disciplined behaviour fascinated everyone. The tribals had also seen so many cars at one place for the first time. One interesting event took place in this gathering. The mothers who had come from Kolkata were fair in complexion and wore make-up and jewellery as they usually wore. The tribals had seen such dressed up and well-toned women for the first time and a canard spread among them that fairies had descended from heaven for the programme. A huge crowd gathered where those women were sitting and everyone was looking at them with wonderment. Nobody had imagined that tribal imagination and belief would work that way. Then, by coincidence, the Kolkata group reached the place where the meal was being served to the tribals. The head of the Kolkata groups suddenly decided that they would also have their meal with the tribals. Though the organising committee had arranged for their dinner at a separate place, the old head of the group insisted on having meals with the tribals. The organisers agreed to arrange meals for them and a row was prepared for their sitting. All the male guests from Kolkata sat there. It was a curious occasion for the tribal society, as they did not expect that the people from the city would eat with them. So, those who were not dining stood around them. Only two items were prepared for the dinner—rice and daal (pulse). The daal was so diluted that it was impossible to separate a grain of pulse. First, the rice was served and then dal was poured on the rice plates. The rice was put on the plate in a way that daal should not flow out of the plate. The people from Kolkata were not accustomed to this kind of dining. Thus, when they started eating, their daal flowed out of the plate (which were made up of plant leaves). The tribals laughed at this scene. Some tribals who were standing, they came to Kolkatans' rescue and arranged their rice and daal in a way that it could not flow out of the plate and they could dine comfortably. Thus, the people from Kolkata could some daal rice. Though, later they went to the place where their dinner had been arranged and they had their meal properly. It left some impression on the minds of people who came from Kolkata. They felt empathy for their tribal brethren. And they decided that they would do something for the tribals.

THE ORGANISATION TEACHES SACRIFICE

The Chakapad programme left its deep imprint on the folks who had gone to attend from Kolkata. It also equally impressed the tribals who had come from different villages. The tribals had so far had a very negative impression of the city people. They thought the city people hated or at least looked down upon them. This was largely because they had been brainwashed by the Church's appointed Popkas. Popkas were in regular touch with them and filled them with poison against people who lived in the cities. The same was the case with the city-dwellers. They were also made to believe in convent schools that the tribals were actually just like animals and they were criminal castes. They were named janjatiya (scheduled tribes) by the Colonial British and it was to denote that the tribals were criminals. The Church was brainwashing both the city people and as well as tribals and were pitting one against the other by propagating hate and disdain. But when the Ekal brought both the societies together on one platform, they came to know that both of them were children born out of the same womb of one mother known as Bharatmata. A bond of love and trust naturally developed between the two societies after the Chakapad programme. Now, the evil designs of the Church seemed in the doldrums. After the Chakapad programme, the whole Phulwani district turned hostile towards the Church and Swami Lakshmanand ji became the undisputed leader of the tribal society. Swam ji gave a clarion call that he would free the whole district of the Church influence. On the other hand, the Church and Maoists threaten to eliminate Swami ji.

It was the misfortune of us Indians that our own state government was sympathetic towards the Church. To combat this challenge, Swami ji launched an aggressive satsang campaign and as part of this, a satsang had to be organised daily in every village. On the other hand, plots were hatched to assassinate Swami ji. The tribal society came to know of such a conspiracy through their own local intelligence. So, some tribal youths were always with Swami ji for his protection whenever he went out of his ashram. Between 1986 and 2007, there were about seven assassination attempts on Swami ji's life, but he was saved every time. With every attempt on Swami ji's life, the anger of tribal society kept rising. On a pleasant note, it united the Hindu society and they became firmly resolved to protect their religion and its honourable figures. This unity enraged the Church and their sympathetic government. They planned something very sinister. In the tribal and rural societies, both Scheduled Castes (SCs) and Scheduled Tribes (STs) had become followers of Swami ji. The government tried to divide both these sections by using the plank of reservation. It actually worked and the local communities divided into SCs and STs. It made one thing clear that the caste was heavier than the combined weight of Hinduism and the rural society took their caste pride or identity as their first priority. It takes years to make people realise the value and importance of their caste, but it even takes longer to draw a bigger line than this. That is that they must be forced to realise that their caste is merely a part of their faith and they must assert their Hindu identity whenever people attempted to divide them along caste lines. Swami ji was successful in invigorating the Hindu rural society to be sensitive towards their religious identity. But his efforts to unite them into one Hindu organisation were in the primary stage.

As a result of these developments, the whole state, especially Phulwani district, had turned into a tinderbox. The atmosphere had become totally vicious.

The Chakapad programme had built momentum, but the formation of a solid organisation takes time. If the fields are not mended with proper fencing in the rainy season, the water not only flows out, it takes the fertile soil of the field along with it. It became a reality in Phulbani. On the day of Krishna Janmmashtami in 2008, when the whole country was celebrating the birthday of Lord Krishna, an illuminating sun of Hinduism went into premature sunset. Swami Laximamnand ji was assassinated with four of his accomplices. He was sleeping in his ashram when the assailants came and brutally killed him. It led to widespread eruption of anger in Phulbani and the whole state of Odisha. The anger turned into a tornado. Violence broke out. Many churches were set on fire in Phulbani alone. The government was with the Church and hence many Hindu tribals were arrested. The army was called in. Around 10 prominent Christian countries of the world put pressure on the Central and state government. The army started a crackdown on protesting Hindus. When men were put in jail, their women came out to protest. The army could not even enter the villages. The most discernible thing in the protest of the women was that they were mostly those women who attended the satsang of Swami ji. Otherwise, even those children who had studied at Swami ji's school and had stayed in hostels built by him and had later joined government service, they stood like silent spectators. In short, in the time of crisis, the service remained silent, but the organisation showed its brave face. From this tragic event, it became clear that the service produces self-interest, but the organisation and its training teach sacrifice and bravery.

SERVICE TURNS INTO TRUST

Shyam ji was touring the South-West areas of Odisha to expand the Sangh network. A densely populated tribal village named Revalkona had organised the meeting of some prominent villagers. When he was on his way to this meeting, a colleague told him on the way that the tribals of this area consume cow meat. Hearing this, Shyam ji felt hurt and a dilemma struck him whether he should visit that village or not. Anyway, he went ahead. By this time, he had learnt enough Odia to converse with the locals. At the meeting, he was introduced to the villagers. People were told that he had come from Cuttack. Then came the turn of Shyam ji to address the gathering. He had already made up his mind to deliver a speech on the evils of eating cow meat. Thus, he shot his salvos against the ills of cow meat consumption. He told the gathering that it was a sin to eat cow meat and that cow must be worshipped. He had not even finished his speech when an old tribal man stood from his place and started speaking in the local language in a high-pitched voice. Shyam ji felt fear-struck. He did not understand anything that the old tribal was saying, he however had the idea that he himself had said something unpleasant and hurtful to that gentleman. He looked at his local colleague who told him that the old tribal man was saying that if Kataki (people from Cuttack) like you were told to quit eating rice, would you follow the diktat? When Shyam ji heard the word Kataki in the address, he grasped the mentality of the villagers. He realised that he must understand them first and then proceeded to speak. He came to realise that his speech on that occasion was perceived to be a demonstration of his pride of being from the city and being knowledgeable. So, he thought it best to apologise to the villagers.

But despite tendering an apology, Shyam ji was determined to find a solution to the cow meat-eating problem prevalent among those tribals. An idea struck him that the Sangh must start a small clinic for the tribals. JK Paper Mill was just in the vicinity of the village. Ashok Singhal ji introduced Shyam ji to its owners and thus, the problem of the place and building was taken care of. A skilled physician also became ready to give his services. Soon, the clinic started and the physician won the hearts of the villagers with his courteous behaviour. When villagers were under his complete control, he started telling them that most of their ailments were because of the consumption of cow meat. In fact, every patient was prescribed to shun eating cow meat to gain sound health. The physician was so persuasive that no patient could resist his prescription. This clinic became popular in all the villages of the area and people slowly moved towards not only a healthy lifestyle but they also quit the habit of eating cow meat. Shyam ji also learnt a lesson from this experiment that people would listen to any advice after their trust would be won first. This way, the service opened the route to winning trust of the tribals.

THE PINNACLE OF TRIBAL'S TRUTHFULNESS?

It was 1978. Shyam ji had until then spent 14 years as RSS pracharak in Uttar Pradesh. Suddenly, he was ordered to go to work in Odisha. Till then, he had only a distant concept of the people of Odisha. He had only read about them in books. He had no person-to-person contact with the tribal people or Odia people. After his arrival in Odisha, he began touring several distant areas in the state. He would always carry a bag that would be locked. His stay was arranged with a tribal family. Since a vanvasi or tribal family lives very simply, it requires almost nothing to intermingle with them. Neither do they themselves feel any hesitation to adopt a stranger among them. However, the lock in the bag of Shyam ji seemed something entirely new to the tribal family. The whole family would look at the lock curiously. One day, the family members asked Shyam ji why he did lock the bag? He said that he locked the bag so that it could be safe from theft. Then, the tribal family asked, 'What is theft?' Shyam ji tried to explain it to them but despite his best effort, he failed to elaborate it. All the skills and values Shyam ji had learnt in cities capitulated here.

Shyam ji shared this episode with a senior colleague Shree Bajrang Lal Bagra. He also shared his own experience. He had spent some time in the tribal areas of South Africa when he was posted there as a duty of his government job. All the houses in the colony there had no latch on the doors to lock them from outside or inside. When he was asked why was it so? He said there was no theft there and that is why there was no requirement of latch or locks. If anyone was hungry, he could go inside any house and eat whatever was left over. Shyam ji felt that it meant the people who live in the lap of nature are naturally free of evils like theft. And this impact of nature on humans was universal worldwide. He also shared his experience with a district-level member. He said that he had a true but unbelievable story to share. Then he narrated, 'Once, a scuffle broke out between two families over some property-related issue. It went out of control. The head of one family killed the head of the other family. It was reported to the police station. The police station in-charge sent out a message to the killer to surrender at the police station. Here, it must be noted that no police officer went to the village to arrest the murderer, he was only informed to come to the police station. As soon as the killer got the message, he was ready to go to the police station. His family accompanied him. The police officer inquired about the murder. He confessed his crime. Then he was asked the reason behind killing the other man. He told the whole story. Then, he was asked how did he murder the other man? Now, he was startled. He did not know what to say. Suddenly, some idea struck him and he took the axe that was hanging on his shoulder and hit it on the neck of his son and told the police officer, 'This is how I killed that man.' The police officer was shocked but the other members of the family who were also there stood emotionless. He was sent to jail. The Sangh district member went to meet him in the jail and asked why he killed his own son. He said, 'I had confessed to killing that man, but the policeman asked me how I did it. When I confessed my crime, why did he ask me again about that? And how could I answer that question without demonstrating it?' Now, you can imagine whether it was the peak of foolishness of that tribe or was it the pinnacle of his truthfulness? Was he at fault or that police officer?

THE STRENGTH OF TRIBAL SOCIETY

One of the most prominent places in South-West of Odisha is Raigarh. It's an industrial district and is home to many industries. It is also full of tribal population and thus it was on the radar of the Church. The Christian priests were active here. So, Shyam ji and other colleagues mulled plans to expand the network of the Sangh here. With the blessing of Almighty, the Sangh began to spread its wings. It was 1982. The Sangh planned a state-level sammelan in Cuttack to infuse energy into its volunteers in the state. The then Chief Minister (JB Patnaik) agreed to attend the programme. The biggest stadium of Cuttack was booked for the programme. The RSS volunteers from across the state thronged to take part in this huge programme. The workers from the Rayagada district were specifically asked to participate in big numbers. A large number of volunteers agreed to this. The Church saw this event as a potential threat to its designs for the state tribals. So, its propaganda machinery became active and they started convincing tribals that the Cuttack programme had been organised in order to bomb all the tribals by assembling them at one place.

The Sangh workers only came to know of the Church propaganda when the expected number of people did not turn up from Rayagada to participate in the Cuttack programme. Anyway, a small number of people still came from Rayagada. Now, when the CM arrived, a small display of firecrackers took place. As the people of Rayagada heard the sound of crackers, they thought it was the trigger of the bomb blast that the Church people had warned them about. They began to cry. They were crying and saying that they made a mistake by not listening to the Church advice and they were going to die. After some time when the cacophony of crackers came to an end, they touched each other to confirm that they were indeed alive. They were unable to believe that they were alive even after the bombing. When Shyam ji and other Sangh workers came to know of these people from Rayagada, they realised how the Church was befooling the innocent tribals. However, at the end of the programme, the same fear-struck Rayagada folks were so impressed that they convinced the Sangh seniors to organise the next programme in Rayagada. Their insistence again demonstrated their innocence. But, the Sangh volunteers were worried about the fact that the Church had filled enormous amounts of venom against the city-dwellers in the hearts of the tribals and this issue warranted immediate resolution.

Anyway, as the people of Rayagada had wished, the 1983 'Sangh Shiksha Varg' (Educational Training Camp) was planned in Rayagada. It was to be organised in a college there and the principal gave his written permission. The Cuttack programme had prepared a ground for more Sangh activities in the state, as the volunteers were full of renewed vigour. They were just waiting for the next Sangh programme so that they could descend in huge numbers. The volunteers from Rayagada were most eagerly waiting for such a programme. The planned programme became the talk of the town. Naturally, the Church also came to know about it. It started fretting about the consequences of such a large Hindu-oriented festival in their backyard. At that time, the state Congress government was friendly towards the Church. Interestingly, the college that had given permission to the Sangh to organise its programme was run by a trust whose head was a Congress MLA. He had won the election with the support of the Church. So, as expected, the Church hatched a conspiracy and just 10 days before the programme, the permission of the college was withdrawn. At that time, there was a veteran Sangh pracharak in Odisha—Deshpande ji. He was around 80 years old. He would mostly rest during the day. However, whenever any crisis would raise its head, he would become ultra-active as a crisis manager. Shyam ji called him and went to Rayagada with him. The local cadres of the Sangh who were overzealous about the programme were extremely sad and their morale was very down. Deshpande ji comforted them all and asked them to keep their spirits high. Then he and Shyam ji started looking for an alternative place to organise the programme. But they realised that the Church had already pressurised everyone in the district to not allow the Sangh programme to occur anywhere. It seemed almost impossible to find an alternative location. Everyone was disappointed. Even the city could not be changed as all the state volunteers had gotten their reservations done for Rayagada. It was also impossible to inform everyone that the permission for the venue of the programme was withdrawn as doing so would create despair in the whole state and the cadres of the Sangh would feel shattered and powerless.

Meanwhile, Deshpande ji was contemplating something seriously. Suddenly, he asked Shyam ji, 'Shyam ji, please call for a motorbike and come with me.' Shyam ji called for a motorcycle and drove it himself. Deshpande ji sat pillion with him and they set out as Deshpande ji guided. The local Sangh workers were puzzled about what those two men were up to. Anticipating some trouble, they also followed them on bikes. Deshpande ji saw a small hillock and he asked Shyam ji to climb it up. All others followed them. When they reached the top of it, they saw a small shivling (statue of Lord Shiva). All of them prayed before that shivling to ease their suffering and show them a way out of their grave crisis. As they opened their eyes, Deshpande ji saw a plateau near the hillock. It was flat. Deshpande ji addressed Shyam ji, 'Shyam ji, we will organise the Sangh Varg here.' Shyam ji thought Deshpande ji was joking. An educational training camp on a plateau! It was unbelievable. But when Deshpande ji insisted, he had to believe him. Then, Deshpande ji started explaining his plan. He said, 'We will build a small village. There will be huts all around here and the guest students will stay in them.'

As he was talking, the Sangh volunteers were listening with patience. When Deshpande ji finished, the volunteers said with confidence that they would really prepare a village there if they were supplied with the required material. Shyam ji was in a catch-22 situation. He had to organise the programme, but within five days and after building a full-fledged village in a hilly area. How? An idea struck his mind as if Mahadev (Lord Shiva) endowed that into his intellect. The JK Paper Mill was nearby and one of its senior officials was a Sangh volunteer. Ashok Singhal ji had already introduced Shyam ji to JK Paper Mill owners and officials. Now, Shyam ji turned to local or tribal Sangh volunteers and asked them that they had to start building the village from the next day early morning. 'Go, and get ready for that,' he asked those volunteers and went to meet Mills officials with Deshpande ji. It is an open secret for Ram ji's devotees that He first tests you in the hardest possible way and if you come through His test, He showers His blessing beyond your expectations. When Shyam ji and Deshpande ji explained the ambitious plan to the senior Mill official-cum-Sangh volunteer, he readily agreed to support it and promised to arrange for the required materials at the earliest. By the next evening, the required materials started arriving at the spot. The tribal workers were already waiting for them there. From the following day, it appeared that a village was taking shape amid the hills. But, another test from Lord Shiva began amidst all of this. An almost a full colony of jungle animals like snakes and scorpions attacked the site. Nobody had seen those many reptiles in their lives. It was as if Lord Shiva had sent His army to invade. However, while everyone was frightened, the local tribal volunteers were busy building the huts and other things for the village as if nothing had happened or if these were routine occurrences. Still, the volunteers and even Shyam ji were afraid of seeing so many snakes and scorpions together. Shyam ji then went to pray to Lord Shiva and by the time he came back, all the reptiles had vanished. The tribal volunteers asked him where he had disappeared? He uttered 'Mahadev' and everybody started laughing. Shyam ji called the local chief of the volunteers and asked him lovingly, 'What's the issue and why are they laughing? Where have all the reptiles disappeared?' He told him that Shyam ji and others had come from Cuttack, so they were afraid of snakes and scorpions. 'And whatever frightens you city people is a sport for us. You know we know the language of these animals. The reptiles that had come here are actually the subject or the citizens of this place. They had only come to know who had suddenly come here. When they saw us, they were relieved and went back.' Shyam ji was stunned to hear this and was still afraid. He asked innocently, 'Will those snakes and scorpions return?' He nodded in affirmation and said, 'But as soon as they will see us, they will go back.' And it happened. Every day, some snake or scorpion would be seen in some hut and people would scream at its sight, but as soon as the local workers would come there, they would go back into the jungle. Seeing all this, the city folk came to know the power of vanvasis or tribal people. Our fear is their sport. And with these memorable and sweet memories, the Sangh Shiksha Varg was organised in the newly built village and ended successfully.

WHY DOES EKAL TEACH VALUE-BASED EDUCATION?

Today, almost every village has a government school and the private schools are mushrooming as well. Even then, parents prefer to send their children to the Ekal schools. Why? Not only this, they also contribute financially to the village committees that run Ekal schools. The attraction in the Ekal schools is their value-based education. Now, the Ekal schools have widened their horizons. They not only teach children but they aim to encompass the whole village development by focussing on the value-based education of the entire village. The value-based education for the tribal society means not only the protection of their local culture and traditions but to help the tribals strengthen them. This is called the civilisation or culture and even the Supreme Court has accepted this in its order on 28 January 2004 (appeal 240/1997). It was after this order that the Central government started weekly value education programmes in village schools. Shyam ji tackles this issue slightly differently. He says, 'Did we ever realise why our past is so glorious and our present so precarious. Why is there so much hopelessness about our future? Eshwar (Almighty) has given this country everything that He could give, why are we then so looked down upon in the world? Try to understand this in this way that a healthy and strong man has kidney or heart failure and he is admitted in a hospital. The same is the condition of our country. Its two systems have failed—the economy and democracy. You make a list of all glaring problems of the country and when you will deeply analyse these problems, you will come to know that the above-mentioned two systems are at the root of all problems. Interestingly, the solution of these two key problems lies in our continued actions.

'Thinkers like Mahatma Gandhi and Pandit Deen Dayal Upadhyay had warned long ago that until every hand in India would have employment and every agricultural field would have irrigation, poverty could not be eradicated from India. They had added that until those two conditions are not fulfilled, development in other sectors would remain ineffective to uplift the poor of India. When our country became free, the correspondence between Nehru ji and Gandhi ji would enlighten us a lot about the future of our country. Gandhi ji wanted the Indian economy to be agriculture or village-centric so that the poor of the country could be brought at par with the well-to-do people living in cities. His advice was not heeded and the consequences are evident before us. Today, as per government records, two farmers commit suicide every hour, as they are unable to pay off their farm loans and thus are not able to lead a life of self-respect. The number of millionaires and billionaires is increasing in the country. However. at the same time, according to the Arjun Sengupta report that was also tabled in the Parliament, around 80 crore Indians earn less than 20 rupees a day. In fact, 30% of them merely earn 9 rupees a day. Neither economists nor industrialists have any solution to tackle such humongous poverty. The government and the so-called civil society are also clueless on this front.

'There is only one solution—we must return to the Gandhian way of economy or turn towards nature. We must serve dhartimata, gaumata and gangamata and they will fill our natural resources again. However, a young farmer will cultivate only when he will be healthy. For this, he must be aware of various health schemes of the government. Similarly, until people will be aware, various welfare schemes of the government will not be successful. Indian Parliament has given the public a weapon named Right to Information, but as per one survey, around 90% villagers have not even heard of it.

'In this gloomy backdrop, the Ekal's four-dimensional programme for the village education—aarogya, gram vikas, jagran shiksha and the literacy of young villagers—seems to show some solution. This is so because the government programmes for the villages mostly remain non-starter or poor-performer because of the lackadaisical attitude of the government officials. The government officials cannot even explain their scheme to the villagers. This is because the villagers understand only the language of religion. The religion is in the soul of Bharat. So, it is necessary that through Weekly Sanskar Classes, the villagers must be taught or allowed to do bhajan kirtan for about one and half an hour and then they must be informed about educational subjects. This way, they will take interest in education and villages can be empowered. This model is briefly called "value-based education".'

Shyam ji says that India has failed miserably on two fronts—one is poverty and the second is internal security. He adds, 'They both depend on good governance. In a democracy, a government is formed on the basis of votes cast by the public. See, in every election, the poor villagers are seen standing in long queues at the polling booths. But, the irony or misfortune of this country is that someone who will become legislator and enforcer of the law sells votes and the poor readily buy them. That too only for a bottle of liquor. Many politicians deliberately distribute free booze in rural areas so that villagers may get addicted to free liquor just before the election. And on the polling eve, they distribute the last cartel of booze bottles on the promise that the next morning, the village votes will be cast in their favour. This is how our democracy gets rotten election after election. What is the solution or counter to this? The answer is a resounding one—value-based education. The addiction of liquor must be replaced with addiction to devotion. This is exactly like the Akbar-Birbal story when Birbal solved the puzzle of drawing a bigger line without erasing the first one—he drew a bigger one. Similarly, the Ekal devised a way to erase the evils of liquor addiction, etc, by organising satsangs and tours of scholarly saints to rural areas.

'Why do tribals of our country drink alcohol? Because he is forced to do this. Why? Imagine his condition. When we work during the day and reach our home in the evening, we have a range of options to entertain us. We can watch TV. We can go to a club, or even to a temple. We can stroll in a park. But, where will our tribal go after toiling the whole day in the field? When he returns after the day's hard labour, he does not have a

TV, club, temple or park. He heads towards the liquor vendor and spends a large amount of his daily wage on getting drunk.

'What is the solution of this malaise among the tribals? Bhakti or devotion. When the tribal heads towards the liquor shop in the evening, his ears must hear bhajans and the melodious words in praise of the Lord, pleading him to leave the path of evil. He must see people dancing in devotion to their Lord. His steps should also match the rhythm of those dancing steps and he should move towards the direction of the Sanskar Kendra.

'This Sanskar Kendra is also called Satsang Kendra and the Ekal is carefully training people who are invited to narrate stories of Bhagwat Katha and other devotional literature. This training is called the Shree Hari Katha training programme.

'According to a rough estimate, around 70% of India's 30 crore population that live in villages is addicted to liquor. One person spends on an average Rs 1,000 on drinking in a month. It means Rs 4,000 crore is burnt in the liquor furnace every month. It totals to Rs 50,000 crore per year. If these tribals or villagers quit drinking alcohol, not only this big amount can be saved, they will stay healthy and help in increasing the annual crop production of India. In economic parlance, if villagers quit drinking, it will mean Rs 1 lakh crore investment into India's villages every year. Imagine it will be like a powerful stimulus into our economy that will uplift it year by year and it will be at par with economies of the developed world soon. This power will beget from the devotion to the Lord. The Ekal's mission is to generate such devotion through value-based education.'

□

10
Turning Adversity into Opportunity

In this world, as per Hindu mythology, there is Jagannath (Lord of the Universe) to take care of the Jagat (Universe). Jagannath resides in Puri, Odisha. There will not be a single family in Odisha where Lord Jagannath will not be present as either a picture on the wall, as a calendar, as a statue or within an entire temple. Odisha seems to be completely soaked in the devotion to Jagannath. It reflects in every aspect of life in Odisha. Hence, it was natural that Shyam ji, who had arrived in Odisha as a Sangh pracharak, felt a sharp urge to know the Odia culture and traditions more closely. The more deeply Shyam ji would dig into Odisha culture, the more he would know about various contours of organisational structure of a well-disciplined society. It was like he was being taught lessons of philosophy of organisation in a monastery. It seemed to Shyam ji that Hindu ancestors would have cared for the future of their society that is why they knitted the society via well-crafted traditions so neatly in an organised form that it would never crumble. It would have ascended to the zenith of its excellence and it would have earned the status of Peeth from Adi Shankracharya.

As a pracharak, Shyam ji could relate to organisational learning in a natural way, but he was mesmerised by seeing the similarities between Jagannatha traditions and the working system of the Sangh. In 1989, when the Sangh celebrated the 100th birth anniversary of honourable Dr Hedgewar, the Sangh founder, one chariot carried the statue of Lord Jagannath, and the other chariot carried the statue of Dr Hedgewar. On this occasion, then state Sangh pracharak, Sree Harihar Nand, explained to devotees that Dr Hedgewar was an avatar of Lord Jagannath and he took birth only to work for the welfare of the Odia people on Jagannath's behalf. He toured places after places in Odisha and said the same thing. The people also believed him. Shyam ji himself admits that his own personality properly took shape in Odisha and the 'Shyam ji' that the world knows is the creation of Odisha. He says that his first birthplace is not in India today (due to the Partition of India), but his second birthplace is Odisha. He also claims proudly that Lord Jagannath actually proved to be the soul of Ekal.

It is believed that a tribal is made the chief priest in the temple of Lord Jagannath in Puri because Lord Jagannath was discovered from the house of a tribal. Only a tribal can enter the dining area of the temple. The offerings at the Jagannath temple are daal chawal (rice and pulse). According to the tradition, devotees, along with their families, are offered daal chawal in Ananda Bazar area in the premises of the temple. If any devotee comes from outside and suddenly on his own starts eating from the same cauldron that serves the devotees, it is considered very auspicious and spiritually rewarding for that devotee. It is also believed that if anyone asks the caste of the new visitor, it is very inauspicious and invites the wrath of the Lord and erases the virtues of the person who commits the mistake of asking the caste. One more interesting aspect of the Jagannath traditions is making friends. If a person feeds another a slice of offering while chanting 'Jai Jagannath' and the other responds in the same vein, they become friends. They become free of any bondage of caste. In fact, this bond is considered greater than even that of familial relation.

When the occasion of a son's marriage comes in any household, the first invitation is sent to that friend in the name of Lord Jagannath. The whole family hails this friend as some elder of the family. This is the reason that while caste determines the selection of chief ministers in other Indian states, chief ministers of Odisha usually come from the caste that has the lowest population in the province. This is all because of the influence of Jagannath ji. We all are citizens of India and call our country 'Bharat Maa' and consider ourselves as her offspring. Similarly, we hail Lord Jagannath as the Lord of the Universe. However, the reality presents a very different picture. Our country is divided into four types of Indians. First are those who are reminded of their country only when they open the newspaper with their morning tea and by the time their teacup is emptied, their concern for their India gets over too. We can only hope that the Lord forgives such Indians! They get to know about their country only the next morning. The second group of Indians is more sensitive. It nitpicks faults in the working of the government and society. It often complains. This group mostly targets the politicians and the plight of the country. However, it forgets that if we point one finger on someone, three fingers always aim at us. It means that we are guiltier than others. May Lord forgive this group as well! The third group is of those people who turn to temples and pray to Lord, 'O Lord, save my Bharat Mata.' One of such devotees once went to a Jagannath temple and prayed, 'Lord, please save my Bharat Mata.' Lord Jagannath replied to him, 'Oh my devotee, can you not see that my feet have been totally exhausted in coming from Lanka to Ayodhya in the Treta Yug (the age of three or triad). Now, I am feet-less. In the Dvapara Yuga (the age of two), my hands are drained of all their energy in handling the reins of the horses. I am handless now. Now, I am left with only eyes. These eyes are round in shape and are without eyelids. It means they remain open day and night. It also means that I will not do anything in the Kali Yuga (the age of darkness). You will have to do whatever has to be done. I will merely monitor the work you are doing your work.'

The devotee was awestruck. He pleaded with Lord, 'Lord, you are Parmatma (Supreme) and I am an ordinary man. How can I match up to you?' Now, Lord explained to him, 'Look, whatever I did in human avatar, I am asking you to do that much only. I had left my home for the vanvas (jungles) in Treta Yuga for 14 years. Cannot you go there even for 14 days once a year? In the Dvapara Yuga, I went to the Vrindavan forests of Tulsi. Why cannot you leave your home and visit forests or tribal areas, which are merely 500 kilometres away from your home and treat the tribals as your brothers? I did all this and I am asking you to just repeat this.' The devotee understood it and thought about ways to make it possible. Shyam ji is also of the opinion that the society has to do what that devotee was asked by Lord Jagannath to do. Will you only keep thinking about yourself and not invest to act upon the command of Lord Jagannath? India is eager to know this.

THE IMPORTANT YEAR OF 1989

The year 1989 was a watershed moment in the journey of the Ekal Abhiyaan. First, it was the year marking 100th birth anniversary of the

RSS founder and its first Sarsanghachalak, honourable Dr Hedegwar. Second, respected Madan Agarwal ji (Madan Babu) founded the Ekal in Dhanbad in the same year. Third, the Vanvandhu Parishad (Friends of Tribals Society or FTS) was established in Kolkata. With this step, at the recommendation of then RSS chief Bhaurao Deoras ji, Shyam ji was appointed the secretary general of the Vanvasi Kalyan Ashram in Ranchi division. He had prior experience of working in various areas of Odisha for 11 years as RSS pracharak. Still, he was somewhat nervous about his new duty. However, there was one relief for him: the chief pracharak in Ranchi then was Shri Shankar Tiwari. Shyam ji was old acquaintance and had experience of working with him. When Shyam ji had joined the Sangh as pracharak in 1964 in Varanasi, Tiwari ji was the district head. Only a senior pracharak knows how difficult it is to handle a new pracharak and train him for the Sangh's work. Tiwari ji treated Shyam ji like his younger brother and trained him in the best possible way. Shyam ji was indebted for this affection and education provided by Tiwari ji. He would become emotional whenever he was reminded of those days. However, he was relieved now as Tiwari ji was in Ranchi and he looked forward to working with him.

First, Shyam ji had to comprehend the working methodology of the Ashram. The state secretary of the Ashram took it upon himself to explain all the modalities of the Ashram. He became his pupil. However, for Shyam ji, Ranchi was an easy place until Tiwari ji was there. As he was transferred to some other place, Shyam ji had to see the real face of the city and its citizens. All the Sangh-related workers were instructed to stay in their respective offices. But the Ashram office was so small that no one could stay there and hence Shyam ji was lodged in a local dharamshala. His food was the responsibility of a nearby Sangh-related family. However, he soon felt bored as there was nothing much to do. He wondered how he should spend his day? The Kalyan Ashram did not have its organisation and there was nobody with whom he could intermingle and discuss work of the Ashram. Then, an idea struck his mind. The local branch of Prabhat Shakha was closed. Shyam ji restarted it and became its 'Mukhya Shikshak' (chief instructor). He began to organise morning jagran and helped RSS volunteers learn prayers. His efforts bore fruits and the local Sangh shakha swelled with an increased number of newcomers. The local in-charge pracharak now became impressed with him and started trusting him. When Tiwari ji returned to Ranchi, he got to know how Shyam ji had spent time in his absence. He was both happy and sad for him. Anyway, Shyam ji was now lost in various tasks of the local Sangh branch.

The state secretary of the Ashram did not live in Ranchi. He would drop in occasionally and teach Shyam ji. Though Shyam ji had spent 11 years as Sangh pracharak and he knew enough about meeting people and getting things done, yet the teachings at the Ashram was avante-garde experience for him. It gave a new direction to his life. Tiwari ji was disappointed that Shyam ji was forced to live in a dharamshala, but he did not talk about it and instead introduced him to other Sangh seniors in Ranchi and helped him to connect more people with the Ashram. Now, Shyam ji was on the right track and people started coming to become members of the Ashram. In the working mechanism of the Ashram, it was imperative to prepare reports and plan projects, hence a senior pracharak chartered accountant promised Shyam ji to teach how to prepare such details. Now, Shyam ji was more engrossed in his work and that is why he shifted his lodging from dharamshala to his office. He also developed relations with some families in the city and the problem of two-time food was also solved. Thus, a small team was formed in the city. One day, Madan Babu arrived in Ranchi. He introduced Shyam ji to some influential families of Ranchi. After that, the Ashram took a flight and even its executive committee was announced. At that time, Madan Babu was the national treasurer of the Kalyan Ashram and the first meeting of the Ashram executive committee was organised in his presidency and it became easy for the Ashram to function in Ranchi. Madan Babu charted a plan for a tour to expand the Ashram in the state. It had to be road travel by car. It was the golden period of training for Shyam ji. As he travelled to various places in Jharkhand, he was reminded of Odisha. Both the places had so many similarities. Only the language was different. This similarity helped him maintain his self-confidence to gel well with local people, as he was familiar with the culture. Once, he happened to visit Dhanbad where Madan Babu had just started the Ekal schools. Shyam ji's introduction to the Ekal was like a devotee sees the beginning of Maa Ganga at Gangotri. Refreshing and rejuvenating! It was thrilling as well. He had earlier seen some night classes being organised in Odisha, but the Ekal school was launched in a proper organised phase in Dhanbad. Still, a question baffled him: 'Why did Madan Babu choose this area for the inauguration of his Ekal project?' He was told that it was the same place where the Jharkhand Mukti Morcha (JMM) originated. The Christian missionaries created the JMM during the British period. Its stated aim was to liberate tribals from the yoke of Hindu society. They had propagated that the Hindu society exploits the tribals and thus the tribals had to be freed from this oppression. They also spread the fake conceptions that the Hindus do not consider tribals as a part of the Hindu society. And thus, the Mukti Morcha (Freedom Front) was floated.

Madan Babu told Shyam ji that the Ekal was a counter to that mentality that had made tribals rebellious against the Hindu society. The Ekal Abhiyaan also had this unique feature that influential Hindu families of Dhanbad had adopted the Ekal schools. They were not merely ready to fund them, they also regularly paid visits to monitor their proper functioning. Madan Babu hailed from one of the most influential business families of Dhanbad. He was owner of coalmines and was the patron and starter of several educational institutes in Jharkhand and thus his family had premier status among the elites of Dhanbad. It was not difficult for him to manage 60 donors or adopters for 60 Ekal schools. When Madan Babu shared his cherished dream with Shyam ji, he first wondered whether its success would be possible. Later, he was convinced that it would definitely succeed. He himself felt that his confidence was inflating. JMM was one of the front-line outfits in the volley of anti-national organisations. Its cadres had demanded a separate Christian state and shown black flags to Nehru ji in 1948. Later, they had also put the proposal for a separate Christian state before PM Morarji Desai in 1979. In Singhbhum district of South Bihar (Jharkhand), violence had erupted after a JMM protest and several people were killed. The Army was called in to quell this violent protest. Thus, the dream to counter such a movement and ultimately free our country of its malignant designs will inspire any patriotic Indian.

If we observe the status of JMM in the last 30 years, we will notice that it has been reduced to a small regional party. This has been possible because of Ekal's efforts. India will always feel proud of the Ekal's achievement of countering outfits like JMM. The second plan that was in the minds of Madan Babu was that if the Sarsanghchalak of the RSS had to call in around 200 cadres at once, the Ekal would be prepared in a way that it would make 200 Ekal members available for the RSS. In other words, the Ekal had to produce Ram Sena (Army for Lord Rama). Today, within 30 years of its existence, this dream has come true. The Ekal is now the world's largest organisation and it has been honoured with the Gandhi Peace Prize by the government of India.

Madan Babu's dream had agitated Shyam ji. His heart and mind were in tumultuous churning of dreams for the future. He felt that the purpose for which he had accepted the life of a pracharak was now in front of him and he only needed to make this purpose his own.

Now, it was decided that Shyam ji would travel to various places with Madan Babu for about a month. Since they were together day and night, the whole charisma of Madan Babu's persona was unveiled before Shyam ji. It was all what Shyam ji needed as a lifetime education. He wondered how a Coal King of Dhanbad suddenly turned into a faqir (mendicant)? First, he got to know that such a living was Madan Babu's heritage. Otherwise, who could dare to become an RSS volunteer during the British period? How would he play an active part in the movement of Mahatma Gandhi? How would he dare shelter the late Guru ji Golwalkar at his home? How would a Coal King agree to become a faqir after the nationalisation of coalmines? How would he balance his duties towards his fully bred family and the life of a social activist? Despite being the eldest in the family, how would he put the future of his sons and daughters at stake for the sake of his brothers so that familial peace should prevail?

A series of such questions took birth in the curious mind of Shyam ji, but he got only one answer—Madan Babu was an industrialist saint. He was known as an industrialist in society, but he led the life of a saint. After his wife died, he was determined that he would first start the vanprastha stage (life in jungles) and then would come the stage of sanyas (complete detachment from the world). This is the good fortune of the Ekal Abhiyaan that such a legendary personality became its founder. There were a myriad of such experiences during the travel with Madan Babu that helped shape Shyam ji's own personality and remained as a guiding light for him throughout his life. In fact, many of them changed the direction of his mindset. Once, both of them went to see a project in a small village. The project was a health clinic, where a physician from Uttar Pradesh was practicing. When they saw a number of patients there during the day, they felt confident that they were able to win the hearts of the tribal society. When night fell, they were urged to stay in the village itself and the house of one of the tribals was selected for this. It was the only available facility in the forested village area. Suddenly, it started raining in the night. Madan Babu and Shyam ji were sleeping in the same room. The roof of the room started leaking. None of them could sleep the whole night. They only spent the night pushing their cots from one side to the other so that they would not get drenched. In the morning, the first advice that Madan Babu gave Shyam ji was not to advise anyone to spend night in the tribal villages. Though there was hardly anyone whom Shyam ji could ask to spend the night in the tribal area, as his circle was miniscule. He was merely a spectator then. However, Madan Babu's direction made sense to Shyam ji, as Madan Babu was concerned about the self-respect of the tribals. The feeling that their guests felt uncomfortable might make them feel inferior. This was the concern of a man who had been living in a palatial house in Dhanbad. His concern became a life-long lesson for Shyam ji.

Once during their tour, they reached a distant village. The villagers were informed of their arrival and they were ready to welcome them. Madan Babu first introduced himself, Shyam ji and the purpose of their visit and then asked them what problems they had been facing. The villagers kept silent. Madan Babu repeated his question. Then, one villager came forward and said, 'Babu ji, many people have come with such types of questions. We also shared our suffering with them and they heard us. However, once they went back, they did not return. So, we doubt you too. You are asking about our problems, but you may not return once you leave. If you come again, then we will share our plight with you.' Madan Babu looked at Shyam ji and then Shyam ji introduced them to Madan Babu. He also told them about the Vanvasi Kalyan Ashram. He also told villagers that Madan Babu was not some petty politician. He then tried to assure villagers, 'We understand and respect your feelings. We will listen to you whenever you wish. You may test us whichever way you want. We will try to learn about your problems only after going through your test.'

The villagers were dismayed to know that they were not politicians and still they were visiting the tribal villages.

They also had the wrong apprehension that the Vanvasi Kalyan Ashram was some political organisation. When they were informed that Madan Babu had started a school for tribals named Ekal school, the villagers were very happy. Then, the same villagers said to them, 'Babu ji, this is our problem. If we get education and medicine for our people, we will not allow Christian priests to enter our villages.' His sentence reminded Shyam ji of Bhaurao Deoras ji's incident with tribals a long time ago. Madan Babu also felt that only education would not be enough for tribals, they also needed healthcare.

THE SYSTEM OF RURAL ORGANISATION

Two Sangh colleagues, Sri Daya Prakash ji (Daya Babu) and Sri Mudrika Prasad Singh (Mudrika Babu) concentrated on developing the working system of the village organisation. Madan Babu focussed on building the urban organisation. First, Daya Babu and Mudrika Babu opened an Ekal school in Gaya district. Mudrika Babu stayed at Sherghati qasbah. It was in the vicinity of Gaya. Hence, Sherghati became the first unit area of Ekal in the state. Now, they had to decide how big should be the working area of the Ekal school established in this unit. Initially, they agreed that a full-time Ekal volunteer, meaning someone who can spend the whole month in the unit, would be appointed. He would spend a night in a village once a month. Finally, they decided to make Sherghati a cluster of 30 Ekal schools. At that time, those volunteers were called full-time workers. They are now known as volunteers (sevavarti). After the formation of the unit, the question was how should the functioning of the Ekal school be monitored and reviewed? Plus, how should the ability of the teachers be evaluated? The organisation then divided the unit into three sub-units of 10 schools each. The teachers of every sub-unit were instructed to assemble at a fixed location every month for 3-hour meetings. One hour of this meeting would be devoted to satsang and the remaining two hours would be reserved for review discussion about the quality of teachers and schools.

Later, the village Satsang Pramukh and the Ekal's Village Committee chief were added to these review meetings. Now, the meeting had around

30 people to verify the quality of Ekal schools and their teachers. The presence of more people meant the satsang became more vibrant and devotional. The review dialogue also focussed on other aspects of the welfare of the villages. The presence of unit in-charges was necessary in these meetings. He was in fact the architect of such meetings. The points of discussion in the review meetings were prepared meticulously by Daya Babu and Mudrika Babu, as both of them had been travelling to the villages for a long time. Initially, this worked but in later stages, when people like Daya Babu and Mudrika Babu were not available, it was decided that a full-time volunteer would be appointed at every sub-unit for the better monitoring of the teachers and schools. Now, the regular training of the teachers was being discussed. After a lot of deliberations, it was decided that the Ekal Abhiyaan would find village youths who might be educated up to Class 9-10. These youth would be trained to become Ekal teachers. However, it would require rigorous training. For this purpose, the training camps of seven days would be organised twice a year and there would be a review meeting for those camps as well. Then a block was conceptualised comprising three units. The zonal head was identified to be the chief trainer. At the unit level, biannual training camps and at the sub-unit level, monthly review meetings were finalised. However, it was found later that was not enough to maintain the quality of the Ekal schools. Every month, Shyam ji and Madan Babu would attend the review meeting with Daya Babu and Mudrika Babu. Since all of them would keep visiting villages and were highly experienced people, their input in the review of the schools was very important.

Then, it was decided that at the unit level, a 24-hour training camp would be organised. The monthly payment to the teachers was also discussed. It was decided that when the teachers assemble for the monthly meeting at the unit centre, they would be paid there. However, how much it would be and who would arrange the money for this expenditure was still a question. And also, who would bring the money? To solve this problem, a committee of three members were constituted and a bank account was opened under their names. The committee members would attend every monthly meeting and would hold a private chat with the teachers and hand them over their honoraria in cash. Though, the formation of the committee and the payment to the teacher was not a very easy issue. There were sharp reservations about it that had to be tackled from the very beginning. The first reservation—could the Ekal find dedicated and honest payment committee members? Who will find them out? If we find worthy people and the Sangh is not functional in their areas, why would they agree to work for the Sangh? But, Daya Babu and Madan Babu solved this puzzle with their experience and skills. They said, 'There are a number of honest people in our society and they also want to contribute for a just cause with sound dedication. If you will trust, you will also be trusted by them.' So, a full-time volunteer of the Ekal tried to contact such people and the committees were formed to solve the problem of payment to Ekal teachers. Later, Madan Babu, Daya Babu and Mudrika Babu themselves started touring committees at the unit level and the rest of committees were also formed to solve the problem once and for all.

After the formation of units and blocks, it was to be decided who would send the reports to the Donation Centre run by the Vanvandhu Parishad (Friends of Tribal Society or FTS) in Kolkata? It had to be so because the FTS was not formed to merely collect money, its primary purpose was to win the confidence of the people and increase the number of members. In short, it had to find new members. The purpose of this membership drive was that a potential member has to be invigorated to work for the organisation with full heart and mind because until he would devote himself fully for the purpose, he could not contribute constructively to the organisation. Daya Babu chipped in with advice to solve this problem. He said if three sanchs can form a sankul, then three sankuls could be merged to form an anchal. And thus, the zonal structure of the Ekal schools came into being. An office of the anchal was established. All the reports coming from the villages had to be collected at the anchal office and an additional account of the FTS was also opened at this office. Madan Babu, Daya Babu and Mudrika Babu started touring the state for the formation of a powerful zonal committee. It was decided that the report about the village schools would be sent directly from the zonal office to the donation centre of the FTS. Three senior full-time volunteers were appointed joint heads of the zonal office. One had to look after the administration of the zone. Others would take care of the training and the third was made in-charge of the office. A special arrangement was made to train these three senior officials. The vigorous campaign of Madan Babu, Daya Babu and Mudrika Babu resulted in success and the influential people of the state started showing serious interest in the Ekal project. The district of Singhbhum was pivotal for the expansion of the Ekal. This was so because it was the same district that was set on fire in 1979 by the protesters while demanding a separate state. The JMM, which was at the forefront of that agitation, was active in almost every village. This district was also the castle of the Church and the missionaries were very active here. The Ekal was determined to win over this district. It was a big challenge and the members were ready to face the challenge with sound guts. Gradually, the Ekal workers expanded the Ekal. They took it to one village after another. The villagers were very enthusiastic about the arrival of the Ekal.

The United Nations announced the year 1993 as the year of original dwellers or aborigines of the earth. They are known by different names in various parts of the world and in India, tribals are considered to be the real natives or original inhabitants of the country. A big programme was organised at Chaibasa in Singhbhum district. It was part of the conspiracy of the Christian society. Even the big Christian countries of the world had manipulated the UN to declare 1993 as the World Native Year. In the Chaibasa programme, the tribals descended in huge numbers. The Christian priests from all over the country had assembled at Chaibasa and when the programme kicked in, they all emphasised only on one point: 'You tribals are slaves of the Hindus. You will have to unite to break the shackles of slavery. The Church is doing exactly that by uniting you.' To drive their point home, all those priests denounced Hindu rituals and deities in whatever terms they could. When those priests were busy declaring the Hindus hardcore enemies of the tribals, one old tribal named Salkhan Hembrum raised his hand to say something. The moderator of the programme allowed him to speak. He said, 'Sirs, recently a board has been installed in our village, it reads "The Ekal School" and the name of some Marwadi businessman from Kolkata has also been mentioned on it. First, we thought that they were our enemies, and we were terrified. But, our children who attended this school were very pleased with the education at the school. We were in a fix about what to do? Suddenly, we found that another was installed. It read "Aarogya Kendra" and the name of some Mumbai's Marwari businessman was with it. We were now more terrified. However, when we approached this centre, we saw that a daughter was distributing medicine to the sick people of the village. We were extremely happy to see this. Still, we were unable to form any opinion about what we should do with them. Meanwhile, someone informed us that some people from Mumbai and Kolkata were coming to meet us villagers. We thought that our enemies were coming to meet us. We called a meeting and prepared a strategy how to tackle our enemies. We in fact divided ourselves into groups to take on the arriving enemies. We were afraid and had informed the whole village that it was a period of emergency for the village. The next day, those people from Mumbai and Kolkata arrived by bus. The bus stopped on a road near the village. From there, there was no road to the village and they had to walk towards us. According to our traditions, we welcomed them with music and dance. As we reached the village, some men from the touring party urged us to hand over our music instruments to them and then they started playing them with full vigour and even danced with us. However, they were neither able to play the music in rhythm nor dance the way we do, so we tribals laughed at them. The females from the city embraced our ladies and started dancing with their hands around one another's waists. It was an unbelievable scene. It was very entertaining for the villagers. The children from the city intermingled with our children and started playing in the soil. Everyone was enjoying those moments. When the city folk got tired, they asked if we could serve them tea. We were surprised. We even did not expect that they would ask for some consumable things from us tribals. We did not even have milk at our homes at that time. As they sensed that we were feeling shy, they asked us to take them to our homes. Now, we had a mother take them to our homes. Since we did not have milk, we only served them hot water. They drank it as if it was better than tea. When they left our homes, we had tears in our eyes and we saw that their eyes were moist as well. We felt as if some of our family members were parting from us. And you tell us that they are our enemies? But our experience tells us that they are our family members. Who should we trust? Our ears that are listening to your words or our eyes who have seen people from the city from so close?'

As he finished his story, a bustle ensued in the gathering. Many people stood up and started sharing their stories. Someone said that a similar delegation from Jamshedpur had come to his village. Someone said that his village was visited by a delegation from Ranchi, and it continued. It turned into a cacophony and the tribals seemed united in expressing their brotherhood for people living in the cities. The Christian priests were now terrified and instead of saying anything, they preferred to save their lives as they feared that excited tribals might even attack them.

Salkhan ji himself told this story to Shyam ji. When he was sharing this story, his eyes were brightening triumphantly. He thanked the Ekal that it ultimately opened the eyes of the tribals. Salkhan ji further told Shyam ji that the Church was playing the divide-and-rule game with the tribals by pitting one group against another. 'But, we will not let their evil designs be successful,' he told Shyam ji with full determination. After this, Salkhan ji devoted himself to the Ekal and visited village after village to advertise it and convince the villagers to take benefit of the Ekal education and blunt the Church's advances. And the Ekal got its first member of the tribal village committee.

OBSERVING DHARMA IN THE FESTIVAL OF DEMOCRACY

The time for Lok Sabha elections had arrived. The Ekal by then had its branches in every district of Jharkhand. If you study the psychology of the tribal society, you will come across a subject or term called Aadivasi Pravirti (tribal instinct). It means that if you do any good or bad to a tribal, the whole village would be affected. And if the village is affected, it has an impact on the whole block. If the block gets affected, the district feels its impact. Hence, now when the Ekal was making so many constructive changes in the tribal belt, it resonated everywhere in the state and the Ekal became a known name. The Ekal's volunteers were also full of enthusiasm. The connection of the Vanvasi Kalyan Ashram also helped in the creation of the tribal leadership. All the political parties were fighting the general election with full force. The main issue in the election was making Jharkhand a separate state carved out of Bihar. The Congress was already on the verge of extinction. The fight was between JMM and BJP. But, the leadership of both the parties were unpopular in the villages. Maoists capitalised on their anger and instigated them against both the parties. Actually, they were brainwashing tribals against the state of India. So, tribals began setting campaign jeeps of both the JMM and BJP on fire. Both the parties stopped entering villages. At this time, the Ekal took up this challenge. It decided to go from door to door in the villages. Since the Ekal was already providing educational services in the villages, it was not difficult to maintain the trust of the villagers. The issue of the Ram Mandir was also at its peak during the election. Kar sevaks who had gone to destroy the Babri Masjid were fired upon in Ayodhya and several of them were martyred in 1991 but in 1992, they had successfully demolished the mosque structure. The whole Hindu society of the country was seething in anger. The political parties split into two parts—while some were opposing the construction of the temple, the BJP was in its favour. So, the Ekal decided to approach tribal villages with a campaign to construct the Ram temple. However, they were stunned to see tribals angry at organisations like RSS, VHP and BJP. They said that the Sanghwallahs call them Hindus but in reality, they did not consider them Hindus. 'The VHP workers chant "Jai Shree Ram" but Ram ji dwells in our hearts. They have never approached us. Similarly, the BJP has behaved like all other selfish political parties and provides only that much access to us that serves its interests. Besides this, its leaders never keep us in their scheme of things,' they complained.

Now the road for the Ekal suddenly became curved and the Ekal volunteers even feared to introduce themselves as an organisation linked to the Sangh. However, the Ekal was respected as it was providing villagers education and its teachers would be a local young man or woman. The Ekal volunteers had to tell villagers that they were just children and that they did not decide the policies of their organisation. The Ekal was then only four or five years old. 'We are not here to talk about any political party. We are here among you to only tell you that in a democracy, elections are like a festival. It is an occasion to worship Bharat Mata. The flowers offered at her feet are called votes and her crown is the Prime Minister of India. Hence, we request you that you should go to polling booths with 100% attendance and cast your vote to the party of your choice with the blessing of Ram ji,' the workers told them very politely and persuasively. Then, the innocent tribals would ask them the name of the party that they had to vote for. At this, the Ekal workers would tell them they had to decide it themselves. The tribals would feel very impressed by such display of honesty by the Ekal workers. Ultimately, the day of the election results came. The result astounded the country. BJP had won 12 out the 14 Lok Sabha seats from Jharkhand. It was unbelievable. The two seats where BJP lost were in the districts where unfortunately the Ekal was yet to expand. Even if there was a single unit in any district, the whole district voted for the BJP as the Ekal campaigned in each and every village. They took Ram ji's message to every village. This was the glaring manifestation of the tribal instinct. It had been possible because the tribal youths connected with the Ekal understood the message of the Ekal and voluntarily roamed around in the villages convincing the other tribal youths to vote for the BJP. Once the tribal youths make up their minds, nobody can shake their resolve. The victory of BJP was its living example. In the meantime, the Church was not sitting idle. It was actively supporting the Congress party. The Congress came at zero. The JMM that had a state-wide network could win only two seats. The morale of the tribals beat the monetary and muscle power of the Church. It was discussed all over India. All the leading parties of India sent their review teams to study this unprecedented election result. Two senior leaders of the BJP, who loved Ekal and Shyam ji like their own children, patted their backs. However, the Ekal was bracing to dig into the last layer of the electoral miracle.

So, it was decided that a meeting should be called for all the prominent members. The same place was chosen for this meeting from where the Ekal had started. Every participant in the meeting was handed a questionnaire about the reasons why the tribals were voting for the BJP. It had points like the effect of the Ekal's services to the villagers and other methods of communicating with them. The participants had to tick one of them. Shyam ji was of the view that since the Ekal was imparting free education and health services to the villagers, it must have been crucial in deciding their electoral choice. However, when the cumulative results of all responses were declared, everyone was stunned that the villagers were impressed by the Ekal workers' tour to villages during the elections. The tribals expressed, 'It was for the first time that the Hindu society made us feel as one of them, so we embraced them in return. The city people who travelled to our villages in huge numbers made us feel that we are their brethren. We were pleased with this and we showed our love for them by voting for the party of their choice.'

Some of the village tribals were also sad that had Hindu society shown such affection for them earlier, some of them would not have become Christians. Some Christians who were present in that meeting said that they would return to their original Hindu faith.

This meeting also proved that affectionate behaviour is more powerful than the service rendered to any group of people, especially rural ones. Thus, the Ekal appointed a vanvasi yatra pramukh (chief to oversee tours to forested villages) in every unit. This official had to organise such a tour once in a month. To make it convenient, Daya Babu gifted a small bus that could carry 10-12 people easily. Slowly, Jharkhand became the nerve-centre of the Ekal's success. Once any city-dweller would visit the villages, he would get so much affection from the villagers that he would soon become a member of the Ekal. He would also share his rural experience with others in the city and thus attract more Ekal members. Similarly, the villagers would be elated to get affection from their city brothers. The Kolkata team was witnessing the same experiment and success. There too, people had developed a penchant for touring tribal villages and a number of tours had been conducted. One thing was certain that whoever visited villages two or three times, he would surely become a donor for the Ekal and if he happened to visit villages more times, he would end up becoming an Ekal member.

Today, the Ekal can claim that all its active members of chapters opened in India or abroad had joined the Ekal because of the tribal village tours.

THE EKAL REINED IN MILITANCY

Sujata Bodo, 32 years of age, is a Bodo tribal woman. She is a resident of the village Thaiguddi in the Kosugaon Unit of Kokrajhar district of Assam. Her father, Ekendra Bodo, runs a small general store and also cultivates a small plot of agricultural land. The Ekal started its school in Thaiguddi village in 2006. Its teacher, Laxmi Bosumatadi, was from the same village. Sujata had studied in the same Ekal school from 2006 to 2009. Sujata has been teaching in the same school since 2016. Around 26 students study in her Ekal school. Prior to 2006, the village was a hotbed of militancy. Only Bodo tribals live in this village. The population of the village is around 200. There are around 35 houses. In this village, there was no government school before 2006 and there is no government health centre even now.

Before 2006, no outsider could enter the village. Since this village is in a deep forested area, the militants would use it as their base camp. If any tribals other than Bodos would enter this village, Bodo militants would suspect him to be a government mole and shoot him down. This village was also completely cut off from the city. In this highly militant-affected village, the Ekal chose Ravi Ram Brahma as the chief of Kokrajhar unit to start an Ekal school in the village. Brahma had earlier been a secretary of All India Bodo Students Union. This organisation had started a movement to safeguard the Bodo language, culture and traditions. So, this organisation had deep connections in the village. Brahma was a leader of Bodos and represented them. It was merely a coincidence that he was chosen to head the Kokrajhar Unit of the Ekal. In his leadership, the Ekal school was opened in Thaikuddi in 2006. This way, the local voluntary members got an entry to the village. A village committee was established and its head was Rakhen Bodo. Besides him, the committee had Ekendra Bodo (satsang chief), Sunil Mushahri, Samar Goyari, etc.

Thus, the Ekal school started in the village. Like all Ekal schools, it did not only focus on the education of the village children, it worked for the development of the villages, organic farming, satsang kendra for value education, health awareness via arogya mahila samiti and awareness campaigns for rural hygiene. Because of all these activities, around 30 children could study in the Ekal school successfully up to Class 5. Then, they got themselves enrolled in the government school. The arogya yojana taught villagers various ways to maintain cleanliness, dig up soak pits for the sewage water, the healthy technique of taking a bath and as part of the value education, satsangs were conducted in the village. Earlier, villagers not only prepared desi liquor, they would also get drunk every evening. After the arrival of the Ekal, around 90% of the villagers quit drinking. Even the production of the liquor as a means of livelihood has reduced and the villagers have turned to farming. Earlier, the Bodo militants would brainwash village youth to join their ranks. They would not only provide them training to use weapons, they would also convert them to other religions. In the last 13-14 years since the Ekal is working in the village, Bodo militancy has been controlled and the conversion has been prevented. Children from three nearby schools come to study in this Ekal school. In 2011, as part of the Sarvashiksha Abhiyaan, the government opened its school in the village. Harmony prevails in the village because of the Ekal.

□

11
Ekal on the Way to Becoming a Mass Organisation

Swami Vivekanand ji is the fountainhead of inspiration for the Ekal. It has kept his thoughts as its guiding light and walked the path shown by Swami ji. The path illuminated by Swami ji leads people to success, prosperity, strength, peace, contentment, glory, vigour and majesty. The Ekal's lodestar, Shyam ji, says, 'The strength of any tree lies in its roots. The visible parts of it like stem, leaves and fruits are just the results of the nutritious mechanism of the root. That is why farmers irrigate the roots and protect them. The condition of our country is the same. It is divided into two parts—one is the visible India that lives in the cities and the second is remote India that thrives in the distant villages. The Ekal's target is to awaken the remote India living in villages. It is like 'awaken the strength of the earth and make India prosperous'. We all know that nature has endowed our country with all resources, yet our country is in the ICU. Why? This is because its kidney and liver have failed. These are two key systems of the country—one is the economy and the second is democracy. If we analyse all the happenings in the country, we come to two conclusions that there is acute poverty and anarchy everywhere. The poverty can be alleviated by the production-based economy and the anarchy can be controlled by apt and alert administration. The administration means the government of the day and it is as powerful and capable as carefully the electorates elect it. Interestingly, the keys of both the systems lie in the hands of distant and poor villagers that form the majority of the Indian population. When our country got independence, Gandhi ji had advised Nehru ji that the path of India's prosperity is through its villages. So, the first priority of the first Indian government must be agriculture. Unfortunately, Gandhi ji did not live long and Nehru did not pay attention to his advice. Today's misery in India is the result of that folly. Today, the country is following the Nehruvian model. But, there has to be someone who must resurrect the Gandhian model and implement it—the Ekal is exactly following this methodology. Nobody can deny the fact that the education of the poor and rural people will form the basis of India's progress. However, even the education is of two types. One is the Nehruvian model that mechanically prepares a student for service (jobs) and then turns him into a consumer. The second is the Gandhian model that turns people into producers and keeps their morale high, as they feel owner of their own labour. The Ekal has chosen the Gandhian model of education.

'Since most of us have been educated in the Nehruvian system of education, our idea of villagers' education is that how many of them have got higher education and how many of them have been placed in various city employments. Gandhi ji was against this. There can be some students who will prefer jobs immediately after the completion of their education and they should not be discouraged from doing so. But, what should the general public do? It is a burning question. They want education so that they are not exploited and yet they prefer living in their villages. For him, agriculture and village-based industries will be the means of income. Sometimes, he also feels competitive with employed city-dwellers and they want their production to increase so much that their income supersedes those of the city-dwellers. He has to become awakened and be able to use his collective wisdom to establish such a democracy that the government must be forced to consider the welfare of the 70% rural population as its first priority. When the villagers will be prosperous, the people who live in the jhuggies of the cities will naturally return to their villages. Then, 25-30% city-dwellers will be contributing to the economy of the country through industries as envisaged by Nehru ji. The remaining 70-75% villagers will strengthen the economy by increasing the agricultural produce and rural industries. But, only those who have deep faith in this land and its people will perform these tasks. The Ekal is doing this and that is why the Ekal is unique.

'Here, we have to keep in mind one more thing that we must shun any sense of arrogance while imparting unnecessary knowledge to rural folks. We do not have to teach them anything, we have to just awaken their self-confidence. They already know more than us about agriculture and cultivation. Plus, their knowledge of rural industries is also better than ours. If we have any suggestion to make their methods better, then it should be okay otherwise we must remain within our limits. This is the clash of two ideologies. Today, the Nehruvian system is ruling the roost, but soon the people will realise the value of the Gandhian model. We have to work on the Gandhian model and have to accelerate it to expand it all across the country. In the end, our efforts will surely taste success. When the city folk would be suffering from the consequences of chemical-based farming and the inequality created by the heavy industrialisation, they would be reminded of the stark realities of the planet earth. It will be a revolution and it will beget from the womb of the self-confidence of those youth who live in small villages, exploited, ignored and away from urban India. This will be the revolution of the Ekal. It will expect only encouragement and affection from the capable and affluent families of the cities. If we will be able to open 100,000 Ekal schools, 200,000 satsang kendras, raise an army of 50 lakh devotees of Lord Ram, maintain lively connection with five crore families and awaken the self-confidence in 30 crore rural people, then there will not be any problem that we will not be able to solve. This is the sole target of the avatar of Ekal. The Ekal has been proving its significance before the society for the last 30 years. This is its destiny.'

Based on Shyam ji deliberation on the Ekal, following conclusions can be drawn:

1) The Ekal has been successful in winning the trust of the villagers.
2) Most of full-time Ekal workers took their jobs as a challenge in life and worked with maniacal spirit.
3) In the journey of the Ekal, both the unit and blocks played pivotal parts.
4) Even the workers have been able to invigorate the committees at the zone level.
5) Gram sanyas (devoting life for the service of the village) instilled enormous amounts of self-confidence in the village youths. It proved to be a personality development training camp for them.
6) Every unit was able to start another unit by managing a self-reliant budget with whatever collection or donation was given to it.

7) The Ekal forms eight samitis with seven members each in the village. A total of 56 members of the gram samitis get involved in the Ekal and its all-round development. In this way, the samitis are formed to take the message of the Ekal to every village doorstep and it has turned out to be a successful venture.
8) All the collection was done in the form of membership of the State Voluntary Organisation (SVO). The collection of every year's membership fee encouraged the self-confidence of the members.

Now, it has been proven that the Ekal Abhiyan is now moving towards becoming a mass organisation. The credit of the journey of the Ekal so far goes to the Rashtriya Seva Sangathan (SPOs). But the future of the Ekal will be shaped by the SVOs.

TWO WHEEL OF THE EKAL CHARIOT

There are two wheels of the Ekal chariot—the rural organisation and the urban organisation. In order to establish the urban organisation, SPOs open their chapters in big cities and influential businessmen are connected to the chapter. This is also called chapter working. To establish the rural organisation, an SVO is first formed. This SVO then forms committees at zone, sub-zone, block, unit and village level so that people can become a part of the Ekal at every step. This is also called zonal working. A chapter that collects the money donates the amount to the zone so that the money could appropriately be used for the welfare of the villagers and it could also satisfy the donor that the money was used for the right purpose. In order to ensure this, the chapter itself monitors this process. The monitoring takes place in two steps—the economic discipline and the quality assessment of the project (the Ekal school and Satsang Kendra). This is to ensure verification of the suitable use of the donor's money. To further ensure this, the chapter, through a coordination committee, oversees the working of the unit where the accounts of the chapter have been opened. The rural organisation is one step ahead in discharging its duties. It has to form groups of dedicated village youths who could roam the villages and work to bring about change in their society. The group of such youths are called Ramsadhak Toli and their work is called Ramkaaj. Shyam ji says that we must communicate with our rural society in the language that it understands. 'It is both natural and practical.'

Eight different kinds of sub-committees are formed in a village to bring about eight types of social change. Each committee has seven dedicated volunteers and thus total 56 volunteers work for Ramkaaj or the desired social change. Besides, the Ekal expects that three villagers from each committee, one village committee head and others should constitute around 25-member Ramsadhak Toli (group). It is noteworthy here that the proper use of donated money is the responsibility of the full-time volunteers and the teacher and they are answerable to the donation kendra. On the other hand, the members of the rural organisation provide donations to the SVO to become its members and thus they have their independent existence. The SPO has to make sure that the villagers must take reins of village development in their own hands and the message that the ownership of the village development is in the hands of the village must reach village after village. This is the purpose of the SPO. The eight sub-committees of the village committee performs following functions:

1) **Shiksha Samiti**

This samiti has to look after three types of schools in the village.

(A) **The Ekal School:** To monitor that the teacher properly runs the school for three hours.

(B) **Parivar Vidyalaya:** To check whether the Ekal students make their parents literate or not.

(C) **Government School:** The government may be offset up by any political party, but it always belongs to us. So, we should also see whether the government teachers teach properly or not. Shyam ji says that if a village remains ignorant in a democracy, the government becomes corrupt, but if a village is awakened, then the government functions. Thus, the villagers have to ensure that the government teachers or other government servants are working properly, even if they have to use tools like the RTI for that.

Result: The result should be a literate village. It means that all the people between the age group 10 to 40 should be literate.

2) **Aarogya Samiti**

(A) The in-charge of the aarogya samiti is a woman. She is given proper training to become aarogya sevika. She then ensures that the village follows basic rules of health and hygiene.

(B) The aarogya sevika also distributes medicine boxes in the village.

(C) The aarogya samiti invites and honour the women workers of three government schemes—Aasha, Aaganvadi and ANM in weekly satsang. It encourages them to work diligently.

Result: A clean and healthy village indicating that the government schemes are functioning purposefully.

3) Vikas Samiti

(A) A campaign against the use of chemical fertilisers. Villagers will be encouraged not to use chemicals in their fields and not let anyone use them. In fact, villagers will be encouraged not to let chemical fertilisers enter villages.

(B) Villagers will be encouraged for organic farming. For this purpose, the students of the Ekal school will be taught techniques like making organic fertilisers so that they could earn and learn the art of self-reliance quite early in their lives.

(C) Water conservation is another responsibility of this committee. It will ensure that the rainwater will not be allowed to flow out of the village and it will be collected in a reservoir.

Result: A developed village that has organic farming, rural employment and water conservation.

4) Jagran Samiti

(A) Forestation or planting trees to protect the environment. Every child and villager will plant a sapling every year and will also ensure that it grows into a tree.

(B) Villagers will have to learn how to make use of RTI so that they can check how effectively the government system is working. For this purpose, the Yuva Jargan Prabhari of the Ekal's local unit will train villagers.

(C) To make villagers aware and organised to make government schemes like MGNREGA, old people pension scheme, public distribution system and mid-day meal, etc., function without any corruption or delay.

Result: Aware village and the proper use of RTI.

5) Satsang Samiti

(A) Organising weekly satsang and arranging the training of the satsang chief.

(B) To ensure the presence of every caste and group in the satsang so that the village can become harmonious and free of social divisions.

(C) Reconversion of villagers to Hinduism (ghar vapsi) and to make the village harmonious.

Result: A harmonious village, that is free of caste and other divisions.

6) Mahila Samiti

(A) To persuade villagers to shun liquor addiction through women's organisations.

(B) To invite some Vyas Kathakaar (storyteller) to make people shun liquor addiction.

(C) To force-shut the liquor shops and liquor factories in the village by uniting people.

Result: Liquor-free villages, meaning that villagers in the age group of 20-40 do not touch liquor.

7) Yuva Samiti

(A) To make an organisation of village youths so that no outsider can enter the village for purposes like conversion or recruitment for anti-national activities.

(B) Organisation the game of kabaddi and the reading of Hanuman Chalisa every Tuesday.

(C) The information that a Lakshman Rekha or strict rules have been imposed in a village should be communicated to neighbouring villages as well.

Result: Safe villages with no conversion or exploitation.

8) Sangathan Samiti

(A) Formation of a mothers' committee to link villages with the country and the country with the villages.

(B) To organise three festivals in the villages annually—Ram Mahaotsav, Krishna Janmashtami and Annual Festival.

(C) Collection through self-reliant ways and make villages self-respectful.

Result: Organised villages and dedicated groups of Ramsadhak youths.

The above committees work for the following social changes:

1) Educated village
2) Healthy village
3) Developed village
4) Aware village
5) Harmonious village
6) Liquor-free village
7) Safe village
8) Organised village

Adopting the above method, a Ramsadhak Toli is expected to approach the neighbouring villages and try to establish similar sub-committees there too. In fact, the whole panchayat is approached to make the 'Mera Bharat, Meri Panchayat' scheme successful. For this purpose, either a former full-time volunteer or the Ekal school teacher is made panchayat prabhari.

As part of Gram Swabhiman Dayitva, every volunteer is given responsibility for five to six villages where he has to tour once in a month. These volunteers are also imparted training in rural education every year in the Anchal Dakshta Varg (Zone Level Training for Capacity Building of Volunteers). A young and educated farmer-villager is chosen as head of the weekly class organised for the villagers. Besides, a gram sangathan chief is selected and he is trained on the very first day during the Aacharya Abhyas Varg twice in a year.

Shyam ji has always believed that the service leads to the formation of an organisation and the organisation results in social change. He says that if a village is developed, the country is developed. If a village becomes aware, the country becomes aware. If we are able to make our gram panchayat an ideal working body, our country will become equally strong and ideal. The Ekal has taken birth as an avatar to realise this dream into reality.

KARYALAYA VIBHAG (OFFICE DEPARTMENT)

The office of any organisation is like the heart in a body. It is a place where all the information about the organisation is assembled and then dispatched to various parts. The Kolkata office of the Ekal Abhiyaan has many achievements under its belt. Meanwhile, the Abhiyaan has also undergone a qualitative change. Now, the flow of information is maintained in every organ of the Ekal about the results of various Ekal programmes and to make it possible, following associate offices have been opened:

1. Ranchi

(A) Gramotthan Karyalaya (Village Development Office)

1) It collects the information about the results brought about by the village development and village awareness departments in an Ekal village.
2) To record the GRC (Gramotthan Resource Centre) achievements.
3) To keep the monthly record of above activities.

(B) Prakashan Karyalaya (Publication Office)

1) It maintains the publication reports of national and state editions of Ekal's monthly magazine, *Ekal Varta.*
2) Annual publication record of *Prerna Pushp* and *Gaurav Gatha.*
3) Publication of achievements and decisions taken by the Ekal Abhiyaan.
4) Half-yearly publication of the handbook edited by the office department.
5) Compilation and publication of the news communicated by the *Ekal Bulletin.*
6) Recording and writing of province-wise history of the Ekal Abhiyaan.
7) Inquiries and planning about publication of personal memoirs.

8) The monthly analysis and compilation of the above-mentioned activities.

(C) Aarogya Karyalaya (Health Department)

1) Compilation of all the activities of the Aarogya Foundation.
2) Recording the achievements of village nurses in every village.
3) The monthly recording of the above activities.

(D) Mahila Bibhag Karyalaya (Women Department Office)

1) Recording and compilation of Upahar Distribution Programmes.
2) Recording and compilation of ghar ghar mandir yojna (schemes at the doorstep).
3) Recording and compilation of Sneh Sampark and Seva Patra Yojna.
4) Recording and compilation of women training camps.
5) Recording and compilation of vanyatras (tribal tours).
6) The monthly description of the above activities.

2. Delhi

(A) Sampark Karyalaya (Communication Office)

1) All types of correspondence like letters, emails, etc.
2) The compilation of news published in the *Ekal Bulletin*.
3) Gyan samanvya and gyan samanvyak sanchaar (knowledge coordination and communication for knowledge coordination).
4) Compilation and publication of all monthly magazines.

(B) Website Updation Office

1) Updation of www.ekal.org
2) Compilation of all sorts of pictorial depictions.
3) The monthly description of the above activities.

(C) Vyavastha Bibhag Karyalaya (System Department Office)

1) The monitoring of all types of financial systems.
2) The monitoring of the self-reliant budget.
3) The analysis of economic discipline.
4) The monthly description of the above-mentioned activities.

3. Lucknow

(A) Gram Sangathan Karyalaya (Village Development Office)

1) The preparation of compendiums on Prantiya Seva Sangathan.
2) Conduct inquiries about swablamban sangrah (collection for self-reliance).
3) The inquiry about legal requirements of the Prantiya Seva Sangathan.
4) Recording and compilation of the eight sub-committees of the Gram Sangathan.
5) The inquiry about all the committees of the unit working.
6) Recording and compilation of weekly analysis.
7) The monthly description of the above activities.

(B) Yuva Bibhag Karyalaya (Youth Affairs Office)

1) Recording and compilation of the Yuva Bharat programme.
2) Recording and compilation of the Youth Affairs Office's work.
3) Recording and compilation of Yuva Jagran Prabhari's work.
4) The monthly description of the above activities.

4. Mumbai

(A) Sri Hari Katha (Sanskar) Karyalaya (Ethic and Values Department)

1) A directory of all types of kathakaars (storytellers).
2) Recording and compilation of the Rath Yatra (Chariot Procession).
3) Recording and compilation of Sri Hari Parv.
4) The inquiry of Ramsadhak list.
5) Recording and compilation of all types of training camps.
6) The monthly recording of all above activities.

In this way, overall, 10 associate offices have been established. Of these, four are in Ranchi, three in Delhi, two in Lucknow and one in Mumbai. The various parts of the Karyalaya Vibhag help all these offices in the collection of information. That is why Abhiyaan Karyalaya Toli visits Ranchi, Delhi and Mumbai after Kolkata for the monthly review. The

Karyalaya Vibhag has been given the key role in the working of the Ekal Abhiyaan. A sizable group of workers has been formed from department to centre level. These workers have not been assigned any other role and thus they are discharging their duties with devoted hearts and minds and their efforts are producing success.

EXPANSION AND DEVELOPMENT

Swami Vivekanand ji used to say that expansion is life and contraction is death. He also used to say that the expansion would be meaningless without development. His famous statement that 'Conquer the World with Your Spirituality' meant that you have to win the world with your spiritual depth or in other words, you have to ensure concurrent expansion and development. The brainchild of Swami ji, the Ekal Abhiyaan, inculcated in its volunteers that they will not only expand their mission, they will not compromise on the question of the development either. Someone may ask why there is such an ambitious plan of development and expansion? Even if it is so, is it practically possible to manage a balance in expansion and development? The answer to the first question lies in the aims of the Ekal. The Ekal aims to establish Ramrajya and whatever Lord Ram did with his subjects, the Ekal will do with tribals or villagers—it will weave a net of affection with them. But, how can Ramrajya be established without freeing Sita, who is the embodiment of self-respect, from the clutches of Ravana? So, there should be an army of Lord Ram in every village. There should be Hanuman in every village. This determines the limit of the expansion of the Ekal.

Even a question arises: Can development and expansion be possible together? At the root of this question, there lies a hint that both of them are perhaps parallel genres. If any organisation can bring about development, it will be incapable of expansion and if it expands, its development will be ruined. This dictum has to be corrected. Expansion and development are not two contrasting genres, rather they are complimentary. Expansion can build upon development and vice versa. They both can be cultivated together as the cultivator is the one and the same. A volunteer can accomplish something only when he is full of inspired spirit and invest his heart and soul into completing his task. Shyam ji explains this beautifully by giving examples from Ramcharitmanas. 'When Tulsidas ji describes the character of Hanuman, he shows him as being capable of expansion as much as that he can measure up to all the seas in the world and if he wishes to develop upward, he can touch the sky. Both of these are possible, when Hanuman in your heart (self-confidence and zeal) awakens and you become capable of performing incredible tasks.'

In the last few years, the Ekal experimented with some of such tasks in Sanch Samman (Honouring the Units) programmes. In 50 units, the Ekal made 100 people members of SVO at the unit level. Then, it prepared a self-reliant budget to create a new unit (sanch) within a unit through a Sangrakshak Mandal comprising members of the unit, block and zonal committees. They constituted eight sub-committees and 30 volunteers were tasked to work for three hours in one village. This experiment proved to be so successful that it created a record. To perform this task, some workers had to go on gram sanyas (rural asceticism) with full vigour ensure the success of their efforts. One more decision was taken that according to the capability of the volunteer, they will be appointed to various roles in different groups like Kendriya Toli, Bhag Toli and Sambhag Toli and they will be assigned some roles at unit sanch, sankul (90 villages) and anchal (270 villages) levels. Rest of the volunteers will be employed in gram committee. Every volunteer has to perform two types of tasks. First is the organising meeting in a month. It does not take more than 9-10 days to make preparations for the meeting. So, for the rest of the 20 days, the volunteers can be employed in some other tasks in some other place. Thus, a concept of unit, block and zone level officers was developed. Since it was known that the Ekal aimed to bridge the gulf between the cities and the villages, it will be a bridge of affection between both of them. It means people must be prepared in so many numbers that they can regard the Ekal school in their area as a pilgrimage place. It means that 30 people in a unit, 120 people in a block and 480 people in a zone should declare the Ekal school as their pilgrimage point. This is the foundation of the harmony upon which India will stand in future.

Despite the rapid growth and development in India, there are still four lakh small villages that are uneducated, undeveloped and unorganised. The Ekal has set a target of making one lakh such villages Ekal villages and each of these villages can influence three of its neighbouring villages and help them develop. In this way, all the left-out four-lakh villages of

India will be educated, healthy, developed, awakened and cultured. Since the Ekal has achieved its target of one-lakh schools, it can focus on these four-lakh villages. The day all these villages will be like Ekal villages, India will proudly claim in the world that it has educated its rural population. In order to achieve this target, every full-time volunteer of the Ekal has pledged to adopt five to seven villages and then help them develop on the Ekal model. These workers are expected to save the last of the month for this task. To fulfil their pledge as part of 'Gram Swabhiman Dayitva', these volunteers decide that they will tour one of their adopted villages once in a month. If these volunteers plan their tours to adopted village in advance, they can stay there for 24 hours, and they can conduct following tasks there:

1. 3 hours for the school
2. 2 hours for the family with whom they will rest
3. 3 hours for the mass communication (gram sabha)
4. 1 hour for the gram sabha (village panchayat)
5. They can use the rest of 15 hours as they think best.

1. In School

They will spend half the time in inspection of the village and half time for teaching.

(A) Vidyalaya Darshan (Inspection of School)

1) Time management
2) Inspection of attendance register
3) Inspection of attendance of those who are registered
4) Hygienic condition of the school and students
5) Capability of the teacher
6) Following the syllabus
7) Vandana Sabha (Prayer)
8) Rhythm and rhyme of the songs
9) Types of physical activities and their practice

(B) Direct teaching

1) With permission of the teacher and students, begin teaching
2) Rhythmic recitation of the prayer
3) Sharing new songs and stories

4) Teaching new games
5) Practice of sports competition and annual function
6) Telling the programmes and aims of next month's programmes to the students

(C) Satsang/Weekly Classroom

1) Obeying time management
2) Teaching new bhajans (devotional songs)
3) Narrating chapters from Mahabharat and Ramayana
4) To share new knowledge about their subject in the weekly classroom
5) Planning for the next month
6) Preparation for the annual festival
7) Review of news
8) Selection of Ekal Varta

2. Gram Sampark (Connecting with Villagers)

1) After the functioning of the Ekal school, a walk in the village to connect with villagers
2) To visit every household in the village with members of the village committee
3) During the interaction with villagers, to discuss relevant issues like education, health and administration.
4) If any villager lives in the city, locate him and if possible, contact him and persuade him to become member of Vidyalaya Sanrakshak Mandal

3. Night Stay

1) Try to avoid night stay in the teacher's home
2) To avoid stay two times with a single family
3) Try to stay in homes of village committee members
4) Try to develop amiable relations with elders and children of the families where you stay
5) To share songs and stories with children. Discuss news of the world with elders and tell them new things about the Ekal Abhiyaan
6) To get up first in the morning

7) Always remember that the worker has arrived to spread word about the Ekal Abhiyaan, and have food there.

4. **Gram Sabha (Village Meeting)**

To ensure that the village meeting is conducted after the noon. Invitation for the meeting should be sent to gram pradhan (village panchayat head) and gram sabha members. Following things should be pointed out in the village meeting:

1) Is your village a Hindu village? Then, arrangement of worship and temple construction.
2) Is your village an Ekal village? Then, asking about the government schools and if possible creating wall posters.
3) Does your home look like a Hindu house? Means are there Tulsi plants in the foreground of your house? Have you written om at the entrance of your house?
4) Is your village literate? Does the student of Ekal school try to make his parents literate?
5) Are you learning something? Is an annual festival organised in your village?
6) Is your village united? Are there sports competitions organised here?
7) Is your village aware of new laws like RTI, etc?
8) Is your village healthy? Do you keep nutrition gardens and do organic farming?
9) Is your village cultured and follows ethics and values? Do you celebrate Ram Navami and Krishna Janmashatmi?
10) Does harmony prevail in your village? Do people behave cordially with each other and shun differences like caste, etc.?

There are two streams of the Ekal Abhiyaan—One Ekal education, and the other value-based education (sanskar or values). These two are like brother and sister in a family. A brother can never become a sister and vice versa. However, they complement each other in the family. This is how the Ekal works. The Yojna Toli of the Ekal assists in the Hari Katha. The vyas kathakaar of Sri Hari Katha implores the villagers to shun alcoholism and help in making villages liquor-free. Thus, the village strides towards complete development.

All the Ekal volunteers take part in gram sanyas for the collection to make villages' education self-reliant and similarly, all of them assist in Hari Parv to make the Hari Katha self-reliant. This mutual cooperation creates the environment of a family.

DETERMINATION OF THE STRONG MIND

There is a Hindi proverb that says 'Man Ke Hare Haar Hai, Man Ke Jete Jeet' (It is the mind which wins or gets defeated). If anyone accepts defeat in his mind, then his defeat is fixed, however strong he is. But, if anyone is willing to win under any circumstances, his victory is fixed as well. Victory and defeat depend on the willpower of the mind. As soon as we hear about Panki Unit (sanch) of Palamu district in Jharkhand, we become terrified. Hills and ravines surround this area. This area is also known as the hotbed of militancy. Not only the public, but also the government was afraid of this area. The menace of militancy has kept this area far from development. Even in such adverse conditions, the Ekal has been running its school in Panki Unit for the last 18 years. In May 2012, the Ekal decided to organise Panki Unit prize distribution programme. The volunteers of the Ekal's Palamu Block began charting out its plan. To make the programme successful, the volunteers from the zone (anchal) also descended to help the local team. This was despite the fact that the circumstances in the area were not suitable for organising such a programme. The Ekal was worried that how could the unit volunteers be encouraged to be free of fear and organise the programme? There would be meetings at various levels to make plans, but their implementation would always remain half-hearted. Things came to such a pass that the unit volunteers decided to postpone the programme and inform the state-level Ekal official about their reluctance. After sometime, another meeting was called in the presence of state-level officials to decide whether the programme will be organised or called off. In the meeting, the unit volunteers shared their assessment: 'Panki is a militancy-infested area. People here reel under poverty, famines and the ever-increasing commodity prices. We have to collect Rs 10,000 from every Ekal school village. How can we manage to collect separate funds for the prize programme?' Rest of the volunteers backed this argument. In this meeting, Shree Kamalkant Jha, a Ranchi zone's senior volunteer and in-charge of Panki Unit Prize programme, and Shree Devkinandan ji, were also present. They got worried when they heard the workers. They knew that the circumstances were no doubt adverse, however the morale of the volunteers was touching ground. This was the defeat.

Both the officials now searched ways to inject confidence back into the volunteers. Kamlakant ji proposed '40 days sanyas' for the volunteers and asked them if they did not see possibility of the prize programme in Panki Unit, they could go to some other unit and perform '40 days sanyas' there. 'Wherever they will complete "40 days sanyas", the prize programme will be conducted there,' he said. It was declared that only that volunteer who will complete '40 days sanyas' would be part of the programme. This declaration worked for volunteers and they decided that they would not go to any other unit and would complete '40 days sanyas' in their unit only. They would also ensure that the prize programme would be held in their unit. Suddenly, the atmosphere in the unit changed. The same volunteers, who sulked a few days before, were now brimming with confidence and determination to hold the programme. They announced that the programme would be held as scheduled. Ultimately, on 14 May 2012, the said programme was organised and Shyam Gupt ji, the inspiration-in-chief of the Ekal, awarded the Panki Unit the prize for its extraordinary work. Everyone agreed that only because of the strong determination of the volunteers, the programme could be organised.

STOPPING COW SLAUGHTER THROUGH KATHA

In Assam province, there are four villages in Kokrajhar district—Basgaon, Yogendrapur, Shatribai and Foqalagi. In these villages, Sri Hari Katha managed to stop cow slaughter. Besides, the incidents of conversions also paused. This situation was possible 2016 onwards. Sri Hari Katha did not succeed in bringing about these mammoth changes in a month or two, it took a total of 10 years. One Ekal village caught the attention of three neighbouring villages and they also tried to implement some of the Ekal reforms in their areas. One example of this is Shatribai village in Saraibil Unit of Kokrajhar zone. The Ekal school of Shatribai was established in 2005. This village is full of Bodo and Rabha tribes. These people depend on agriculture for their living. They manufacture liquor at their home and consume meat. Most of the people of these villages are Hindus. Overall, this region is Hindu-dominated. Christians among Bodo and Rabha people would slaughter cows and consume their meat before 2016. These irreligious people had also persuaded Hindus villagers to eat cow meat and drink liquor.

The Ekal zone of Kokrajhar organised the Sri Hari Katha on 25 December 2016 in the Kali Temple of Saraibil Unit for seven days. Following this, vyas kathakaar of North-East chapter of the Ekal Abhiyaan, Rupali Hazarika, came to narrate Sri Hari Katha for seven days. It was the first experience for that village to listen to Sri Hari Katha. Many people including those who were Bodo, Rabha, Bengali and Bihari assembled to listen to the Katha. In this Katha, the storyteller emphasised to tell villagers that the cow, like the earth, is the mother of devotees and that Parmatma resides inside cows. Apart from milk, cow's gaubar (dung) and mutra (urine) are also beneficial and are used for many purposes. They were also told how a cow can support a family and could be the source of prosperity. The Katha had its effect and the villagers pledged in groups that they would not slaughter cows, and not let anyone do so. And whoever will be found guilty of cow slaughter, he would be punished with a heavy fine. After the Katha of Rupali Hazarika, not a single cow was slaughtered in the village. Instead, Bodo people constituted a committee of around 25 people for the development of their tribe. This committee remains ultra-alert to protect cows and stop conversions in the village.

BENEFITS OF THE GOVERNMENT SCHEMES

In the Saho Unit of Samba Block of Himachal Pradesh, the Ekal school was established in 2006. This village is situated in the most difficult terrain and the villagers are utterly impoverished. They hardly had any knowledge about various government schemes. Even if some people were about to get some benefits, the gram pradhan (panchayat chief) and his acolytes would block it in several ways so that they themselves usurped all the government grants for the village. So, the corruption was rampant in the village. As the Ekal became active in the village, it organised meetings of the villagers through the village committee and told the villagers to use information tools like RTI. The villagers, under the guidance of the Ekal, have become aware of their rights and the village paints a different picture now. Now, only deserving people get benefits of the government schemes. In 2013, information was received through an RTI that the pradhan was not releasing the daily wage money of the workers. All those needy 30 labourers were paid their wages. Similarly, the construction material for paving a road was being used in short measure, so the villagers intervened and thus the road was constructed with appropriate measure. Since the government schemes were implemented properly, the villagers were happy that finally development was coming to their village. The Ekal has changed the village so much that now no panchayat member or government officer dares to indulge in corruption.

The central government's 'Ayushman Bharat Scheme' and state government's 'Himcare Yojna' is also now reaching the village. The members of the village committee and volunteers of the Ekal have ensured that no villagers should be deprived of such schemes' benefits. They planned to organise camps at sub-unit level to inform villagers about these schemes. They appointed some volunteers 'lok mitra' (friends of people) and they approached all villagers and made their 'health cards' on the spot. Thus, within a month, all the villagers had their health cards, which ensured that they could get treatment up to Rs 5 lakh free of cost. In this way, under Ayushman Bharat Yojna, around 1,065 people and under Himcare schemes, around 2,283 families were benefited through 1,218 health cards.

LESSONS FROM THE CORONAVIRUS PANDEMIC PERIOD

In the annals of known human history, the coronavirus pandemic will be counted as the largest and most gruesome. Many countries, including India, had to impose total lockdown for some months. So, all the activities of government and non-government groups came to a pause. The Ekal Abhiyaan has been no exception. But, as it is said, 'Where there is a will, there is a way.' The Ekal, under the leadership of Shyam ji, took to social media and did not let its march stop for more than a few days. For this purpose, some volunteers were specially trained. These volunteers later went to various places and trained the Ekal volunteers active on the ground. They took Ekal messages to every village. If some villages did not have the Internet facility, the required communication material was provided to them in a downloaded format from the neighbouring villages. The Vichar Kranti Team (VKT) played an important role in this. Now, the VKT has been turned into a war room and is working rigorously. It has following duties:

Padaav (Halt or Camp)-1

1) Voluntary dialogue
2) Gram Sangathan dialogue
3) Mothers empowerment dialogue
4) Nagar Sangathan dialogue
5) Youth brigade dialogue

Padaav-2

To organise the groups in a way that only those people can be their members who work at the lowest level. Besides, there will be a review of the working of such groups.

1) **Voluntary Dialogue:** In this group, only group chief, group development chief, division and subdivision level voluntary members could be part of this group.
2) **Gram Sangathan Dialogue:** Only group and division commander can be part of this group.
3) **Mothers Empowerment Dialogue:** Group and division level mothers can be part of this group. Besides, Hanuman Parivaar Sanyojak and Gau Parivaar Sanyojak can also be part of this group.
4) **Nagar Sangathan Dialogue:** Only divisional custodian, divisional organiser of Gau Palak Parivaar and chapter organiser can be parts of this group.
5) **Youth Group Dialogue:** Only group in-charges of Shabri Youth Brigades can be parts of this group.

Padaav-3

All divisional chiefs list Telegram/WhatsApp numbers in a voluntary group so that the VKT can maintain the group properly.

Padaav-4

Administrator of each group sends the report of attendance of the members of each group every week. Those who remain absent are warned once so that they may return. If they still do not pay attention, they are removed from the group. All the groups of the Ekal have to be managed well and similarly important is to make them devoted to the group. This could be understood from the following lines of a bhajan:

Ja Par Kripa Ram Ki Hoi
Ta Par Kripa Keren Sab Koi
Ramkaaj Lagi Mam Avtara
Ekalmay Ho Jeevan Sara
Ekal Seva Dharm Hamara
Ekal Puja Karm Hamara

It means that if you want cooperation of everyone in the organisation for the sake of Lord Ram, you will have to make Ekal the mission of your life and working for the Ekal should be your daily worship. The Ekal seeks only one hour of 24 hours in the life of its volunteer. Those who do not have even this much dedication for the Ekal, they will be counselled to prepare themselves. And those who can devote one hour daily for the Ekal will be considered eligible for being a member of the VKT and only these people will be part of the Central group.

Let us discuss here how each one should be utilised:

Padaav-1

In the VKT, any position is given to any member according to his eligibility. They might be shouldering any other responsibility as a regular executive of the organisation, only one-hour dedication will be the sole criterion.

Padaav-2

VKT is formed on three levels:

1) Prabhaag (consists of two to three Sambhags) level
2) Sambhaag (consists of 4-5 Bhags or divisions) level
3) Group level

VKT only contacts the Prabhaag level members. Prabhaag level team has to activate the Sambhaag level team. Similarly, Sambhaag team activates Group level teams.

Padaav-3

There are two Ekal schemes which it is focussing on now:

1) Vratt Nivedan (**Reporting Request**)
    a) Daily
    b) Weekly
2) C.N.C. Vaarta (**Telephonic Dialogue**): Held once or twice a week.

The division commander to take care of Reporting and the Conference Call (CNC) is the responsibility of a division level mother (Bhag Ma).

Padaav-4

Prabhaag Commander (PBC) and Prabhaag Mother (PBM) are appointed by VKT based on its own experience. There are PBC1 and PBC2 and PCM1 and PCM2.

Padaav-5

Vritta (Reporting) Nivedan is done through the central WhatsApp group and the CNC is telecast through the Telegram group.

Padaav-6

As a part of the VKT, volunteers were used till 30 September 2020. After that, the members of the committee did all reporting requests and central-level communication.

Padaav-7

Administrators of various Telegram groups review the presence of their members and make their weekly report public in their groups, which are as following

1. Voluntary dialogue—Ramesh Limbu ji
2. Gram Sangathan dialogue—Shree Bulakee ji
3. Mothers Empowerment dialogue—Mrs Madhu Gupta ji
4. Nagar Sangathan dialogue—Mahesh Mittal ji
5. Youth Brigade dialogue—Shree Durgesh ji

Padaav-8

Based on the group administrator's report, only VKT members can remove any member.

VKT also shoulders other responsibilities which are as following:

Padaav-1

For every area, one Vichar Kranti Sampark Pramukh (VKSP) has been appointed. They can only contact following members of the Prabhaag Team:

1. Prabhaag President
2. Prabhaag Secretary
3. Prabhaag Vikas Pramukh
4. Prabhaag Commander-1
5. Prabhaag Commander-2
6. Prabhaag Mother-1
7. Prabhaag Mother-2

Padaav-2

Any problem in the Prabhaag is solved by the Prabhaag Team. The Prabhaag Team records even the daily presence of the Prabhaag member. Prabhaag Team is connected to all Samvaad groups so that they can examine members of those groups.

Padaav-3

It is expected that if any member has difficulty reading the message of any member, he can contact his VKSP over phone. Similarly, if he has any difficulty in communicating any suggestion or experience, he can also send his message directly to the war room through VKSP.

Padaav-4

The members who are removed because of their absence from the group are contacted to re-join by the Prabhaag Team only. Thus, the Prabhaag Team ensures that such members will not remain absent again in future.

Padaav-5

Every day, a classroom is held in the war room of VKT and all messages of the day are discussed in this classroom. Therefore, the VKT is able to answer any query about its functioning.

Padaav-6

Daily reporting requests are reviewed. In this, they are asked to achieve their daily targets. It is also expected that it will be discussed in the CNC.

When the Ekal had launched the Vichar Kranti (VK), it had assumed that the Ekal had reached every village. And then, to take it forward, the entire Ekal ideology must reach those villages. However, the COVID-19 pandemic changed the entire scenario. It forced the Ekal to redefine its priorities. So, the Ekal made the safety of the village its target and the safety of families its priority. People still do not have any clear picture how long the pandemic will stay. Meanwhile, to take the message of the Ekal to villages, the Announcement (Udghosh) Campaign was launched.

The Announcement Session was divided into two parts:

1) Lecture (45 minutes)
2) Hanuman Chalisa, songs, music (15 mins)

The song and chalisa were included so that the session can be converted into a satsang session. However, during the coronavirus pandemic, no group activity has been possible. Yes, for the city volunteers of the Ekal, the 45-minute lecture is very important. It has come to the notice that volunteers are regularly listening to the lecture session, but the response from village teams has been quite weak. There is hardly anyone from the Nagar Sangathan who will answer the questions asked after the lecture. It is an issue of grave concern. If the people who have to lead the Ekal will show such lethargy, how will the Ekal reach all Indian villages? And in such a case, how can we expect simple villagers to respond properly and associate with the Ekal? If the powerhouse is generating electricity and our house is in the dark, it means there is no connection between the powerhouse and our house. So, the people whose responsibility is to take the central message of the Ekal to villages have to be trained meticulously. Thus, it was decided that on every Sunday, the announcement lecture of Saturday must be telecast in the Telegram group so that all the members could listen to it and post their remarks in the group.

The announcement also has its working mechanism that is as following:

Padaav (Stage)-1

The subject matter of Saturday's announcement lecture is divided into three following parts the next week:

1) Aastha Vaarta (Faith Dialogue)
2) Aastha Sandesh (Faith Message)
3) Aastha Sanket (Faith Indication)

Padaav-2

Aastha Vaarta (Faith Dialogue): Saturday's lecture is divided into seven parts and short videos (2.5 mins) are prepared and then sent in the group to all members.

Padaav-3

Aastha Sandesh (Faith Message): The subject matter of the Saturday lecture is briefed into a short note and sent to rural areas so that villagers who might not download the videos can read it.

Padaav-4

Aastha Sanket (Aastha Indication): A short note based on the announcement lecture is made and post on Twitter.

Padaav-5

CNC: In every conference call, the announcement lecture should be discussed so that its message reaches all the villages. It is the responsibility of the CNC team that they should ensure that the message reaches the village units, and they should be held accountable for this.

Padaav-6

Parivarik Satsang (Family Satsang): Since the group satsang is not possible due to the pandemic, families gather at the Hanuman Mandir on every Saturday and hold a family satsang.

Padaav-7

Every Sunday, the video of Saturday's lecture is uploaded in the Telegram group and the members are expected to listen to it and then communicate their views.

Padaav-8

If members feel they can send the video of Saturday's lecture to their friends so that they could also be aware of the Ekal's mission. This video can also be shared on Facebook and YouTube.

Plan for 2025

With the Parinaam Kumbh (Festival of Result) in Dhanbad in 2015, the Ekal had started thinking about plans for the next 10 years till 2025. In this regard, a questionnaire of 20 questions was sent to the Nagar Sangathan and Gram Sangathan volunteers. They organised meetings at various levels. The Ekal got around 1,000 responses or suggestions. Then, a grand all-India meeting was called in the presidentship of Shyam ji in Coimbatore to analyse and draw conclusions from these responses. Later, based on the analysis of this meeting, a meeting was called by the Ekal Abhiyaan Trust to draw final conclusions.

First and foremost, it was realised that the Ekal would not dilute its mission by considering any option. The success of any missionary work depends on the faith of its leadership in its determination. The stated aim of the Ekal is that it will build 100,000 Shakti Kendras (Power Centres), 200,000 Sampark Kendras (Communication Centres), will link 400,000 villages and will use the energy of 40-45 crore energetic Indians to make India an economically and democratically powerful country. The Ekal has achieved its target set for the last 30 years. There should not be an iota of doubt about that. How the Ekal will move towards its future target, it will depend on the workability of the workers and blessing of Lord Ram. Any faith demands utmost devotions from its followers who put their trust on the Shradha Kendra (Devotion Centre). The internal strength and the life of any organisation depends on the fact that its cadres themselves do not attack and neither let anyone strike its Shradha Kendra. Since the Ekal is a forever-developing organisation, it will always remain open to the suggestions. Making no compromise with its fundamental principles and keep making progress in the light of new suggestions is called progress. Any discussion that sows seeds of discord among volunteers and breaches the trust of affection between them will be considered a crime. So, everyone has to remain alert of the virus of criticism.

The purpose of the future plans of the organisation means that we must discern our weaknesses first and then develop will to remove them and then assemble resources and manpower to implement new plans. This project is built on the internal strength of the organisation and it depends on the mutual trust, affection and cumulative enthusiasm to move towards destination. For this purpose, every worker will have to do following tasks:

1) Our volunteers from Gram and Nagar Sangathan should be absolutely active to achieve the target set for them.
2) All of them should be committed to maintain quality and credibility.
3) Everyone should be enthusiastic to expand the organisation.
4) There should be provision for strong action against any breach of discipline.

Shyam ji says that Singhavlokan (overview) means that the lion first looks backward and then jumps forward. So, when we look back, we count our mistakes and then get ready to proceed. Meanwhile, we realise:

1. The Karyakarta Vibhaag (workers' department) has to be made more active in following ways:
   a) Prepare them for communication with families.
   b) Gram Swabhimaan Dayitva Yojna
   c) Discussion with village committee members during the tour to villages.
   d) The guardians must regularly take care of volunteers and evaluate their financial well-being on monthly basis.
   e) The monthly review of senior volunteers whether they are taking the messages from the centre to the villages or not.
2. We should also make it our priority that our training camps get better. The base of the evaluation of these camps should be judged through enthusiasm of the participants who take part in these camps and get ready to work with dedication. To improve the syllabus training, the efforts will be made from the above. We will have to improve the regularity and quality of these camps with religious zeal.
3. Everyone should contribute money and time, only then the families connected with the Ekal will realise that it is their organisation and the organisation will become powerful. In order to make this experiment successful, the village development committee will have to collect money from the village itself twice in a year so that the teacher can be paid his/her honorarium. It will be possible when the members of the unit will start going to meet villagers at their houses daily. So, one solution for this is that the number of voluntary organisations can be increased at the unit level. The only way to maintain the quality and credibility of the Ekal is that villagers must be aware.
4. There should be a second review of the Gram Sangathan (SVO). Any lapse in the legal requirements proves very costly. We read about it daily in the newspaper. So, as the circumstances demand, the Gram Sangathan should be reconstituted. So long as we have decided to pay workers through online banking, it has been realised that a new organisation should be formed in this regard. Besides, the way we have taken the services of the volunteers, we will have to soon keep the records in writing for the legal requirements. The basis of

reorganisation of the village team should be that new members would be legally literate and active.

5. The pivot of the Ekal's success so far has been the strength of the Nagar Sangathan. To make it stronger and friendlier for the Ekal, the reporting about the Ekal activities should be more clear, transparent and credible. For this, workers from senior to junior levels will have to make tours to various areas on a regular basis to monitor the working at every section. If they find repeated breach of discipline, they will have to take stern action. Only then, the credibility of the organisation will be maintained.
6. In the Abhiyaan, anyone is judged by their work, and not by their post. The basis of the measurement of the result is organisation, meaning how many new members joined as voluntary and committee members. Those who can raise an alternative can have the moral right to punish anyone. The base of any volunteer's activeness is the ability to contact as many people as possible. Organising meetings and other programmes are necessary for mass contact, but if a volunteer thinks that they are the only methods, they cannot earn respect in the organisation. Only an energetic person can infuse energy in an organisation. The source of the Ekal's energy is its trust on the capability of village level volunteers because the village works as its powerhouse. The more closely the Ekal will link to the village, the more power will be supplied to the Ekal.

The main points about the future proposal for the Ekal are as following:

1. The appointment of selected volunteers for primary education, activity department and sanskar education at sanch, anchal, bhag and sambhag level.
2. Weekly Satsang (That is also called weekly classroom and gram shiksha kendra) will now be the responsibility of the Sri Hari Katha Kendra.
3. Volunteers of the primary education will train the teacher. Volunteers of the activity department will train the village committee head and the volunteers of Sri Hari Katha will train the satsang chief.

4. All three—Gramotthan, Gram Swarajya and Aarogya Yojna—will be a part of the activity department.
5. Like the sanch, anchal and bhag chiefs take care of the Prathmik Shiksha volunteers, the vyas kathakaar will take care of volunteers connected with their yojna.
6. At every stage of the Sri Hari Katha, vyas kathakaar and satsang chiefs will be appointed so that satsang can also be organised in villages other than Ekal villages.
7. Workers of Sri Hari Katha will constitute a Hari Katha Committee at sanch, anchal and bhag level. It will be considered sub-committee of the Prantiya Seva Sangathan.
8. Ekal Prasikshan Kendras (EPKs) will be established for the development of training chiefs of all genres.
9. Gramotthan Prasikshan Kendra (GRC) and Aarogya Prasikshan Kendras (ARC) will be considered centres of both these schemes. A target has been set that first one GRC and ARC will be made in every sambhaag and then similar ones in the bhaag the next year.
10. To achieve the Digital Ekal, the computer education will be expanded.
11. To make use of available resources, the Corporate Social Responsibility (CSR) of various companies will be approached.
12. For Gramotthan Yojna, suitable government schemes will be explored to check if they can be beneficial.
13. All the necessary steps will be taken to make Ekal a success in the society.

The Parinaam Kumbh in Dhanbad proved that Ram ji's blessings are with the Ekal. Now, it is the turn of the Ekal to do its share of labour to prove worthy of Ram ji's blessing.

□

12
Vanvasi Ka Shyam

I always bow before the traditional ideology of becoming pracharaks of the Rashtriya Swayamsevak Sangh (RSS). A pracharak shuns every joy of life, leads an ascetic life, does not marry and immerses himself in the service of the matrubhumi. The mere mention of such sacrifices fill one with utter respect for RSS pracharaks. Honourable Shyam Gupt ji is a lodestar of the same sacrificial tradition. His life has been the embodiment of service to society. We have been talking to him since we started writing this book. He has emerged as a missionary, who has been toiling indefatigably to uplift the weakest in society, applying all his capabilities to achieve the targets of his team. However, amid highlighting his qualities and the journey of his work, the account of his early life has been lost. His story that transformed him from 'Shyam' to 'Vanvasi ka Shyam' has remained untold.

It has always been considered an uphill task to sum up anybody's personality, traits, achievements and weaknesses in few words. And when a person is as illustrious as Shyam ji, the task becomes tougher. However, I have tried to utilise all of my abilities to weave a short story of his life based on interviews with him and comments and anecdotes about him shared by his colleague and followers.

Shyam ji was born in West Punjab (now Pakistan). His father was an established businessman in the area. His father was the youngest of three brothers. His elder tau ji worked in a bank and younger tau ji was a businessman like his father. During the riots of 1947, Shyam ji suffered a trauma when the son of his younger tau ji was killed on the day of Holi. The mental condition of his widowed sister-in-law deteriorated and the sadness it brought upon the family affected young Shyam ji a lot. Thereafter, his family never celebrated Holi. His younger tau ji turned to spirituality after suffering a period of grave grief. As the violence was turning severe in 1947, his family, like many others, felt increasing pressure to leave Pakistan and migrated to India. The people connected with the bank where his elder tau ji worked, helped the family to safely leave Pakistan. Shyam ji's family left their roots, but his father stayed back. After a few days, his father returned with some belongings, evading a massacre. The train that left Pakistan just before his was intercepted by the rioters and every Hindu aboard was killed. Though his father came to India safely, the whole family was trauma-struck. Shyam ji was merely four years old then. Still, his young mind was wrestling with the question—what wrong did we do? Why did we have to leave our land? Why did our own people not stand with us? Why did I lose my cousin brother in the riots?

In India, his widowed sister-in-law started living in the Barsana town of Mathura, UP. His family had to start anew from scratch. Shyam ji was later admitted to Ram Krishna Mission School, Kanpur. It was during his school days that he pondered over the reasons behind his family's tragedy in Pakistan. He realised that his family merely focussed on the family business and stayed cut off from the rest of society. So, when the time of crisis came, the family found itself isolated. The wisdom dawned upon him that we should never forget our society and maintain regular contact with everyone. At RK Mission School, he also got to read Swami Vivekanand ji. One of Swami ji's sentences rattled him and taught him the lesson of life—'The society that will not follow its samaj dharma (maintaining social relations as a religious duty) will be punished hardest by the history as history is brutal.' However, some questions still disturbed him. He felt that reading Swami Vivekanand and living his life ideals were two different things and it could only be possible when you had access to the last person in the society. When Shyam ji entered Banaras Hindu University, its atmosphere hardened his resolve. He joined the RSS as pracharak and toured places like Agra, Mainpuri, Mathura and Kanpur. He came in close contact with society. He lived among people and got to know their problems. However, when he went to the Kalahandi area of Odisha, the direction and purpose of his life changed forever. When he spent time among the tribals, he realised that the climax of satisfaction for him lay in the service of these tribals. He wished to bring education, health services and other requirements of development to the tribal society. Thus, he set out on a voyage, where the shloka '*Sarve Bhabantu Sukhina, Sarve Santu Niramaya, Sarve Bhadrani Pashyantu, Maa Kashchid Dukh Bhagbhabet*' was a guiding flag and filled him with the emotions needed to push his spirit up. His was a path where '*Ayan Nije Parovaiti Gadna Laghuchetsaam, Udaarchritannatu Tu Vasudeva Kutimbkam*' fills your heart with sense of compassion and care.

Today, Shyam ji is 78 years old, but he still lives for the Vanvasi Samaj. Whenever you meet him, you hear him discuss that this has to be done for the tribal society, that has still not been done for tribals, etc. It is not a hyperbole if we call Shyam ji 'Vanvasi ka Shyam' because his life has unarguably been devoted to the tribals and their welfare.

SAVING VILLAGES DURING CORONAVIRUS PANDEMIC

The coronavirus pandemic has brought innumerable sufferings to human society. It is not doubt being called the greatest catastrophe in human history. Our country has also suffered enormously. The disease was controlled by timely efforts of the Modi government. However, India being a huge country, the relief could not be sent to distant villages. The peculiarity of this disease is that if a person gets it and he does not isolate himself, he passes it on to the whole village. Not only this, even if a person gets infected in a neighbouring village and he conceals his disease, he can still infect the neighbouring villages. There is one more problem: an infected person does not get to know that he is infected for about seven to eight days. And by the time it is found that he is COVID-19 positive, he has already transmitted the virus to a number of people who came into his contact. Thus, the Ekal villages have decided that not only will they protect their own village, but also protect all the villages in the panchayat area. In this way, the Ekal has prevented the outbreak of virus in a number of villages by the activeness of its village organisation on time. In the time of crisis, the Ekal proved that it took birth only to protect villages.

The Ekal has pledged to wipe tears from the eyes of Bharatmata and we know that Bharatmata lives in the villages. The Ekal's devotion, since its inception, has been for the tears of Bharatmata.

In the time of the coronavirus pandemic, the Ekal has taken following decisions in favour of the villagers and villages:

1. First of all, the Ekal established contact with the administrative officials of the area. It provided them necessary cooperation and sought their help for the sake of the villagers.
2. In the second step, the Ekal inspired the villagers to guard the entrance of the village so that no stranger or coronavirus positive person could enter the village.
3. A barrier was erected on the entrance of the village and a soap and sanitiser was kept at the barrier. So, if anyone came from outside, it was mandatory for them to wash their hands with soap and then sanitise themselves before entering the village.
4. The Ekal contacted the administrator and convinced them to sanitise the whole village.
5. If any person, even though they might be from the village itself, came from the city, they were considered a potential spreader of coronavirus. First, the local administration was informed about their arrival. Then, they underwent the COVID-19 test and if the report was negative, only then were they allowed to stay near the village.
6. If there was no isolation centre or place in or near the village, then the Ekal school premises or any other secluded place was turned into the isolation centre.
7. The villagers were instructed to communicate with the person who had returned from a city by maintaining at least six feet distance. The villagers were asked that they must have respect for the person in their hearts, but they had to maintain the required distance. The villagers were told that such measures were put in place for only some days.
8. All the Ekal workers wore masks and the villagers were also encouraged to do so.
9. The women of the villages were trained to make masks. Their masks were bought and distributed in the villages.
10. The Ekal workers earmarked such village households, which needed immediate ration relief, and they were provided all required items. Even the government schemes were used to provide relief to the villages.
11. If there was information about anyone coming to the village, they were asked to download the Aarogya Setu app on their phone.

12. The Ekal workers followed discipline like military regimen and encouraged the villagers to do so.

THE FUTURE WITH THE EKAL

Today's scenario is one of intellectual debates. On one side is the Hindu ideology, while on the other side is the anti-Hindu ideology. It is very saddening that the people of the martial race living in distant Indian villages have been facing the onslaught of anti-Hindu ideology for several years. The only solution to this problem is that we have to disseminate the Hindu ideology among the villagers so that they can understand the reality. Fortunately, the Ekal has reached one-lakh villages and every Ekal village has connections with two to three neighbouring villages. The Ekal school is the body and its ideology is its soul. Imagine what is the body without the soul? It is dead. The same is the condition of a society without ideology. Today, the Ekal is standing at a roundabout. One reality about the Ekal is that its experienced voluntary members worked hard to take the number of Ekal schools to one lakh, but as far as the ideology of the Ekal is concerned, it can be disseminated only through the village committees. That is why in every Ekal Committee Kendra, a monthly discussion takes place to discuss the Ekal ideology. All the members of the village committee attend these meetings. The Ekal has many audio and video clips that can effectively communicate the ideology of the Ekal to the villagers. Then, committee members convey the Ekal message to village volunteers in their own languages and thus it reaches every villager. Using the same method, the Ekal is now working on future schemes to generate harmony, self-reliance and self-respect in the villages. The Ekal's arrival in one-lakh villages is the foundation that is yet to rise into a giant building. Honourable Shyam ji says, 'No house can be built without a foundation and the foundation is no use if it does not rise into a building. We have to offer all our achievements gained so far at the feet of Bharatmata. Now, the test will be whether those who have put the sword on the neck of Bharatmata will prevail or those who are lying on her feet. Therefore, whatever experiments have been conducted through Vichar Kranti, they have to be inducted into the Ekal Abhiyaan gradually.'

The Ekal's proposal for the future is that the first three schemes of the

'Chatushpadi' Yojna (Four-legged Plan) will be part of the Sri Hari Katha Department and the fourth one will be part of the Jagran Department.

The Hari Katha schemes are:

1) Hanuman Parivaar Yojna
2) Shabri Basti Yojna
3) Gau Gram Yojna

The Jagran scheme is:

4) Sainik Samman Yojna

In the Hari Katha department, one Hari Katha chief will be appointed in every Sambhag (zone). His responsibility will be to oversee above-mentioned three schemes. The Sambhag Vyas will take care of the vyas kathakaars who come under it. Similarly, there will be one Gram Swaraj Pramukh in Sambhag of Gram Swaraj Vibhaag who will take care of Sainik Samman Yojna along with his own responsibilities. The members trained by Vichar Kranti Vibhaag will help all these just-mentioned Sambhag Pramukhs. In other words, all these steps are being taken to make the Ekal a mass movement. It will prepare an army of volunteers who will be ready to avert any threat to Bharatmata and this should be and will be the ultimate aim of any Ekal worker.

1. **Hanuman Parivaar Yojna:** The Sri Hari Katha Satsang Samiti of Mumbai has found an unerring mantra to guide the Ekal towards Gram Swaraj (village self-rule). In the inaugural session of the February 2020 Parivartan Kumbh at Lucknow, Honourable Saint and Life Management Guru, Shree Vijay Shankar Mehta ji, emphatically said that the Hanuman Chalisa is a proven mantra. Once it is proven or its true meaning is exposed to the devotee, he does not need to pray to any other god. Goswami Tulsidas ji had composed it 500 years ago. In it lies the whole summary or subject matter of Ramayana and with this mantra on their lips, Indians have protected themselves for hundreds of years. The kind of crisis India is facing today is nothing compared to the mammoth crisis the country faced when this mantra was created. We get following solutions from this mantra:

1) What should we become?
2) What should the Ekal do?
3) What is the concept of Ramrajya?

So, Honourable Shyam ji thought out a plan: let us turn the crisis into an opportunity. The crisis is that everyone is besotted with an unknown inner fear. Thus, we must take shelter of this mantra and free ourselves from the fear by the blessing of Hanuman ji. We all have to become the Hanuman of Lord Ram's army. We must strive that our family becomes a Hanuman Parivaar. Every family member should sit together in the evening and read the Hanuman Chalisa at least five times. It will take around 35 minutes, but we will feel a difference in our family. Families usually care the most about the youngest members of the family. It becomes very difficult to devise ways to control or help them. However, if we recite Hanuman Chalisa, we will see miraculous changes.

Hence, the proposal is that all the members of the Ekal—whether rural or city-dwellers—will recite Hanuman Chalisa five times a day and will make it a part of their daily routine. It is also possible that the Ekal will be able to expand because of recital of this mantra. If it happens, this will be the greatest blessing of Hanuman ji. Every Hanuman Parivaar is expected to make other families Hanuman Parivaar.

Sankalp (Determination):
Hanuman Parivaar Banayenge, Dushman Se Desh Bachayenge
10 Karor Hon Hanuman Parivaar, Utne Ho Hanuman Taiyyar
Ghar-ghar Mein Ho Gau Mata, Aangan Mein Ho Tulsi Mata
Gau Mata Ba Bharatmata, Sada Rahe Hamara Nata
Bharat Maa Ki Hum Santaan, Bharat Ko Banayeinge Desh Mahaan.

2. **Shabri Basti Yojna:** In the story of Lord Ram, it is clear that had Shabri not told Him the address of Sugreev, He would not be worshipped in temples in India today. So, every Ram Bhakt should make sure that he should visit the Shabri Basti (Jhuggi or Poor Colonies) of his city and say thanks or honour one family there. He must spend time with them, accept their tea and refreshments. In short, he must prove himself to be a Ram Sevak instead of a Ram Bhakt. Shabri

Bastis are usually those colonies that are considered untouchable and people avoid visiting them. The Ekal first wants people to say the names of the Shabari Bastis with honour. With this concern in mind, these colonies were named Shabri Colony and the food packets to be distributed among them were called Shabri Aahaar at the Lucknow Kumbh. In this Kumbh, the residents of such colonies participated in huge numbers. Seeing their enthusiasm, the Ekal announced that in the Ekal parlance, these colonies would always be referred to as Shabri Basti. Experience tells us that the youths who have genetic traits to struggle in their blood and struggle in their life as well, they know how to sweat for their living. These are called martial societies. These societies were originally rural, but because of faulty schemes of the government, the villages in the East were emptied and the villagers migrated to cities in search of living. They colonised the Shabri colonies in the city. So, the city families will have to develop affectionate connections with them to win their trust. The base of such connections will be the Hanuman Parivaar Yojna. The youths and mothers in urban families will have to come forward and play pivotal roles. The prominent plan of the Ekal now will be to make Hanuman Parivaars in Shabri colonies. This will be done through the Sri Hari Satsang Samiti. Its reports will be collected by Mumbai-based Mahila Samiti. The Ekal has decided to make Gram Sangathan Samiti (Village Organisation Executive) in every small and big city. Among them will be one sub-committee for Sri Hari Katha. After discussing with all Sambhaag chiefs, conveners will be appointed in all cities for making Hanuman Parivaar.

Before the arrival of the British, there was no caste discrimination in our country. All the castes were known via their professions. The British sowed the seeds of divisions and clashes based on castes. They divided people in our service sector into SC, ST, OBC and MBCs. However, in Ramayana, this society was known as Shiv Samaj. We have accepted this society as tribal society. However, people in the ST category feel insulted if they are called tribals. They take it as if they are being called the junglee samaj. So, the Ekal has re-started the tradition of calling them Shiv Samaj. If the Nagar Sangathan feels that it is easy to introduce them as tribals to their donors, they can call them so for the sake of convenience, but the Gram Sangathan will use the word Shiv Samaj strictly. Shiv Samaj does not dwell only in villages, it also resides in cities for the livelihood of its families. Indian society can be divided into two categories—one is shant samaj (peaceful society) and the other is shaurya samaja (brave or warrior society). The second one is the Shiv Society of the Ramayan era. The self-respect of this society, whether it is thriving in cities or living in villages, will ensure the guaranteed protection of India. The Ekal calls members of this society Ram ji's Sena (Army of Lord Ram). This is the working area of the Ekal to prepare such a society. In cities, the Shiv Samaj mostly lives in Shabri colonies. Some of the people from this society have got educated and are doing jobs in the government sector or with private companies. They lead lives of luxury and have forgotten the struggle of their original society. But, the people, who are struggling for their livelihood, will also struggle for their country. That is why the Ekal calls them with Shiv Samaj honorific. In the simple language, this society can also be called poor society.

There is mention of Shiv Samaj at many places in the Ramayana. One notable mention is in the Rameshwar episode. At the time of the installation of the Shivling, Ram ji called Sugreev and asked him to invite all the munis (scholarly saints) of the country. When everyone was present, Ram ji said, 'I love those who love and respect the Shiv Samaj. Those who look down upon the Shiv Samaj and still worship me, they are doomed for hell.' What more could Ram ji say in respect of the Shiv Samaj? Ram ji made one more announcement, 'Someone who will offer water on Rameshwar Shivling will become like Him, meaning he will become Ram.' This is also the introduction of the Ekal. The Ekal aims to win over the Shiv Society through affection and this is nothing but obeying Lord Ram. We know that the Shiv Samaj is not limited to the villages, they are found in abundant numbers in Shabri colonies in the cities as well. So, the Ekal thinks that like the importance of the self-respect of the villages, it is equally important to ignite people of Shabri colonies to develop self-respect. Therefore, it has been decided that the responsibility of the villages will be on the shoulders of the voluntary members and the youths will work on Shabri colonies. The Ekal Gram Sangathan will form small executive committees in cities as well. Every family in Shabri colonies needs social security as much as families in the villages do. In every Shabri colony, a team of young warriors (or members) who will pledge to take care of 10 families will be formed. In the future, these Shabri families will be urged to become self-dependent families. In short, the Ekal is now expanding. It is now taking responsibility of maintaining self-respect of village as well as the Shabri families in the cities at the same time.

3. **Gau Gram Yojna:** It must be a matter utter shame for Indians who revere cows as their mother and still thousands of cows are slaughtered in slaughterhouses of the country daily. What will be Gau Mata be thinking about its children who see it being slaughtered in a halal way and still hail her. On one hand, there is a huge crowd in the temple of Gopal (son of cow) Krishna and in the same country, the blood of Gau Mata flows in the drains daily. What will the souls of those gau rakshaks think who laid down their lives to protect their mothers? What will the world have opinion about India where so many avatars of Lord took birth to protect cows and Indians worship these avatars and at the same time stay silent on the question of slaughter of cows? On this issue, Honourable Shyam ji says, 'Put your hand on your heart and imagine that if your real mother is being killed in front of you, will you still stay silent? Will you call yourselves her son? In the same way, Lord has given Gau Mata to nourish us and we remain silent when it is killed barbarously. Do we deserve to be called Hindus? When the world calls us anti-Hindu, why do we object? Should not people, who merely run a gaushala (cow shed), and someone who keeps a bread apart daily for the cow, be called karmkandi Hindus (Hypocrite Hindus)? Anyway, the question remains what should we do about it? There is a simple logic: if Gau Mata is not sold, it will not be slaughtered. But who sells the cows? The farmers of our country. They do so because the policies of the government are not beneficial for them and they are unable to eke out a living for their families and thus how will they manage expenses of the cows in their homes? If every gau bhakt vows to adopt one cow in every rural household and convince the family that it should only care about itself, the expenses of the Gau Mata is his responsibility, I can say with 100% certainty that not a single cow will be sold in the market. If Gau Mata is not sold, it will not go to the slaughterhouses to be killed by butchers.'

The Ekal has included in its plans for the future proposals about Gau Kranti. Though it is only in the proposal stage, as the decision will be taken after rigorous consultations from every quarter. One decisive committee of the Ekal will be formed in this regard and this committee will seek responses from every organ of the Ekal about the proposal and then it will review those answers to come to any conclusion. Two names have been proposed for the proposed committee. The first is Shree Sunil Mansinghka, chief of the Go Vigyan Anusandhan Kendra, Nagpur. He is also associated with many Cow Research Institutes in India. Fortunately, he is elder of brother of Mumbai-based Anil Mansinghka and thus he can be considered a part of the Ekal family. The second name is of Mumbai's Shree Narayan Aggarwal ji, who himself has nodded to head this project. He is also an old and devoted member of the Ekal family.

In this regard, the proposed points are as following:

1. The youth brigade will visit every Hanuman Parivaar in the villages and will urge them to adopt one cow (or its calf) and whichever family will agree, it will be provided one cow.
2. Every gaushala (cow shed) will be approached and its managers will be asked to donate those cows that are post their milking phase, and also some calves, so that they can be provided to Hanuman Parivaars in the villages.
3. The Ekal's Gram Sangathan will be expected to bear expenses of the food of that cow for only one year. In the meantime, the family will be assisted to make use of cow dung and urine to help it financially.
4. The family will be linked to Gramotthan Yojna and taught ways to make organic fertilisers from cow dung and urine.
5. This scheme will be one dimension of the Sri Hari Satsang Samiti and it will be named gau seva or gau sanskar. To manage the fodder for cows, some gau-palak parivaar will be found among city-dwellers.
6. A committee of central-level interested workers will be formed to supervise the whole scheme.
7. A sub-committee of every chapter in cities will be formed and these committees will monitor the scheme in their areas.

8. In the later stage of the scheme, cow dung and cow urine banks will be established at the unit and sub-unit level so that both these items will be used to make ayurvedic medicine and other items.
9. The sale of the above-mentioned items will be done through Gramotthan Yojna and the city Hanuman Parivaars will play key role in this sale.
10. Ramsadhak group of villages will ensure that farmers do not sell cows. The responsibility of protection of cows will be of Ramsadhak Toli.

Is there any Hindu who does not revere the cow as his mother? But, is there also a Hindu who, when he sees his Gau Mata being slaughtered, feel agitated within himself and consider himself a criminal because he is unable to do anything? Until Gau Mata, which is blessed by 33 koti (ranks) of gods and goddesses, keeps getting killed, will any of her gods and goddesses bless us, the devotees? Now, the time has come that every Hindu has to wipe this mark of insult from his forehead and the Ekal has taken an initiative in this direction. The slaughter of Gau Mata will stop when it will not be sold in the market. And it will be possible when post-lactase phase (non-milking) cows and other bovines will be adopted by village families. It means there will be ghar vapsi (home return) of gau vansh (neat cattle). And the urban Hindu families will have to help in this project. The Ekal has pledged that not a single drop of Gau Mata's blood will be spilled on the ground where Gopal (her son) is worshipped. With this pledge, the Ekal is starting Gau Gram Yojna. It means that every Ekal village will turn into Gau Gram and every family in it will have to honourably adopt a cow. The urban families will help cow-adopting families financially so that at least for a year, the adopting village families will feel no economic burden. Then, the Ekal members will teach adopting families to produce organic fertilisers from the cow dung and urine so that the families can earn extra money for themselves and slowly they will become self-dependent. The Gau Gram Yojna was unveiled on Gopashtami (22 November 2020) at the Govardhan Teerth. Initially, as an experiment, it was to be launched in 16 units of Jharkhand and Bengal.

In the meeting of the Ekal Abhiyaan Trust, the Gau Gram Yojna was discussed and the following decisions were taken in this regard:

1. This yojna will be operated by the Sri Hari Satsang Samiti and the entire Abhiyaan will support to make it successful.
2. At first, it will be launched in 10 units of Jharkhand and 6 units of Bengal and based on the success of the experiments there, it will be started elsewhere.
3. Sri Hari Satsang Samiti was established in 1996. On 6-7 March 2021, it was decided to celebrate its silver jubilee.
4. The cow-adopting families, which were till now called Gau Mata Parivaar (village families), will now be addressed as Gau Sevak Parivaar. And the urban families, which were called Gau Bhakt Parivaar, will now be called Gau Palak Parivaar.
5. Every Gau Palak Parivaar will be urged to donate Rs 25,000 per year for rearing one cow. As an experiment, around 8,000 cows will be provided to Gau Sevak Parivaars in the 16 units.
6. The distribution of the cows was to take place after March 2021. By that time, all the cowsheds would have been contacted for making cows available. A target of collecting Rs 20 crore was set to be collected from the Gau Palak Parivaars. Both these works will be done by city organisations.
7. Vyas Kathakaars will handle the duty of training the Gau Sevak Parivaars, and the supervision of such families and their review. We do not consider cows as our mother from the point of view of economy. We revere cow as our mother from the point of view of reverence and as per our traditions. Only the vyas kathakaars can teach these things to villagers.
8. Initially, two vyas kathakaars will be appointed in the experimental units (sanch). They will be trained in making various products from cow dung and urine.
9. In the experimental units, Sri Hari Katha chiefs will be appointed so that they can handle the works related with this Yojna.
10. The initial list of the central committee of the Yojna was made public on 22 November 2020 in Gokulashtami programme at Govardhan. This Samiti is empowered to take all decisions and formulate policies regarding this Yojna.

Honourable Shyam ji says about Gau Gram Yojna, 'It was 1998. I was attending an All-India Meeting of the Sangh. Some untoward incident had happened and there was atmosphere of despair everywhere. In that meeting, Honourable Ashok Sighal ji had said that there was no need to feel worried. Gau Mata will save this country and the Ekal will protect Gau Mata. I was flabbergasted. Then, Ashok ji gave the target of one-lakh schools for the Ekal. Whatever the Ekal has achieved today is the result of tapasya of Ashok ji and today, we are facing that moment when we have to protect Gau mata. We will have to make sure that the claim of Ashok ji comes true.'

4. **Sainik Samman Yojna:** There is no doubt that our soldiers are our pride. The government trains them and supports them financially. But, is it enough for the jawan who has been posted at the border and has put his life at stake for the sake of his country? Similarly, the soldiers who have laid down their lives, will the honour from the government be sufficient for them? Does society hold no responsibility for them? Former or retired soldiers live in almost every other village. Should society not honour them while it sees their disciplined nature and heightened degree of patriotism? Should not they get respect in the society, as they are one of the most important parts of it? It is not merely salary that draws our jawans towards military services, they choose this service for the love of their country. Now, it is the duty of the society that it must honour the retired and working soldiers so that the youth should be motivated to join the military services. The Ekal has decided that such families should be selected when someone has been in the military and they should be honoured from time to time on some occasion. One proposal is that such army families can be honoured on the occasion of Independence Day on 15 August. And it can be made a tradition. The form of the honour should be left to the local committee and circumstances.

Following three types of soldiers can be honoured in different ways:

1) The family of the soldier posted on the border
2) The family of the martyred soldier
3) Retired soldiers, who live in villages
4) Future soldiers

The Ekal is lucky that everyone is upbeat about this Yojna. Once the family of a soldier is selected for honour, the ceremony can be organised in a well-managed way. That day should be the birthday of the current soldier and the martyrdom day of the martyred soldier. This way, the whole programme can be planned very well. Now, even the soldiers have been divided into three categories:

1. The first category is of those soldiers who are posted on the border. To mark the birthday of this soldier, the villagers are asked to go and meet his mother and wife and honour them. If possible, they should organise a group satsang with them. Even the aarti of Bharatmata (the worship of Bharatmata) will create a patriotic atmosphere. When this soldier comes home during holidays, his friends and villagers can invite him and his family for lunch or dinner.
2. Ex-soldiers can be given some role in the village committee and even their birthdays can be celebrated by organising a group satsang at their homes.
3. The soldiers who have laid down their lives, their martyrdom day should be a day of pride and tribute for the whole village. This day should be observed as Gaurav Divas. In a public programme, their mother and wife should be honoured. Even some high-ranking government official should be invited for the occasion. It should be checked whether the family is getting the prescribed government services or not. The qualities and bravery of the martyred soldier should be narrated on the occasion.
4. The Ekal wishes to prepare the youths for the future so that they should always be ready to protect the country. For this purpose, there is a plan to organise sports and other physical activities for the youths. This will help youths stay healthy, fit and ready to serve their nation.

Similarly, the efforts are being made to honour the soldiers whose families have been living in cities. The modality of the honouring programme will be the same here. However, all the nationalist organisations active in the city will be urged to take part in it and the programme will be organised on such a grand scale that the whole city will notice that soldiers are the real heroes of the nation and they deserve their due respect. People should be told that every martyred soldier is more important than the politician, social worker or any saint of the country. That is why they should be accorded their due honour in the society. The government should do whatever it has to do for the families of the martyred soldiers, but the real responsibility lies on the shoulders of the society. Even, the birthday of the serving soldier should be celebrated with his family by the society. Similarly, the retired soldiers should be adjusted in the Ekal's city committees as per their abilities.

The implementation of this scheme is the responsibility of mainly the Nagar Sanagathan and the youth brigade of the Gram Sangathan. Both of them have to chart out the plan for the programme as this programme targets the youths and aims to inspire them to join the military services. So, the Gram Sangathan's Yuva Bibhaag will form the Ekal Future team and the youths of Nagar Sangathan will form Ekal Yuva team and both these teams will together form an organising committee. One thing has to be ensured here that no political person should be part of this committee. It would be best for some administrative officer to head this committee. Similarly, in the honouring programme for the martyred soldier, only the administrative officer should be present with the family members of the martyred soldier on the stage. If youth are given the opportunity to deliver a speech on the occasion, it will be most appropriate. However, it should be kept in mind that no politician should be allowed to speak on this occasion. This programme should be purely social in nature.

THE DREAM OF EKAL

When Honourable Shyam ji speaks about the future of the Ekal, his eyes brighten with hope. He says, 'In the coming four to five years, when we will be able to make eight crore families of Shiv Samaj and two crore families of Shabri Basti Hanuman Parivaar and thus 10 crore families will have Tulsi in their premises, our India will change as following:

1. **Liquor Free:** When every heart will have Hanuman ji and every house will have Tulsi plant, who will dare touch liquor?
2. **Poverty Free:** When half of the income of every household will be saved because of being liquor-free, it will automatically lift everyone above the poverty line.
3. **Corruption Free:** When nobody will sell his vote for a bottle of

liquor, the politicians will not need crores of rupees to contest elections and it will plummet the level of corruption.

4. **Conversion Free:** When every village and colony has groups of Shiv Warriors, which Christian priest would dare to enter such villages and colonies?
5. **Violence Free:** When youths from the two crore Shabri families will be alert to avert any untoward incident, who will dare to launch violent attacks on them? Or how can the terrorist organisations find recruits?
6. **Untouchability Free:** When 20 lakh Shabri colonies will get respect and love from Shabri Mitra Parivaar, who would say that untouchability exist in our country?
7. **Cow Slaughter Free:** When two crore cows will get adopting families and cows will not be sold in the market, they will not be slaughtered.
8. **Economy:** When every village youth will prepare products to sell in the market, who will stop India's prosperity?
9. **Literacy:** When every villager will be literate, no one can befool him or her.
10. **Hindu Pride:** When 50 crore Hindus of 10 crore Hindu families will be ready to act united in the name of Ram ji and Hanuman ji, which political party will dare to say anything disrespectful about Hindus?

Today, there are around 25 lakh current and former Ekal teachers and volunteers. They will spread like seeds in every field and if they are cultivated properly, they will sprout in a larger number of plants. Then the dream of the Ekal will not merely remain a dream, it will become a reality.'

Swami Vivekanand ji used to say that one who does not have any dream in his life is like a dead man. The real dream does not happen in your sleep, the real dream is the one that does not let you sleep. So, the lifeblood of any individual or organisation is his/its dream. When there was no ray of hope, Shivaji dreamed of a Hindu Rajya and achieved it. Dr Hedgewar dreamed of a Hindu nation and perhaps no one had the idea that it will be realised within 100 years. The Ekal is also following the footsteps of these great men and blowing the bugle for Swaraj.

□

13
Address of Prime Minister Narendra Modi

(Video Address on the Inauguration of the 100,000th Ekal School, 2019)

All the office-bearers of the Ekal Abhiyaan, all the dignitaries present on this occasion, students, teachers and my dear brothers and sisters, namaskar (salutations) to all of you!

I would have been happier had I been present among you physically and addressed you face-to-face. I am really grateful to all of you that you have made me a part of this important milestone achieved by the Ekal Abhiyaan. Today is, no doubt, a glorious day for the one-lakh schoolteachers and three lakh volunteers associated with Ekal. For me too, this is an occasion of great joy. The joy arises from the fact that you are not only teaching more than 28 lakh rural and, more importantly, adivasi (forest-dwelling) children, but through them you are also contributing to the noble task of nation-building.

I vividly remember that around three to four years ago, during a program, I had urged you to take the number of Ekal schools to one lakh by 2022. It gives me the greatest happiness that you have achieved this target in 2019, three years earlier than the deadline of 2022. This achievement demonstrates the fact that if we believe strongly in ourselves, and work in a planned and systematic manner towards our objective, infusing it with passion, dedication and commitment, then no goal in the world is impossible to achieve. I congratulate each and every member of the Ekal family for their efforts and for being able to fulfil this aim. It is because of efforts such as these that your Abhiyan has been awarded with the Gandhi Peace Prize and various other honours.

Friends, the story of Ekal has been inspiring for the country at each stage. To connect this movement with the masses, many dedicated and noted compatriots of the Movement, many inspirational figures have been our guides and mentors. Today, we remember their contribution also, with the utmost respect. We salute their sacrifice, devotion and Herculean efforts. Coincidentally, today is also the death anniversary of a great man who had devoted his entire life to uplifting the lives of tribals, the deprived sections and backwards—the creator of our Constitution, Dr Bhimrao Ambedkar. He had once written to a friend about the significance of education. Today, on this special occasion, I would like to tell all of you about that letter. He had written, 'We will progress faster, if we give equal emphasis to the education of our boys and girls. So, make it the goal of your life that you will spread awareness about the importance of education, especially among those close to you.' Baba Saheb had written that letter to his friend, but today I can say with great satisfaction that if there is one organisation that is following his advice a 100%. That honour goes to you, the Ekal Abhiyaan, that has implemented on the ground the dreams and aspirations of Baba Saheb.

Friends, today, you might be standing victorious on the pinnacle of one more achievement, but the trials and tribulations that you have overcome in your journey of almost three decades are becoming obvious to more and more people. Ekal has taken on the mantle of imparting education and life-sustaining skills to those living in the most difficult and inaccessible terrains of Bharat, and in distant tribal areas where I think even governments have been unable to reach. This movement, which took birth in Jharkhand, has now expanded to every corner of our 27 states. And so, it is not only a watershed moment in your journey, but also a matter of great pride for all Indians.

Friends, the Ekal Abhiyaan is, in itself, a commendable example of an out-of-the-box idea. It gives me the greatest pleasure to know that you do not keep education limited to classroom study and bookish knowledge; rather, you strive to work for the holistic development of the children. You have developed the concept of poshan vatika (plantations of nutrition-rich fruits and vegetables) to promote good health among the vanvasi children, taught farmers to make organic fertilisers for chemical free farming and given training for making ayurvedic medicines with herbs. You have made available to the village folk primary education, the tenets of basic hygiene and various employment skills. You have also educated them on social self-reliance and on awareness of their roles as citizens. This five-dimensional model of education is proving to be a huge success. It has been found to be instrumental in uplifting the lives of tribals, and making them aware of their rights and duties. Today, when you come to know that the children who once studied in Ekal Vidyalayas are now working as teachers in your own schools, serving the society as employees of the police force, serving the nation in the armed forces or participating in industry and business as entrepreneurs, you must surely be feeling a great sense of pride and satisfaction. Seeing your hard work paying such rich dividends, you must be feeling inspired to do even more.

Friends, the zeal and good intentions with which you are working in the tribal areas, is being emulated by the Central government too, our main focus being on education and the development of skills. We have made the scholarship programme for Scheduled Tribes children more effective and transparent, and at the same time opened new avenues for teaching opportunities. For this purpose, we are developing an extensive, countrywide network of 'Eklavya Model Residential Schools'. We are planning to open more than 400 such schools throughout the country by 2022. In these schools, we are paying attention to minute details like the scheduling of holidays in accordance with the timing of tribal festivals. This has resulted in minimising the rate of school dropouts, and given the tribal children the opportunity of enjoying their festivals at home. Besides this, sports facilities are being upgraded in these schools, so that the intrinsic sportive skills of tribal kids can be honed.

Friends, I believe that for bringing about any change in society, the government's efforts alone are not sufficient. It is when the government and society coalesce that their combined efforts bring manifold and extraordinary results. The Indian Government is implementing many schemes like Mission Indradhanush (Mission Rainbow), Poshan Abhiyaan (Movement for Nutritious diet) and Ayushman Bharat (Promoting Health and Longevity in Bharat) for poor children and their families. To bring about increased awareness about these schemes among the tribal people, united and organised efforts are necessary. On their part, the Ekal

Vidyalayas can inculcate in the rural population the awareness of both their duties as well as responsibilities, and develop in them a new, more emancipated pattern of thinking. I have been told that you are working on a multitude of projects for the future. Awareness of issues like water conservation and afforestation is of immense importance in present times. I hope that you will progress a lot in this direction too.

Friends, you know very well that I hold your sense of service, sacrifice and devotion in the highest esteem. You have always showered your affection on me, and because of these bonds of love, I feel free to offer you my suggestions whenever we meet. Even today, as I stand before committed volunteers like you, knowing that I am addressing dedicated, hard-working and austere stalwarts, I am naturally tempted to suggest a few ideas to you. Friends, in 2022, India will complete 75 years of its Independence. If we look back at our history from 1857 to 1947, we will know that our tribal communities contributed enormously to the struggle for Independence. Who can forget Birsa Munda? History is replete with inspiring tales of the tribal society's sacrifices and devotion to the country. Therefore, my suggestion is that Ekal must initiate research on this subject, viz 'Azadi ki Jung Mein Adivasi (Tribals' Role in the Freedom Struggle)'. My suggestion to all of you is that teachers, students and Ekal volunteers should unearth true tales of tribal heroes in your own regions. In the memory of these brave hearts, they should prepare and stage plays, compose songs, hold contests for both the genres, organise discussions, elocution competitions and debates. These should begin in 2020 and continue for two years until in 2022 a grand finale must be organised at the national level in all the categories.

Friends, your organisation can similarly organise a mahakumbh (grand festival) of all the traditional sports of the country. Since ages, India has possessed a veritable treasure of traditional sports activities that have helped in enhancing intellectual and physical strengths, promoting team spirit, and awakening sensitivity towards the society. However, these traditional sports are gradually becoming extinct because of general ignorance and apathy. We have to refurbish our ancient games, and present them to our people in modern and scientific formats. In our villages and tribal hinterlands, we have the kind of sporting talents that can match up to any international standards. By organising competitions of our traditional games, we will gain the twin advantages of giving our local games recognition and renown, as well as discovering talents from the rural areas. Organising district-level or state-level competitions could be a big step in this direction.

One more thing can be done in cooperation with the administration and the many sports training institutes—Ekal Vidyalayas should be paired with renowned schools in cities, private or government-run, for organising sports competitions and other purposes. For this, a project called 'Sahyatri' (co-traveller) should be instituted, and as part of this, once a year, students of Ekal Vidyalayas should be invited to their partner schools in the cities to spend some time there and learn about the city environment. It should be ensured that the Ekal students get to stay at the homes of the students of city schools. Similarly, students of city schools should visit their partner Ekal Vidyalayas once in a year, spend at least one night at a village home, and experience their rituals and overall culture.

You can imagine the many outcomes that are possible from such efforts—the making of Ek Bharat, Shrestha Bharat (A United and Supreme Bharat), the propagation of social harmony, the awakening of sensitivity in every section of the society, and many others. I understand that such efforts will benefit and enrich students of both city schools and Ekal Vidyalayas. At the same time, their families will also gain myriad hues of experiences, which will always remain with them as memories. Later, these experiences are sure to play a major role whenever they make important decisions in their lives.

Friends, I have learnt that you have also tried to imbibe modern techniques of education in your vidyalayas and have focussed on e-education, for which you deserve the highest accolades. You do not want tribal children to live a life of backwardness, but rather to become a part of modern India. Your plans and efforts for this are indeed venerable. I just have one request regarding this—that all the one-lakh Ekal schools should be brought on to one digital dashboard by combining the individual dashboards of each school. All your systems from the central, state, and up to the village level must be on the same dashboard. This dashboard should be designed in a way that it should have real-time information, real-time monitoring and real-time top-to-bottom guidance.

Friends, in the 75th year of Independence in 2022, it is successes such as the ones you have won, that will help fulfil the dreams of Mahatma Gandhi's Gram Swaraj, Baba Saheb's Social Justice, Deendayal Upadhyay's Movement for Social Harmony and Swami Vivekanand ji's resolve for the creation of a glorious India. They will become a powerful force, a significant contributor towards these ends. I congratulate you once again for your achievements and extend to you my unlimited good wishes for the future. I am grateful that you have given me this opportunity to be present in your midst, and even though I have interacted with you through technology, I will never forget the love given to me by all of you.

Once again, I extend my heartfelt good wishes to all of you. Thank you very much!

□

Details of Statistics about Ekal Abhiyan (Till November 20, 2020)

As Per Ekal Abhiyan, Kolkata, Report

Sequence No	Activity/Detail	Numbers
1.	**Ekal School/Volunteer**	
	Number of Schools/Teachers	102,702
	Number of Students	2,784,806
	Number of Boy Students	1,393,069
	Number of Girl Students	1,391,737
	Number of Volunteers	8,207
2.	**Structure of Ekal Abhiyan**	
	Number of Divisions (A Group of 4 to 6 Sub-divisions)	8
	Number of Sub-divisions (A Group of 2 to 4 Areas)	27
	Number of Areas (A Group of 3 to 8 zones)	77
	Number of Zones (A Group of 3 to 16 Units)	401
	Number of Units (A Group of 30 Schools)	3,550
3.	**Computer Bus (Ekal-on-wheels)**	
	Number of Buses	36
	Number of Involved States	16

	Number of Trained Youth	13,629
4.	**Women Empowerment Centres** (Sewing Centres)	
	Number of Centres	33
	Involved States	15
	Number of Trained Women	9,739
5.	**Computer Training Centres**	
	Number of Centres	27
	Involved States	13
	Number of Trained Youth	3,036
6.	**Gramotthan Sansadhan Kendra**	
	Number of Centres	16
	Involved States	10
	Trained Farmers	150,000
	Number of Farmers Doing Organic Farming	11,000
7.	**Samgra Gram Vikas**	
	Number of Units	12
	Involved Villages	360
	Involved States	5
8.	**E-shiksha**	
	Number of Units	39
	Involved Villages	1,170
	Involved States	11
9.	**Poshan Vatika (Nutrition Nursery)**	
	Total Number	29,844
	Number of Beneficiaries	790,938
10.	**Aarogya Sansadhan Kendra**	
	Number of Anaemia Control Villages	1,110
	Number of Beneficiaries	1,192,330

11.	**Telemedicine Centres**	
	Involved States	2
	Number of Beneficiaries	5,370
12.	**Soaking Pits**	
	Number of Villages	102,090
	Number of Soaking Pits	944,135
13.	**Waste Pits**	
	Number of Villages	1,056
	Number of Waste Pits	13,089
14.	**Sanskar Kendra**	
	Number of Centres	69,406
	Number of Vyas Kathakaar	999
	Number of Video Chariots	48
	Number of States Where Chariots Visit	17

□

References

1. Shree Shyam Gupt ji (Founding Member, Ekal Abhiyan)
2. Shreemati Manju ji (Chairperson, Ekal Sansthan)
3. Prerna Pushp (Part 1-7)
4. Ekal Gaurav Gatha
5. Ekal Abhiyan (Janm Se Jan Andolan Tak)
6. Kahani Ekal Ki

□□□